Innovations

Innovations essays on art & ideas edited by Bernard Bergonzi

Macmillan London
Melbourne Toronto 1968

Published by
MACMILLAN & CO LTD
Little Essex Street London WC2
and also at Bombay Calcutta and Madras
Macmillan South Africa (Publishers) Pty Ltd Johannesburg
The Macmillan Company of Australia Pty Ltd Melbourne
The Macmillan Company of Canada Ltd Toronto

Printed in Great Britain by
ROBERT MACLEHOSE AND CO LTD
The University Press, Glasgow

Contents

Acknowledgements 7
Preface 9
Introduction 11
LESLIE A. FIEDLER The New Mutants 23
LEONARD B. MEYER The End of the Renaissance? 46
FRANK KERMODE Modernisms 66
IHAB HASSAN The Literature of Silence 93
E. H. GOMBRICH Art at the End of its Tether 109
MORSE PECKHAM A Reply 119
MARSHALL McLUHAN The Relation of Environment to Anti-Environment 122
RICHARD KOSTELANETZ Marshall McLuhan 134
JOHN SIMON Norman Brown's Body 150
MARTIN GREEN British Marxists and American Freudians 158
BERNARD BERGONZI Thoughts on the Personality Explosion 185
DAVID LODGE Objections to William Burroughs 200
EDWIN MORGAN Concrete Poetry 213
WILLIAM VARLEY Art as art as Art etc. 226
ELENORE LESTER Happenings and Happiness 238
Contributors 245
Index 247

Acknowledgements

The editor and publishers wish to thank the following, who have kindly given permission for the use of this copyright material:

Encounter for 'Thoughts on the Personality Explosion', copyright Bernard Bergonzi, 1967; the author and *Partisan Review* for 'The New Mutants', copyright *Partisan Review*, 1965; the author for 'Art at the End of its Tether', reprinted from the *New York Review of Books*, copyright *New York Review*, 1966; the author for 'British Marxists and American Freudians', copyright Martin Green, 1968; the author and *Encounter* for 'The Literature of Silence', reprinted by permission of Alfred A. Knopf Inc., from *The Literature of Silence*, copyright Ihab Hassan, 1967; the author and *Encounter* for 'Modernisms', copyright Frank Kermode, 1966; the author, *Commonweal* and *Twentieth Century* for 'Marshall McLuhan', copyright Richard Kostelanetz, 1967; the author and *Commonweal* for 'Happenings and Happiness', copyright Elenore Lester, 1966; the author and *Critical Quarterly* for 'Objections to William Burroughs', copyright David Lodge, 1966; the author and *University of Windsor Review* for 'The Relation of Environment to Anti-Environment', copyright Marshall McLuhan, 1966; the author and the *Hudson Review* for 'The End of the Renaissance?', reprinted from the *Hudson Review*, XVI, no. 2 (Summer 1963), copyright Leonard B. Meyer, 1963; the author and *Peace News* for 'Concrete Poetry', copyright Edwin Morgan, 1965; the author for 'A Reply', reprinted from the *New York Review of Books*, copyright *New York Review*, 1966; the author and the *Hudson Review* for 'Norman Brown's Body', reprinted from the *Hudson Review*, XIX, no. 3 (Autumn 1966), copyright the *Hudson Review* Inc., 1966; the author and *Stand* for 'Art as art as Art etc.', copyright William Varley, 1966.

Preface

The principal debt I incurred in compiling this book was to the authors of the essays included in it: without their generous co-operation it could never have come into existence. I am particularly grateful to Martin Green for substantially revising his contribution, which was originally delivered as a lecture in America and is now published for the first time. I am also obliged to Richard Hoggart, Jan Gordon and Clive Bush for putting me in the way of items I might otherwise have missed. And, finally, I owe a special debt to Frank Kermode for the encouragement he gave me when this book was in the planning stage, as well as for the unfailing intellectual stimulation offered during several years of friendship.

Introduction

With one exception, the essays collected in this book were first published in British, American and Canadian magazines between 1963 and 1967. I came across most of them in the course of my own fairly random reading of current periodicals, and I have gathered them together because they seem to me to converge illuminatingly on a number of questions which have been often raised during the past ten years, in several areas of cultural activity: aesthetic theory, artistic practice, psychological attitudes and social behaviour. It is noticeable that certain names tend to recur like running motifs throughout this material, particularly those of the socio-cultural critic Marshall McLuhan, the composer John Cage, the novelist William Burroughs, and the neo-Freudian evangelist Norman O. Brown. Taken together, they should do something to indicate the scope of this book, and the kind of issues raised in it. Some of these essays were also written with deliberate reference to each other: Leslie Fiedler's 'The New Mutants' advances a thesis which Ihab Hassan refers to approvingly, but which Frank Kermode attacks; and Kermode's essay is also mentioned by Hassan and David Lodge and the present writer.

In some ways the material might be conveniently summarized as dealing with aspects of the contemporary avant-garde; several of the contributors do in fact use this term, but I resisted it for a number of reasons. In the first place, the 'avant-garde' label has come to seem a little old-fashioned, as it must inevitably do, having been in continuous use for about sixty years, and although a basic avant-garde tenet is the desirability of 'perpetual revolution' this concept is too paradoxical to convey much meaning to a sceptical mind. The distinction that Frank Kermode makes between 'paleo-modernism', referring to the great ferment of innovation that dominated all the arts between 1900 and 1930, and 'neo-modernism', which describes recent attempts at radical experiment, seems to me more useful and accurate. A further objection to the use of 'avant-garde' is that although it may still convey some general meaning in the area of aesthetics, it becomes unmanageably vague if one tries to apply it to those kinds of cultural manifestation that are fairly remote from questions of art. So I have settled for 'innovation', an innocuous but precisely descriptive term.

The extent to which there has been any real innovation is discussed at length in the opening essays, which are the most wide-ranging and theoretical. Leslie Fiedler is convinced that the changes currently visible, not only in art but in the socio-psychic attitudes and behaviour of young people in western societies, are so radical and disturbing that he is prepared to talk, in science-fiction terms, of 'mutants' who are moving towards a 'post-human future'. Leonard Meyer restricts himself to a searching analysis of the most advanced attitudes in the music and painting, and to a lesser extent, the literature, of the late fifties and the sixties; he also decides that they indicate a truly revolutionary break with past work, including that of the paleo-modernists. Ihab Hassan is similarly impressed with the evidence of discontinuity in all forms of contemporary art and draws a vivid picture of a literature tending towards silence and an art dominated by the goal of an impossible concreteness, an atmosphere in which man is reduced to the status of an object. Ranged against these three critics is Frank Kermode, who argues that whatever seems revolutionary in the present scene was already implicit in the basic attitudes of the great paleo-modernists, and that the neo-modernists are entertaining but insignificant schismatics in a well-established tradition. He dismisses all talk of radical breaks, and still more of a 'post-human future', as unhistorical apocalypticism, and whilst admitting the anti-humanism of the recent avant-garde, claims that this is nothing new: 'the anti-humanism of early modernism (anti-intellectualist, authoritarian, eugenicist) gives way to the anti-humanism (hipsterish, free-sexed, anti-intellectualist) of later modernism'. Professor Kermode makes a very convincing case as long as he stays close to the theory and practice of art, but in his zeal to preserve continuity I feel that he does not give sufficient weight to changes in the extra-artistic context over the years. The anti-humanism of the paleo-modernists was a conscious reaction against a widespread and rather weary liberalism; on the other hand, neo-modernist anti-humanism exists in a world of generally totalitarian societies, differing from each other only in degree, where public violence is taken very much for granted: in such a context, it seems to me, contemporary anti-humanism will be received in significantly different ways from the earlier variety. Again, Mr Kermode, in playing down the social behaviour that Leslie Fiedler draws attention to, is perhaps being too insistent that *plus ça change* . . . Granted, drug-taking has always been part of bohemian fringe existence; nevertheless, when such activities are said to be regarded as normal in a large segment of the American student population, one may reasonably suggest that this is a new phenomenon rather than the extension of an old one. There comes a time, as Marx suggested, when quantitative change becomes qualitative. I am not inclined to take a partisan role in this debate, although the title of this book and the fact that I thought it worth compiling at all, shows that I think there is *something* genuinely new going on in the neo-modernist camp, even though, like Kermode, I feel that apocalyptic alarmism is not called for. That these essays have been assembled means, I hope, that the reader will be able to make up his own mind.

Mr Kermode has valuably emphasized the difference between 'order' as a traditional goal of art, pointing in the direction of an ultimate transcendence, and 'an order', which can be something local, small-scale, provisional, and perhaps established by random means, like the patterns perceptible in ink blobs. What is most noticeable about neo-modernist art is its lack of concern with overall 'order', with goals or ends. Professor Meyer describes it as 'anti-teleological'; its main function is simply to exist, to catch a perceiver's attention, and not to move in any particular direction, or manifest any ultimate purpose. 'Order', it seems, is rejected as part of an obsolescent metaphysical view of the world, and with this rejection goes the traditional notion of the artist as someone who imposes form and order on 'life' or the raw flux of experience. Instead, 'life' is looked on as inherently superior to art, and the artist tries to work, as Robert Rauschenberg puts it, in the gap between art and life; hence, the extraordinary development of the technique of collage from a modest device of the easel-painter's into the art of the assemblage, where complicated arrangements are made of fragments of the 'real' world. Again, there is the celebrated or notorious musical composition by John Cage, referred to by several of the contributors to this volume, in which a performer sits in front of a closed piano for a given period of time, whilst the audience pays attention to whatever random noises drift into the concert hall. There is also the art – if one may describe it as anything so definite – of the 'Happening', which tries to fuse elements of painting and the theatre with the unpredictability of life itself.[1] Cage has gone a long way in his rejection of 'order' and in his eager embrace of randomness, as has William Burroughs in developing the 'fold-in' technique of his recent fiction. At this point the reader who has always assumed that art is essentially about the imposition of order on disorder may protest that the phenomena under discussion might have great cultural interest but can hardly be regarded as art. It is to meet such objections that the American philosopher and critic Morse Peckham has written a long, closely argued book called *Man's Rage for Chaos*, which might be described as a treatise in behaviourist aesthetics. Professor Peckham dismisses out of hand the notion that art has anything to do with order. Our ordinary everyday perception, he argues, projects too much order on the world, and we are liable to become stuck in the grooves of habitual living. Art, on the other hand, involves us in surprise,

[1] There is a good essay on 'Happenings' in Susan Sontag's *Against Interpretation* (N.Y. and London, 1967), and a less useful one by Jean-Jacques Lebel in *New Writers 4: Plays and Happenings* (London, 1967).

shock, discontinuity, enabling the biological organism to adapt itself with greater vigilance to an uncertain world where it can never really be at home. For Mr Peckham 'art' is not a question of ontological qualities, but of cultural agreement. He claims that, in connection with art, there are two necessary roles to be played: that of the artist, and that of the perceiver. The artist's role is to establish a perceptual field, and the perceiver's is to learn to perceive it properly. Mr Peckham is very hard on the idea that being an artist involves 'creating' anything (indeed, he banishes from his discourse not only the term 'creative mind' but 'mind' itself), for the 'perceptual field' need not be created at all. It can be quite well established by switching a fragment of the 'ordinary' world into the kind of special context in which we are accustomed to exercise perception (or, to use the distinction of Marshall McLuhan's to which I shall subsequently refer, by turning the environmental into the anti-environmental). Here we see a justification for the cult of the 'ready-made' and the *objet trouvé*; we cannot say that an art-object need exhibit any essential difference from other kinds of objects, for the difference lies in the use made of them. For Peckham the only true differentiating feature of art is that it exhibits what he calls 'non-functional stylistic dynamism'; in other words, that it is always changing. In the world of contemporary neo-modernism, where styles change with tremendous rapidity, as though in conscious rivalry of the never-ending transformations of modern technology, the conscientious perceiver must do an immense amount of work. Susan Sontag has observed, 'artists have had to become self-conscious aestheticians: continually challenging their means, their materials and methods'. This is also true of the perceiver; he has to come to terms with a considerable volume of aesthetic theory – such as Mr Peckham's – before he can decide whether what he is offered can be regarded as art, let alone whether or not he likes it. Mr Peckham's approach is original and highly provocative, but it contains many evident difficulties; they are discussed in Professor Gombrich's review in the present volume, to which Peckham has appended a reply.

Leaving questions of art and aesthetics, one can see the concept of the 'anti-teleological' at work in patterns of socio-cultural behaviour. Leslie Fiedler dwells on the abandonment of rationality and purposiveness by many of the American young, and Marshall McLuhan has seen the end of the traditional kind of goal-orientation as an inevitable result of the Electric Age:

> I had a friend visiting from Harvard the other day who said: 'You see, my generation does not have goals.' (He is a young architect.) 'We are not goal-oriented. We just want to know what is going on.' Now that means not a point of view but total ecological awareness. I was reading aloud from *Finnegans Wake* for a moment, and he said: 'When you take L.S.D., the whole world takes on a multidimensional and multisensuous character of discovery, and when I listened to *Finnegans Wake* I got the same experience as L.S.D.' (Perhaps *Finnegan* would be safer, and also more rewarding.)
>
> The point this person was making was that it is absurd to ask us to pursue fragmentary goals in an electric world that is organized integrally and totally. The young today reject goals – they want roles – R-O-L-E-S that is involvement. They don't want fragmented, specialized goals, or jobs. Now that is not easy to explain or to prescribe for.[1]

Professor McLuhan is referred to in several of these essays, and he is discussed by Richard Kostelanetz in one of the few serious attempts at critical assessment that I have come across. One could wish that there had been more, for McLuhan is in the unfortunate position of being a cult figure without being properly understood, and as such he is all too apt to receive both naïve praise and uninformed abuse. Undoubtedly he tends to formulate his ideas before they are properly thought through, and his habit of thinking in slogans means that bright half-truths all too readily get the wrong kind of circulation. Despite the prolixity of his style, McLuhan is essentially an aphorist who uses his formulations, not to establish 'truth', but as what he calls 'probes'. Unfortunately, since McLuhan tends not to advance arguments, he is

[1] Marshall McLuhan, 'Address at Vision 65', in *American Scholar* (Spring 1966).

difficult to argue with, which means he is liable to be accepted or rejected *in toto*. I think he is saying some important things about the state of our culture and its probable development and that the dangers of ignoring them are greater than those of uncritically accepting them; nevertheless, one wishes that they were better formulated, and that McLuhan had been subjected to the right kind of critical attention from the beginning. Presumably he is not happy about the label of 'high priest of pop' that is sometimes applied to him, and the common assumption that he is in sympathy with the processes he describes. Admittedly he aims at a neutral tone, but there are unmistakable hints of enthusiasm in some of his accounts of the more spectacular implications of the electronic media. (The use that is made of McLuhan in a pop context is described by Elenore Lester in her lively account of the 'psychedelic' scene of the New York discothèques.) In a recent interview, however, McLuhan gave an unusually frank statement of his personal attitudes:

> I want observations, not agreement. And my own observation of our almost overwhelming cultural gradient toward the primitive – or the involvement of all the senses – is attended by complete personal distaste and dissatisfaction. I have no liking for it.
>
> Since however, this new cultural gradient is the world – the milieu in which I must live and which prepares the students I must teach – I have every motive to understand its constituents, components, and operations. I move around in these elements (as I hope any scientist would) through a world of disease and stress and misery. If a doctor or surgeon or scientist were to become personally agitated about any phenomenon whatever, he would be finished as an explorer or observer. The need to retain an attitude of complete clinical detachment is only necessary for survival in this kind of work.[1]

McLuhan's reference to a 'world of disease and stress and misery' may surprise those who have been struck by the rather heartless aphoristic cheerfulness of *Understanding Media*. At the

[1] Interview with G. E. Stearn, in *Encounter* (June 1967).

same time, one may reasonably doubt whether the claim to scientific rigour is appropriate to one who is so inclined to ride his hunches and whose magpie-like attitude to evidence is far removed from scientific method as it is usually understood.

Mr Kostelanetz is, I think, on the right lines in describing McLuhan as a technological determinist (or, more specifically, as an 'informational technological determinist'), which means that we can give his insights the same degree of partial assent that we give to other attempts at a deterministic explanation of reality, whether economic, psychological or biological. In his essay Kostelanetz interestingly traces the parallels between McLuhan and Norman O. Brown, the neo-Freudian speculator whose work, though hardly known in England, has an immense following in America. Just as McLuhan sees the electronic media as leading man away from the linearity and successiveness that characterized the print era, towards simultaneity and total involvement, so Brown's concept of 'polymorphous perversity' aims at the generalized sexuality of the infant and the down-grading of the linear, tension-orgasm-release pattern of genital sexuality. We would arrive, in short, at anti-teleological sex, analogous to the anti-teleological art discussed in earlier chapters, though its practical enactment is hard to envisage. It is, I hope, one of the virtues of this book that it looks at the same phenomena from opposed points of view; and in a subsequent essay John Simon accepts the similarities between McLuhan and Brown, but damns them both.

Of the slogans emanating from McLuhan, the most notorious is 'The Medium is the Message'. This is at best half-true, or true about half the time (though I keep realizing how much it applies to unsuspected aspects of modern society; like those forms whose purpose is to be filled in, rather than filled in meaningfully); but, as Mr Kostelanetz shows, even with reference to the electronic media there are many occasions when it simply does not apply. Again, I feel that McLuhan's distinction between 'cool' and 'hot' media is so slippery and tenuous as to be unusable: here we have a clear example of a hunch that was pushed into a premature formulation. On the other hand, the concept of 'Environment versus Anti-Environment' that Marshall McLuhan develops in his own contribution to this book seems to me both straightforward and genuinely fruitful. As he shows, it can explain such a typical manifestation of the contemporary cultural world as Pop art: 'the use of some object in our own daily environment as if it were anti-environmental'. It can also, I think, help us to understand the *raison d'être* of another artistic mode discussed in this book, namely, concrete poetry. With the advent of the electronic media, print ceases to be simply an environment (and therefore invisible to everyone except typographers) but becomes an object of conscious attention, like an art-work. On McLuhan's terms, the concrete poet may be trying an innovatory blend of media; but he is also cherishing in an anti-environmental way a particular medium – print – that is already acquiring a faint flavour of obsolescence.

Although McLuhan is a Canadian, his ideas have found their principal channels of diffusion in the United States, where most of the activity discussed in this book is taking place. For West Europeans, and particularly for the English, America is the future (just as, for the eastern United States, California is the future). At the same time contemporary Britain is already a good deal more like America than many English people like to think. Thus, although Miss Lester's study of New York discothèques, which was first published in 1966, must in one sense have become obsolescent soon after it was written, so quickly do styles change, I am assuming it will have a considerable documentary interest for the English reader, since similar phenomena will undoubtedly have established themselves in this country by the time this book is published. On the intellectual plane, the common language and the free traffic of ideas and persons means that it is reasonable to think of an Anglo-American cultural area, as do many continental Europeans; certainly the differences between, say, British and American literary criticism look quite insignificant in comparison with the contemporary French variety, which seems to exist on another planet, with no point of contact at all with the English-speaking world.

Nevertheless, once one has admitted the extent of the common ground, the differences, when looked at more closely, do exist and are important. Martin Green's essay is devoted to discussing these differences, particularly in relation to those groups in Britain and America which have a claim to be radical in their socio-cultural attitudes. The British he sees as thinking in social and communal categories, deriving much of their impetus from the non-dogmatic Marxism of the New Left; the Americans, on the other hand, are still basically in the Freudian tradition, concerned with the liberation and emancipation of the individual, and regarding Marxism as a largely conservative and irrelevant view of reality. (One should, perhaps, add that the stress on the courageous lonely individual, whilst making a good deal of sense in terms of American tradition, can also be regarded as an act of rebellion against the conventional neo-Freudianism that upholds the virtues of socialization and acculturation in respect of the prevailing norms of American society.) Susan Sontag has used the phrase the 'New Sensibility' about this kind of American attitude, and in her writings its intimate connection with the aesthetics of neo-modernism is apparent. Mr Green includes Miss Sontag, McLuhan and Brown in his discussion, which ranges widely and goes in, as he admits, for a good deal of confident generalization. But by setting British and American attitudes in a sharp polarity he has, I think, enabled one to get a salutary impression of the virtues and limitations of each approach: one might conceive of the opposition in an emblematic way by comparing Raymond Williams and Norman Mailer as social critics.

The essay by the present writer is concerned with cultural forces that are evident throughout the western world, and is an attempt to trace the way the concept of 'personality' is used in widely differing contexts. It suggests, in a speculative fashion, that the inclination towards extreme concreteness and impersonality in neo-modernist art may well have the complementary effect of making personality an opposed and absolute goal in its own right. The remaining essays deal with particular manifestations of neo-modernism. David Lodge takes a strongly critical view of William Burroughs, who is one of the most admired figures in the canon of the New Sensibility, and for whom large claims have been made. Burroughs has been seen as a pioneer of aleatory or chance-oriented forms of composition, a rebel against outmoded concepts of literary and moral order, and a courageous explorer of 'inner space': this strange term, which I have difficulty in finding meaningful, also occurs with some frequency in the writings of R. D. Laing, who has affinities both with the New Left and the New Sensibility.

Edwin Morgan writes of concrete poetry both as a sympathetic exponent and as a practitioner; Frank Kermode refers admiringly to Mr Morgan's talents in this area in 'Modernisms'. William Varley discusses the development of Pop art in both its American and British aspects, but remains critical of its apparent acceptance of cultural exploitation:

> Of course, artists and intellectuals remote and socially isolated have had this privilege of creating works of art with other men's misery as their subject-matter for centuries, but for the first time they celebrate, by implication, their 'humbler fellows'' insufficiency and the forces which create it.

It is this note of urgent moral criticism that one associates with the attitudes of the New Left in England, and which contrasts so strongly with the general acceptance of all phenomena and all experience that marks so much American neo-modernism.[1]

The last of the essays, Miss Lester's entertaining but sharp-eyed survey of discothèques, shows just how complicated the relations between 'highbrow' and 'mass' culture have become of late. She takes us back to Mr Fiedler's mutants, and the science-fiction future they seem to forebode. But she also remarks in passing on

[1] Cf. Robert Rauschenberg: 'Towards all these materials, however, his attitude has always been one of cheerful and nearly total acceptance. He is unfailingly surprised when someone regards an object in one of his works as ugly. He never thinks that anything he uses is ugly at all, and sometimes he finds his salvaged objects strikingly beautiful' – Calvin Tomkins, *The Bride and the Bachelors* (New York and London, 1965) p. 194. For a fruitful encounter between British criticism and American acceptance, see Richard Hoggart's exceedingly fair and discriminating review of Tom Wolfe's *The Kandy-Kolored Tangerine-Flake Streamline Baby* (New York, 1965; London, 1966), in *Encounter* (Aug. 1966).

something that not many of the contributors to this volume have noted, and which one does not need to be very much of a Marxist to see the importance of: the economic foundation for the 'non-functional stylistic dynamism' of so much contemporary culture: 'The little *fleurs du mal* are frugging in nothing more *mal* than the old American pay dirt.'

The aim of this volume is basically a very simple one: to provide information and different points of view about a number of related cultural phenomena that are becoming increasingly noticeable in the modern world. The data can be used in different ways by different readers: those who are sympathetic to neo-modernism and its associated attitudes can discover more about it; while those who are hostile can use this book to become informed opponents (and it is hardly worth being any other kind). The editor may seem unnaturally detached, but he is in the position – which cannot be so very unusual – of being deeply interested in a good many things he does not particularly like; he is also inclined to find the aesthetic theories of neo-modernism more interesting than the works of art they are intended to explain and justify. Left to himself, he would want to endorse the vigorous rationality expressed by Mr Simon and Mr Lodge, and he is optimistic enough, ultimately, to believe that rationality and humanism will survive even in the predicted 'post-human future'. But in such a world survival will involve unusual alertness and a great deal of information about what, at any moment, is really happening.

B. B.

Warwick
July 1967

Leslie A. Fiedler The New Mutants

A realization that the legitimate functions of literature are bewilderingly, almost inexhaustibly various has always exhilarated poets and dismayed critics. And critics, therefore, have sought age after age to legislate limits to literature – legitimizing certain of its functions and disavowing others – in hope of insuring to themselves the exhilaration of which they have felt unjustly deprived, and providing for poets the dismay which the critics at least have thought good for them.

Such shifting and exclusive emphasis is not, however, purely the product of critical malice, or even of critical principle. Somehow every period is, to begin with, especially aware of certain functions of literature and especially oblivious to others: endowed with a special sensitivity and a complementary obtuseness, which, indeed, give to that period its characteristic flavor and feel. So, for instance, the Augustan Era is marked by sensitivity in regard to the uses of diction, obtuseness in regard to those of imagery.

What the peculiar obtuseness of the present age may be I find it difficult to say (being its victim as well as its recorder), perhaps toward the didactic or certain modes of the sentimental. I am reasonably sure, however, that our period is acutely aware of the sense in which literature if not invents, at least collaborates in the invention of time. The beginnings of that awareness go back certainly to the beginnings of the Renaissance, to Humanism as a self-conscious movement; though a critical development occurred toward the end of the eighteenth century with the dawning of the Age of Revolution. And we may have reached a second critical point right now.

At any rate, we have long been aware (in the last decades uncomfortably aware) that a chief function of literature is to express and in part to create not only theories of time but also attitudes toward time. Such attitudes constitute, however, a politics as well as an esthetics; or, more properly perhaps, a necessary mythological substratum of politics – as, in fact, the conventional terms reactionary, conservative, revolutionary indicate: all involving stances toward the past.

It is with the past, then, that we must start, since the invention of the past seems to have preceded that of the present and the future; and since we are gathered in a university at whose heart stands a library[1] – the latter, like the former, a visible monument to the theory that a chief responsibility of literature is to preserve and perpetuate the past. Few universities are explicitly (and none with any real degree of confidence) dedicated to this venerable goal any longer. The Great Books idea (which once transformed the University of Chicago and lives on now in provincial study groups) was perhaps its last desperate expression. Yet the shaky continuing existence of the universities and the building of new college libraries (with matching Federal funds) remind us not only of that tradition but of the literature created in its name: the neo-epic, for instance, all the way from Dante to Milton; and even the frantically nostalgic Historical Romance, out of the counting house by Sir Walter Scott.

Obviously, however, literature has a contemporary as well as a traditional function. That is to say, it may be dedicated to illuminating the present and the meaning of the present, which is, after all, no more given than the past. Certainly the modern or bourgeois novel was thus contemporary in the hands of its great inventors, Richardson, Fielding, Smollett and Sterne; and it became contemporary again – with, as it were, a sigh of relief – when Flaubert, having plunged deep into the Historical Romance, emerged once more into the present of Emma Bovary. But

[1] 'The New Mutants' is a written version of a talk given by Mr Fiedler at the Conference on the Idea of The Future held at Rutgers in June 1965. The conference was sponsored by *Partisan Review* and the Congress for Cultural Freedom, with the cooperation of Rutgers, The State University.

the second function of the novel tends to transform itself into a third: a revolutionary or prophetic or futurist function; and it is with the latter that I am here concerned.

Especially important for our own time is the sense in which literature first conceived the possibility of the future (rather than an End of Time or an Eternal Return, an Apocalypse or Second Coming); and then furnished that future in joyous or terrified anticipation, thus preparing all of us to inhabit it. Men have dreamed and even written down utopias from ancient times; but such utopias were at first typically allegories rather than projections: nonexistent models against which to measure the real world, exploitations of the impossible (as the traditional name declares) rather than explorations or anticipations or programs of the possible. And, in any event, only recently have such works occupied a position anywhere near the center of literature.

Indeed, the movement of futurist literature from the periphery to the center of culture provides a clue to certain essential meanings of our times and of the art which best reflects it. If we make a brief excursion from the lofty reaches of High Art to the humbler levels of Pop Culture – where radical transformations in literature are reflected in simplified form – the extent and nature of the futurist revolution will become immediately evident. Certainly, we have seen in recent years the purveyors of Pop Culture transfer their energies from the Western and the Dracula-type thriller (last heirs of the Romantic and Gothic concern with the past) to the Detective Story especially in its hard-boiled form (final vulgarization of the realists' dedication to the present) to Science Fiction (a new genre based on hints in E. A. Poe and committed to 'extrapolating' the future). This development is based in part on the tendency to rapid exhaustion inherent in popular forms; but in part reflects a growing sense of the irrelevance of the past and even of the present to 1965. Surely, there has never been a moment in which the most naïve as well as the most sophisticated have been so acutely aware of how the past threatens momentarily to disappear from the present, which itself seems on the verge of disappearing into the future.

And this awareness functions, therefore, on the level of art as well as entertainment, persuading quite serious writers to emulate the modes of Science Fiction. The novel is most amenable to this sort of adaptation, whose traces we can find in writers as various as William Golding and Anthony Burgess, William Burroughs and Kurt Vonnegut, Jr, Harry Matthews and John Barth – to all of whom young readers tend to respond with a sympathy they do not feel even toward such forerunners of the mode (still more allegorical than prophetic) as Aldous Huxley, H. G. Wells and George Orwell. But the influence of Science Fiction can be discerned in poetry as well, and even in the polemical essays of such polymath prophets as Wilhelm Reich, Buckminster Fuller, Marshall McLuhan, perhaps also Norman O. Brown. Indeed, in Fuller the prophetic–Science-Fiction view of man is always at the point of fragmenting into verse:

> men are known as being six feet tall
> because that is their tactile limit;
> they are not known by how far we can hear them,
> e.g. as a one-half mile man
> and only to dogs are men known
> by their gigantic olfactoral dimensions. . . .

I am not now interested in analyzing, however, the diction and imagery which have passed from Science Fiction into post-Modernist literature, but rather in coming to terms with the prophetic content common to both: with the myth rather than the modes of Science Fiction. But that myth is quite simply the myth of the end of man, of the transcendence or transformation of the human – a vision quite different from that of the extinction of our species by the Bomb, which seems stereotype rather than archetype and consequently the source of editorials rather than poems. More fruitful artistically is the prospect of the radical transformation (under the impact of advanced technology and the transfer of traditional human functions to machines) of *homo sapiens* into something else: the emergence – to use the language of Science Fiction itself – of 'mutants' among us.

A simpleminded prevision of this event is to be found in

Arthur C. Clarke's *Childhood's End*, at the conclusion of which the mutated offspring of parents much like us are about to take off under their own power into outer space. Mr Clarke believes that he is talking about a time still to come because he takes metaphor for fact; though simply translating 'outer space' into 'inner space' reveals to us that what he is up to is less prediction than description; since the post-human future is now, and if not we, at least our children, are what it would be comfortable to pretend we still only foresee. But what, in fact, are they: these mutants who are likely to sit before us in class, or across from us at the dinner table, or who stare at us with hostility from street corners as we pass?

Beatniks or hipsters, layabouts and drop-outs we are likely to call them with corresponding hostility – or more elegantly but still without sympathy, passive onlookers, abstentionists, spiritual catatonics. There resides in all of these terms an element of truth, at least about the relationship of the young to what we have defined as the tradition, the world we have made for them; and if we turn to the books in which they see their own destiny best represented (*The Clockwork Orange*, say, or *On the Road* or *Temple of Gold*), we will find nothing to contradict that truth. Nor will we find anything to expand it, since the young and their laureates avoid on principle the kind of definition (even of themselves) for which we necessarily seek.

Let us begin then with the negative definition our own hostility suggests, since this is all that is available to us, and say that the 'mutants' in our midst are non-participants in the past (though our wisdom assures us this is impossible), drop-outs from history. The withdrawal from school, so typical of their generation and so inscrutable to ours, is best understood as a lived symbol of their rejection of the notion of cultural continuity and progress, which our graded educational system represents in institutional form. It is not merely a matter of their rejecting what happens to have happened just before them, as the young do, after all, in every age; but of their attempting to disavow the very idea of the past, of their seeking to avoid recapitulating it step by step – up to the point of graduation into the present.

Specifically, the tradition from which they strive to disengage is the tradition of the human, as the West (understanding the West to extend from the United States to Russia) has defined it, Humanism itself, both in its bourgeois and Marxist forms; and more especially, the cult of reason – that dream of Socrates, re-dreamed by the Renaissance and surviving all travesties down to only yesterday. To be sure, there have long been anti-rational forces at work in the West, including primitive Christianity itself; but the very notion of literary culture is a product of Humanism, as the early Christians knew (setting fire to libraries), so that the Church in order to sponsor poets had first to come to terms with reason itself by way of Aquinas and Aristotle.

Only with Dada was the notion of an anti-rational anti-literature born; and Dada became Surrealism, i.e. submitted to the influence of those last neo-Humanists, those desperate Socratic Cabalists, Freud and Marx – dedicated respectively to contriving a rationale of violence and a rationale of impulse. The new irrationalists, however, deny all the apostles of reason, Freud as well as Socrates; and if they seem to exempt Marx, this is because they know less about him, have heard him evoked less often by the teachers they are driven to deny. Not only do they reject the Socratic adage that the unexamined life is not worth living, since for them precisely the unexamined life is the only one worth enduring at all. But they also abjure the Freudian one: 'Where id was, ego shall be', since for them the true rallying cry is, 'Let id prevail over ego, impulse over order', or – in negative terms – 'Freud is a fink!'

The first time I heard this irreverent charge from the mouth of a student some five or six years ago (I who had grown up thinking of Freud as a revolutionary, a pioneer), I knew that I was already in the future; though I did not yet suspect that there would be no room in that future for the university system to which I had devoted my life. Kerouac might have told me so, or Ginsberg, or even so polite and genteel a spokesman for youth as J. D.

Salinger, but I was too aware of what was wrong with such writers (their faults more readily apparent to my taste than their virtues) to be sensitive to the truths they told. It took, therefore, certain public events to illuminate (for me) the literature which might have illuminated them.

I am thinking, of course, of the recent demonstrations at Berkeley and elsewhere, whose ostensible causes were civil rights or freedom of speech or Vietnam, but whose not so secret slogan was all the time: *The Professor is a Fink!* And what an array of bad anti-academic novels, I cannot help reminding myself, written by disgruntled professors, created the mythology out of which that slogan grew. Each generation of students is invented by the generation of teachers just before them; but how different they are in dream and fact – as different as self-hatred and its reflection in another. How different the professors in Jeremy Larner's *Drive, He Said* from those even in Randall Jarrell's *Pictures from an Institution* or Mary McCarthy's *Groves of Academe.*

To be sure, many motives operated to set the students in action, some of them imagined in no book, however good or bad. Many of the thousands who resisted or shouted on campuses did so in the name of naïve or disingenuous or even nostalgic politics (be careful what you wish for in your middle age, or your children will parody it forthwith!); and sheer ennui doubtless played a role along with a justified rage against the hypocrisies of academic life. Universities have long rivaled the churches in their devotion to institutionalizing hypocrisy; and more recently they have outstripped television itself (which most professors affect to despise even more than they despise organized religion) in the institutionalization of boredom.

But what the students were protesting in large part, I have come to believe, was the very notion of man which the universities sought to impose upon them: that bourgeois-Protestant version of Humanism, with its view of man as justified by rationality, work, duty, vocation, maturity, success; and its concomitant understanding of childhood and adolescence as a temporarily privileged time of preparation for assuming those burdens. The new irrationalists, however, are prepared to advocate prolonging adolescence to the grave, and are ready to dispense with school as an outlived excuse for leisure. To them work is as obsolete as reason, a vestige (already dispensible for large numbers) of an economically marginal, pre-automated world; and the obsolescence of the two adds up to the obsolescence of everything our society understands by maturity.

Nor is it in the name of an older more valid Humanistic view of man that the new irrationalists would reject the WASP version; Rabelais is as alien to them as Benjamin Franklin. Disinterested scholarship, reflection, the life of reason, a respect for tradition stir (however dimly and confusedly) chiefly their contempt; and the Abbey of Theleme would seem as sterile to them as Robinson Crusoe's Island. To the classroom, the library, the laboratory, the office conference and the meeting of scholars, they prefer the demonstration, the sit-in, the riot: the mindless unity of an impassioned crowd (with guitars beating out the rhythm in the background), whose immediate cause is felt rather than thought out, whose ultimate cause is itself. In light of this, the Teach-in, often ill understood because of an emphasis on its declared political ends, can be seen as implicitly a parody and mockery of the real classroom: related to the actual business of the university, to real teaching only as the Demonstration Trial (of Dimitrov, of the Soviet Doctors, of Eichmann) to real justice or Demonstration Voting (for one party or a token two) to real suffrage.

At least, since Berkeley (or perhaps since Martin Luther King provided students with new paradigms for action) the choice has been extended beyond what the earlier laureates of the new youth could imagine in the novel: the nervous breakdown at home rather than the return to 'sanity' and school, which was the best Salinger could invent for Franny and Holden; or Kerouac's way out for his 'saintly' vagrants, that 'road' from nowhere to noplace with homemade gurus at the way stations. The structure of those fictional vaudevilles between hard covers that currently please the young (*Catch 22, V., A Mother's Kisses*), suggest in their brutality and discontinuity, their politics of mockery something of the spirit of the student demonstrations; but only Jeremy Larner, as far as I know, has dealt explicitly with the abandonment of the classroom in favor of the dionysiac pack, the turning from *polis* to *thiasos*, from forms of social organization traditionally thought of as male to the sort of passionate community attributed by the ancients to females out of control.

Conventional slogans in favor of 'Good Works' (pious emendations of existing social structures, or extensions of accepted 'rights' to excluded groups) though they provide the motive power of such protests are irrelevant to their form and their final significance. They become their essential selves, i.e. genuine new forms of rebellion, when the demonstrators hoist (as they did in the final stages of the Berkeley protests) the sort of slogan which embarrasses not only fellow-travelers but even the bureaucrats who direct the initial stages of the revolt: at the University of California, the single four-letter word no family newspaper would reprint, though no member of a family who could read was likely not to know it.

It is possible to argue on the basis of the political facts themselves that the word 'fuck' entered the whole scene accidentally (there were only four students behind the 'Dirty Speech Movement', only fifteen hundred kids could be persuaded to demonstrate for it, etc., etc.). But the prophetic literature which anticipates the movement indicates otherwise, suggesting that the logic of their illogical course eventually sets the young against language itself, against the very counters of logical discourse. They seek an anti-language of protest as inevitably as they seek anti-poems and anti-novels, end with the ultimate anti-word, which the demonstrators at Berkeley disingenuously claimed stood for FREEDOM UNDER CLARK KERR.

Esthetics, however, had already anticipated politics in this regard; porno-poetry preceding and preparing the way for what Lewis Feuer has aptly called porno-politics. Already in 1963, in an essay entitled 'Phi Upsilon Kappa', the young poet Michael McClure was writing: 'Gregory Corso has asked me to join with him in a project to free the word FUCK from its chains and strictures. I leap to make some new freedom. . . .' And McClure's own 'Fuck Ode' is a product of this collaboration, as the very name of Ed Saunders' journal, *Fuck You*, is the creation of an analogous impulse. The aging critics of the young who have dealt with the Berkeley demonstrations in such journals as *Commentary* and the *New Leader* do not, however, read either Saunders' porno-pacifist magazine or *Kulchur*, in which McClure's manifesto was first printed – the age barriers eparating readership in the United States more effectively than class, political affiliation or anything else.

Their sense of porno-esthetics is likely to come from deserters from their own camp, chiefly Norman Mailer, and especially his recent *An American Dream*, which represents the entry of anti-language (extending the tentative explorations of 'The Time of Her Time') into the world of the middle-aged, both on the level of mass culture and that of yesterday's ex-Marxist, post-Freudian avant-garde. Characteristically enough, Mailer's book has occasioned in the latter quarters reviews as irrelevant, incoherent, misleading and fundamentally scared as the most philistine responses to the Berkeley demonstrations, Philip Rahv and Stanley Edgar Hyman providing two egregious examples. Yet elsewhere (in sectors held by those more at ease with their own conservatism, i.e., without defunct radicalisms to uphold) the most obscene forays of the young are being met with a disheartening kind of tolerance and even an attempt to adapt them to the conditions of commodity art.

But precisely here, of course, a disconcerting irony is involved; for after a while, there will be no Rahvs and Hymans left to shock – anti-language becoming mere language with repeated use and in the face of acceptance; so that all sense of exhilaration will be lost along with the possibility of offence. What to do then except to choose silence, since raising the ante of violence is ultimately self-defeating; and the way of obscenity in any case leads as naturally to silence as to further excess? Moreover, to the talkative heirs of Socrates, silence is the one offence that never wears out, the radicalism that can never become fashionable; which is why, after the obscene slogan has been hauled down, a blank placard is raised in its place.

There are difficulties, to be sure, when one attempts to move from the politics of silence to an analogous sort of poetry. The opposite number to the silent picketer would be the silent poet, which is a contradiction in terms; yet there are these days non-singers of (perhaps) great talent who shrug off the temptation to song with the muttered comment, 'Creativity is out'. Some, however, make literature of a kind precisely at the point of maximum tension between the tug toward silence and the pull toward publication. Music is a better language really for saying what one would prefer not to say at all – and all the way from certain sorts of sufficiently cool jazz to Rock'n'Roll (with its minimal lyrics that defy understanding on a first hearing), music is the preferred art of the irrationalists.

But some varieties of skinny poetry seem apt, too (as practised, say, by Robert Creeley after the example of W. C. Williams), since their lines are three parts silence to one part speech:

My lady
fair with
soft
arms, what
can I say to
you – words, words . . .

And, of course, fiction aspiring to become Pop Art, say, *An American Dream* (with the experiments of Hemingway and Nathanael West behind it), works approximately as well, since clichés are almost as inaudible as silence itself. The point is not to shout, not to insist, but to hang cool, to baffle all mothers, cultural and spiritual as well as actual.

When the Town Council in Venice, California was about to close down a particularly notorious beatnik café, a lady asked to testify before them, presumably to clinch the case against the offenders. What she reported, however, was that each day as she walked by the café and looked in its windows, she saw the unsavory types who inhabited it 'just standing there, looking – nonchalant'. And, in a way, her improbable adjective does describe crime against her world; for non-chaleur ('cool', the futurists themselves would prefer to call it) is the essence of their life-style as well as of the literary styles to which they respond: the offensive style of those who are not so much *for* anything in particular, as 'with it' in general.

But such an attitude is as remote from traditional 'alienation', with its profound longing to end disconnection, as it is from ordinary forms of allegiance, with their desperate resolve not to admit disconnection. The new young celebrate disconnection – accept it as one of the necessary consequences of the industrial system which has delivered them from work and duty, of that welfare state which makes disengagement the last possible virtue, whether it call itself Capitalist, Socialist or Communist. 'Detachment' is the traditional name for the stance the futurists assume; but 'detachment' carries with it irrelevant religious, even specifically Christian overtones. The post-modernists are surely in some sense 'mystics', religious at least in a way they do not ordinarily know how to confess, but they are not Christians.

Indeed, they regard Christianity, quite as the Black Muslim (with whom they have certain affinities) do, as a white ideology: merely one more method – along with Humanism, technology, Marxism – of imposing 'White' or Western values on the colored rest of the world. To the new barbarian, however, that would-be post-Humanist (who is in most cases the white offspring of Christian forebears), his whiteness is likely to seem if not a stigma and symbol of shame, at least the outward sign of his exclusion from all that his Christian Humanist ancestors rejected in themselves and projected mythologically upon the colored man. For such reasons, his religion, when it becomes explicit, claims to be derived from Tibet or Japan or the ceremonies of the Plains Indians, or is composed out of the non-Christian sub-mythology that has grown up among Negro jazz musicians and in the civil rights movement. When the new barbarian speaks of 'soul', for instance, he means not 'soul' as in Heaven, but as in 'soul music' or even 'soul food'.

It is all part of the attempt of the generation under twenty-five, not exclusively in its most sensitive members but especially in them, to become Negro, even as they attempt to become poor or pre-rational. About this particular form of psychic assimilation I have written sufficiently in the past (summing up what I had been long saying in chapters seven and eight of *Waiting for the End*), neglecting only the sense in which what starts as a specifically American movement becomes an international one, spreading to the *yé-yé* girls of France or the working-class entertainers of Liverpool with astonishing swiftness and ease.

What interests me more particularly right now is a parallel assimilationist attempt, which may, indeed, be more parochial and is certainly most marked at the moment in the Anglo-Saxon world, i.e. in those cultural communities most totally committed to bourgeois-Protestant values and surest that they are unequivocally 'white'. I am thinking of the effort of young men in England and the United States to assimilate into themselves (or even to assimilate themselves into) that otherness, that sum total of rejected psychic elements which the middle-class heirs of the Renaissance have identified with 'woman'. To become new men, these children of the future seem to feel, they must not only become more Black than White but more female than male. And it is natural that the need to make such an adjustment be felt with especial acuteness in post-Protestant highly industrialized societies, where the functions regarded as specifically male for some three hundred years tend most rapidly to become obsolete.

Surely, in America, machines already perform better than humans a large number of those aggressive-productive activities which our ancestors considered man's special province, even his *raison d'être.* Not only has the male's prerogative of making things and money (which is to say, of working) been pre-empted, but also his time-honored privilege of dealing out death by hand, which until quite recently was regarded as a supreme mark of masculine valor. While it seems theoretically possible, even in the heart of Anglo-Saxondom, to imagine a leisurely, pacific male, in fact the losses in secondary functions sustained by men appear to have shaken their faith in their primary masculine function as well, in their ability to achieve the conquest (as the traditional metaphor has it) of women. Earlier, advances in technology had detached the wooing and winning of women from the begetting of children; and though the invention of the condom had at least left the decision to inhibit fatherhood in the power of males, its replacement by the 'loop' and the 'pill' has placed paternity at the mercy of the whims of women.

Writers of fiction and verse registered the technological obsolescence of masculinity long before it was felt even by the representative minority who give to the present younger generation its character and significance. And literary critics have talked a good deal during the past couple of decades about the conversion of the literary hero into the non-hero or the anti-hero; but they have in general failed to notice his simultaneous conversion into the non- or anti-male. Yet ever since Hemingway at least, certain male protagonists of American literature have not only fled rather than sought out combat but have also fled rather than sought out women. From Jake Barnes to Holden Caulfield they have continued to run from the threat of female sexuality; and, indeed, there are models for such evasion in our classic books, where heroes still eager for the fight (Natty Bumppo comes to mind) are already shy of wives and sweethearts and mothers.

It is not absolutely required that the anti-male anti-hero be impotent or homosexual or both (though this helps, as we remember remembering Walt Whitman), merely that he be more seduced than seducing, more passive than active. Consider, for instance, the oddly 'womanish' Herzog of Bellow's current best seller, that Jewish Emma Bovary with a Ph.D., whose chief flaw is physical vanity and a taste for fancy clothes. Bellow, however, is more interested in summing up the past than in evoking the future; and *Herzog* therefore seems an end rather than a beginning, the product of nostalgia (remember when there were real Jews once, and the 'Jewish Novel' had not yet been discovered!)

rather than prophecy. No, the post-humanist, post-male, post-white, post-heroic world is a post-Jewish world by the same token, anti-Semitism as inextricably woven into it as into the movement for Negro rights; and its scriptural books are necessarily *goyish*, not least of all William Burroughs' *The Naked Lunch*.

Burroughs is the chief prophet of the post-male post-heroic world; and it is his emulators who move into the center of the relevant literary scene, for *The Naked Lunch* (the later novels are less successful, less exciting but relevant still) is more than it seems: no mere essay in heroin-hallucinated homosexual pornography – but a nightmare anticipation (in Science Fiction form) of post-Humanist sexuality. Here, as in Alexander Trocchi, John Rechy, Harry Matthews (even an occasional Jew like Allen Ginsberg, who has begun by inscribing properly anti-Jewish obscenities on the walls of the world), are clues to the new attitudes toward sex that will continue to inform our improbable novels of passion and our even more improbable love songs.

The young to whom I have been referring, the mythologically representative minority (who, by a process that infuriates the mythologically inert majority out of which they come, 'stand for' their times), live in a community in which what used to be called the 'Sexual Revolution', the Freudian-Lawrentian revolt of their grandparents and parents, has triumphed as imperfectly and unsatisfactorily as all revolutions always triumph. They confront, therefore, the necessity of determining not only what meanings 'love' can have in their new world, but – even more disturbingly – what significance, if any, 'male' and 'female' now possess. For a while, they (or at least their literary spokesmen recruited from the generation just before them) seemed content to celebrate a kind of *reductio* or *exaltatio ad absurdum* of their parents' once revolutionary sexual goals: The Reichian-inspired Cult of the Orgasm.

Young men and women eager to be delivered of traditional ideologies of love find especially congenial the belief that not union or relationship (much less offspring) but physical release is the end of the sexual act; and that, therefore, it is a matter of indifference with whom or by what method one pursues the therapeutic climax, so long as the climax is total and repeated frequently. And Wilhelm Reich happily detaches this belief from the vestiges of Freudian rationalism, setting it instead in a context of Science Fiction and witchcraft; but his emphasis upon 'full genitality', upon growing up and away from infantile pleasures, strikes the young as a disguised plea for the 'maturity' they have learned to despise. In a time when the duties associated with adulthood promise to become irrelevant, there seems little reason for denying oneself the joys of babyhood – even if these are associated with such regressive fantasies as escaping it all in the arms of little sister (in the Gospel according to J. D. Salinger) or flirting with the possibility of getting into bed with papa (in the Gospel according to Norman Mailer).

Only Norman O. Brown in *Life Against Death* has come to terms on the level of theory with the aspiration to take the final evolutionary leap and cast off adulthood completely, at least in the area of sex. His post-Freudian program for pan-sexual, non-orgasmic love rejects 'full genitality' in favor of a species of in-discriminate bundling, a dream of unlimited sub-coital intimacy which Brown calls (in his vocabulary the term is an honorific) 'polymorphous perverse'. And here finally is an essential clue to the nature of the second sexual revolution, the post-sexual revolution, first evoked in literature by Brother Antoninus more than a decade ago, in a verse prayer addressed somewhat im-probably to the Christian God:

> Annul in me my manhood, Lord, and make
> Me woman sexed and weak . . .
> Make me then
> Girl-hearted, virgin-souled, woman-docile, maiden-meek . . .

Despite the accents of this invocation, however, what is at work is not essentially a homosexual revolt or even a rebellion against women, though its advocates seek to wrest from women their ancient privileges of receiving the Holy Ghost and pleasuring men; and though the attitudes of the movement can be adapted to the anti-female bias of, say, Edward Albee. If in *Who's Afraid of Virginia Woolf?* Albee can portray the relationship of two homosexuals (one in drag) as the model of contemporary marriage, this must be because contemporary marriage has in fact turned into something much like that parody. And it is true that what survives of bourgeois marriage and the bourgeois family is a target which the new barbarians join the old homosexuals in reviling, seeking to replace Mom, Pop and the kids with a neo-Whitmanian gaggle of giggling *camerados*. Such groups are, in fact, whether gathered in coffee houses, university cafeterias or around the literature tables on campuses, the peace-time equivalents, as it were, to the demonstrating crowd. But even their program of displacing Dick-Jane-Spot-Baby, etc., the WASP family of grade school primers, is not the fundamental motive of the post-sexual revolution.

What is at stake from Burroughs to Bellow, Ginsberg to Albee, Salinger to Gregory Corso is a more personal transformation: a radical metamorphosis of the Western male – utterly unforeseen in the decades before us, but visible now in every high school and college classroom, as well as on the paperback racks in airports and supermarkets. All around us, young males are beginning to retrieve for themselves the cavalier role once piously and class-consciously surrendered to women: *that of being beautiful and being loved.* Here once more the example of the Negro – the feckless and adorned Negro male with the blood of Cavaliers in his veins – has served as a model. And what else is left to young men, in any case, after the devaluation of the grim duties they had arrogated to themselves in place of the pursuit of loveliness?

All of us who are middle-aged and were Marxists, which is to say, who once numbered ourselves among the last assured Puritans, have surely noticed in ourselves a vestigial roundhead rage at the new hair styles of the advanced or – if you please – delinquent young. Watching young men titivate their locks (the comb, the pocket mirror and the bobby pin having replaced the jackknife, catcher's mitt and brass knuckles), we feel the same baffled resentment that stirs in us when we realize that they have rejected work. A job and unequivocal maleness – these are two sides of the same Calvinist coin, which in the future buys nothing.

Few of us, however, have really understood how the Beatle hair-do is part of a syndrome, of which high heels, jeans tight over the buttocks, etc., are other aspects, symptomatic of a larger retreat from masculine aggressiveness to female allure – in literature and the arts to the style called 'camp'. And fewer still have realized how that style, though the invention of homosexuals, is now the possession of basically heterosexual males as well, a strategy in their campaign to establish a new relationship not only with women but with their own masculinity. In the course of that campaign, they have embraced certain kinds of gesture and garb, certain accents and tones traditionally associated with females or female impersonators; which is why we have been observing recently (in life as well as fiction and verse) young boys, quite unequivocally male, playing all the traditional roles of women: the vamp, the coquette, the whore, the icy tease, the pure young virgin.

Not only oldsters, who had envisioned and despaired of quite another future, are bewildered by this turn of events, but young girls, too, seem scarcely to know what is happening – looking on with that new, schizoid stare which itself has become a hallmark of our times. And the crop-headed jocks, those crew-cut athletes who represent an obsolescent masculine style based on quite other values, have tended to strike back blindly; beating the hell out of some poor kid whose hair is too long or whose pants are too tight – quite as they once beat up young Communists for revealing that their politics had become obsolete. Even heterosexual writers, however, have been slow to catch up, the revolution in sensibility running ahead of that in expression; and they have perforce permitted homosexuals to speak for them (Burroughs and Genet and Baldwin and Ginsberg and Albee and a score of others), even to invent the forms in which the future will have to speak.

The revolt against masculinity is not limited, however, to simple matters of coiffure and costume, visible even to athletes;

or to the adaptation of certain campy styles and modes to new uses. There is also a sense in which two large social movements that have set the young in motion and furnished images of action for their books – movements as important in their own right as porno-politics and the pursuit of the polymorphous perverse – are connected analogically to the abdication from traditional maleness. The first of these is non-violent or passive resistance, so oddly come back to the land of its inventor, that icy Thoreau who dreamed a love which '... has not much human blood in it, but consists with a certain disregard for men and their erections....'

The civil rights movement, however, in which nonviolence has found a home, has been hospitable not only to the sort of post-humanist I have been describing; so that at a demonstration (Selma, Alabama will do as an example) the true hippie will be found side by side with backwoods Baptists, nuns on a spiritual spree, boy bureaucrats practicing to take power, resurrected socialists, Unitarians in search of a God, and just plain tourists, gathered, as once at the Battle of Bull Run, to see the fun. For each of these, nonviolence will have a different sort of fundamental meaning – as a tactic, a camouflage, a passing fad, a pious gesture – but for each in part, and for the post-humanist especially, it will signify the possibility of heroism without aggression, effective action without guilt.

There have always been two contradictory American ideals: to be the occasion of maximum violence, and to remain absolutely innocent. Once, however, these were thought hopelessly incompatible for males (except, perhaps, as embodied in works of art), reserved strictly for women: the spouse of the wife-beater, for instance, or the victim of rape. But males have now assumed these classic roles; and just as a particularly beleaguered wife occasionally slipped over the dividing line into violence, so do the new passive protestors – leaving us to confront (or resign to the courts) such homey female questions as: *Did Mario Savio really bite that cop in the leg as he sagged limply toward the ground?*

The second social movement is the drug cult, more widespread among youth, from its squarest limits to its most beat, than anyone seems prepared to admit in public; and at its beat limit at least inextricably involved with the civil rights movement, as the recent arrests of Peter DeLissovoy and Susan Ryerson revealed even to the ordinary newspaper reader. 'Police said that most of the recipients [of marijuana] were college students', the U.P. story runs. 'They quoted Miss Ryerson and DeLissovoy as saying that many of the letter packets were sent to civil rights workers.' Only fiction and verse, however, has dealt with the conjunction of homosexuality, drugs and civil rights, eschewing the general piety of the press which has been unwilling to compromise 'good works' on behalf of the Negro by associating it with the deep radicalism of a way of life based on the ritual consumption of 'pot'.

The widespread use of such hallucinogens as peyote, marijuana, the 'mexican mushroom', LSD, etc., as well as pep pills, goof balls, airplane glue, certain kinds of cough syrups and even, though in many fewer cases, heroin, is not merely a matter of a changing taste in stimulants but of the programmatic espousal of an anti-puritanical mode of existence – hedonistic and detached – one more strategy in the war on time and work. But it is also (to pursue my analogy once more) an attempt to arrogate to the male certain traditional privileges of the female. What could be more womanly, as Elémire Zolla was already pointing out some years ago, than permitting the penetration of the body by a foreign object which not only stirs delight but even (possibly) creates new life?

In any case, with drugs we have come to the crux of the futurist revolt, the hinge of everything else, as the young tell us over and over in their writing. When the movement was first finding a voice, Allen Ginsberg set this aspect of it in proper context in an immensely comic, utterly serious poem called 'America', in which 'pot' is associated with earlier forms of rebellion, a commitment to catatonia, and a rejection of conventional male potency:

America I used to be a communist when I was a kid I'm not sorry.
I smoke marijuana every chance I get.
I sit in my house for days on end and stare at the roses in the closet.
When I go to Chinatown I . . . never get laid . . .

Similarly, Michael McClure reveals in his essay, 'Phi Upsilon Kappa', that before penetrating the 'cavern of Anglo-Saxon', whence he merged with the slogan of the ultimate Berkeley demonstrators, he had been on mescalin. 'I have emerged from a dark night of the soul; I entered it by Peyote.' And by now, drug-taking has become as standard a feature of the literature of the young as oral-genital love-making. I flip open the first issue of yet another ephemeral San Francisco little magazine quite at random and read: 'I tie up and the main pipe [the ante-cobital vein, for the clinically inclined] swells like a prideful beggar beneath the skin. Just before I get on it is always the worst.' Worse than the experience, however, is its literary rendering; and the badness of such confessional fiction, flawed by the sentimentality of those who desire to live 'like a cunning vegetable', is a badness we older readers find it only too easy to perceive, as our sons and daughters find it only too easy to overlook. Yet precisely here the age and the mode define themselves; for not in the master but in the hacks new forms are established, new lines drawn.

Here, at any rate, is where the young lose us in literature as well as life, since here they pass over into real revolt, i.e. what we really cannot abide, hard as we try. The mother who has sent her son to private schools and on to Harvard to keep him out of classrooms overcrowded with poor Negroes, rejoices when he sets out for Mississippi with his comrades in SNCC, but shudders when he turns on with LSD; just as the ex-Marxist father, who has earlier proved radicalism impossible, rejoices to see his son stand up, piously and pompously, for CORE or SDS, but trembles to hear him quote Alpert and Leary or praise Burroughs. Just as certainly as liberalism is the LSD of the aging, LSD is the radicalism of the young.

If whiskey long served as an appropriate symbolic excess for those who chafed against Puritan restraint without finally challenging it – temporarily releasing them to socially harmful aggression and (hopefully) sexual self-indulgence, the new popular drugs provide an excess quite as satisfactorily symbolic to the post-Puritans – releasing them from sanity to madness by destroying in them the inner restrictive order which has somehow survived the dissolution of the outer. It is finally insanity, then, that the futurists learn to admire and emulate, quite as they learn to pursue vision instead of learning, hallucination rather than logic. The schizophrenic replaces the sage as their ideal, their new culture hero, figured forth as a giant schizoid Indian (his madness modeled in part on the author's own experiences with LSD) in Ken Kesey's *One Flew Over the Cuckoo's Nest*.

The hippier young are not alone, however, in their taste for the insane; we live in a time when readers in general respond sympathetically to madness in literature wherever it is found, in established writers as well as in those trying to establish new modes. Surely it is not the lucidity and logic of Robert Lowell or Theodore Roethke or John Berryman which we admire, but their flirtation with incoherence and disorder. And certainly it is Mailer at his most nearly psychotic, Mailer the creature rather than the master of his fantasies who moves us to admiration; while in the case of Saul Bellow, we endure the theoretical optimism and acceptance for the sake of the delightful melancholia, the fertile paranoia which he cannot disavow any more than the talent at whose root they lie. Even essayists and analysts recommend themselves to us these days by a certain redemptive nuttiness; at any rate, we do not love, say, Marshall McLuhan less because he continually risks sounding like the body-fluids man in *Dr Strangelove*.

We have, moreover, recently been witnessing the development of a new form of social psychiatry[1] (a psychiatry of the future

[1] Described in an article in the *New Left Review* (Nov.–Dec. 1964) by R. D. Laing, who advocates 'ex-patients helping future patients go mad'. [It has since been reprinted in Laing's *The Politics of Experience and the Bird of Paradise* (Harmondsworth, 1967), *Ed.*]

already anticipated by the literature of the future) which considers some varieties of 'schizophrenia' not diseases to be cured but forays into an unknown psychic world: random penetrations by bewildered internal cosmonauts of a realm that it will be the task of the next generations to explore. And if the accounts which the returning schizophrenics give (the argument of the apologists runs) of the 'places' they have been are fantastic and garbled, surely they are no more so than, for example, Columbus' reports of the world he had claimed for Spain, a world bounded – according to his newly drawn maps – by Cathay on the north and Paradise on the south.

In any case, poets and junkies have been suggesting to us that the new world appropriate to the new men of the latter twentieth century is to be discovered only by the conquest of inner space: by an adventure of the spirit, an extension of psychic possibility, of which the flights into outer space – moonshots and expeditions to Mars – are precisely such unwitting metaphors and analogues as the voyages of exploration were of the earlier breakthrough into the Renaissance, from whose consequences the young seek now so desperately to escape. The laureate of that new conquest is William Burroughs; and it is fitting that the final word be his:

> This war will be won in the air. In the Silent Air with Image Rays. You were a pilot remember? Tracer bullets cutting the right wing you were free in space a few seconds before in blue space between eyes. Go back to Silence. Keep Silence. Keep Silence. K.S. K.S. . . . From Silence re-write the message that is you. You are the message I send to The Enemy. My Silent Message.
>
> The Naked Astronauts were free in space. . . .

Leonard B. Meyer **The End of the Renaissance?**

Notes on the Radical Empiricism of the Avant-Garde

I

No aspect of contemporary art has received so much publicity and so much attention from critics, professional and amateur, as the fact that it is often created by accidental or random means. Nor have the artists themselves discouraged such publicity – the storms of protest, the raillery, and the cries of outraged anguish. For, after all, notoriety, even when based on misunderstanding, is perhaps better than neglect.

While the use of random techniques in the plastic arts has received more publicity, the use of chance in music has been much clearer and more systematic. For though Jackson Pollock dripped his paint on a canvas from a considerable height and the French painter, Mathieu, hurls paint at his canvas from a safe distance, one cannot be sure how much was *really* accidental and how much was governed by an inspired spontaneity – an unconscious control of line, color, and texture arising out of the artists' past training and discipline.

In the composition of music no such doubts arise. For here chance procedures have been employed explicitly and systematically. This has been done in three basic ways: In the first, the composer uses a technique for randomization to create a fully written-out score. As John Cage put it:

> Those involved with the composition of experimental music find ways and means to remove themselves from the activities of the sounds they make. Some employ chance operations derived from sources as ancient as the Chinese *Book of Changes* or as modern as tables of random numbers used also by physicists in research. Or, analogous to the Rorschach tests of

> psychology, the interpretation of imperfections in the paper upon which one is writing may provide a music free from one's memory and imagination.[1]

In the second way of randomizing music, the composer merely indicates, by means of a graph or schematic drawing, approximate pitches, time relationships, textures, dynamics, and so forth. The realization of this 'score' is left to the performer or, if there is an ensemble, the performers. This method has been used by the Italian composer, Sylvano Bussotti, and the U.S. composers, Morton Feldman and John Cage. Peter Gradenwitz describes the score of Bussotti's *Piano Piece for David Tudor* as consisting of 'a line-drawing made up of straight and curved lines, arrows, vertical and diagonal signs of direction, ornaments, and so forth. This drawing is to inspire the pianist to whom the composer leaves every freedom to interpret the "signs" of the "score".'[2] Where several players are involved in such a performance, the result may be random indeed. For not only are the particular pitches and the precise time relationships not stipulated in the parts played by the performers but, since these are indeterminate, their synchronization is also random. The coincidence of pitches is purely accidental. The third way of creating so-called indeterminate music is somewhat less random. In this case the composer writes down in detail several separate snippets of music, each lasting for only a few seconds. But the order in which these snippets is played is left to the whim of the performer. Karlheinz Stockhausen's *Piano Piece No. 11* is an example of such a work. Here are Stockhausen's instructions to the pianist:

> The performer looks at random at the sheet of music and begins with any group, the first that catches his eye; this he plays, choosing for himself tempo . . . dynamic level, and type of attack. At the end of the first group, he reads the tempo, dynamic, and attack indications that follow, and looks at random to any other group, which he then plays in accordance with the latter indications.

[1] *Silence*, Middletown, Conn. (1961) pp. 10–11.
[2] 'The Performer's Role in the Newest Music', in *Chesterian*, XXXIV 62.

> 'Looking at random to any other group' implies that the performer will never link up expressly-chosen groups or intentionally leave out others.
>
> Each group can be joined to any of the other 18: each can thus be played at any of the six tempi and dynamic levels and with any of the six types of attack . . .
>
> When a group is arrived at for the third time, one possible realization of the piece is completed. This being so, it may come about that certain groups are played once only or not at all.

Random or indeterminate music must be distinguished from electronic music and from computer music. Electronic music is simply music composed *directly* on tape. That is, the composer begins with either natural sounds or those produced by a frequency oscillator, puts them on tape and then by rerecording these sound fragments at faster or slower tempi, higher or lower pitches, louder or softer volumes, backwards or forwards, upside down, and so forth, constructs a piece of music. Such a work may involve chance elements or it may be completely pre-planned. In other cases a pre-planned set of time, pitch, volume, and tone-color relationships activated by an electronic mechanism may be put directly on tape. This kind of music has been written by Stockhausen, Boulez, Luciano Berio, Milton Babbitt and others. Though the composition of 'computer music' often *begins* with a series of random numbers corresponding to a series of pitches, the finished piece is not usually random. In computer music a set of rules or instructions – they might be the rules for writing a Bach fugue (if we really knew those well enough) or the rules for writing a popular tune – are fed into a computer which, following these instructions, selects appropriate notes from the random series and thus 'composes' a piece of music. Depending upon the nature of the instructions fed into the computer, the compositions it produces can be either highly determined or completely random.

In discussing works of art, the critic can focus his attention upon the work itself – its organization, inter-relationships, process of development, etc. or he may concern himself with the *way* in which the work was created, or he may deal with the cultural beliefs and attitudes which led the artist to employ a particular means in a particular way. Since completely random or indeterminate music is avowedly and purposefully without any organization, it is impossible to analyze or discuss its form or process. I cannot, therefore, deal with the structure and organization of this music – with the music itself. Nor will I be concerned with the random procedures themselves. For while such procedures have received considerable publicity, they are more interesting as symptoms of a new aesthetic than as techniques for creating works of art. In other words, random procedures are a means to an end and their real significance begins to appear when one asks *why* – for what purpose – they are employed. This distinction between means and ends is also important because in music, as well as in other arts, the same ends have been achieved in different ways. In fact, as George Rochberg has pointed out, the aesthetic effects produced by random methods of composition are, paradoxically, the same as those realized by totally ordered music.[1] Hence it is not surprising to find that sometimes the same composer writes both kinds.

It is easy, of course, to ridicule art created by accident – by asking 'What does it represent?' or asserting that 'my little child could have done that'. And perhaps the child could. But for these artists that is not the point at all. If we take what they are doing seriously – and, as I shall try to show, their position is a consistent and tenable one – then precisely because the art and aesthetic of the avant-garde represents a radical break with our common cultural convictions, we shall be forced to examine and make explicit those fundamental assumptions about the nature of man, the universe and man's place in it, which are so much a part of our habitual modes of thought and perception that we unconsciously take them for granted.

II

What characterizes the music with which most of us are most familiar – the music of Bach or Haydn, Wagner or Bartók? Their

[1] 'Indeterminacy in the New Music', in *Score* (Jan. 1961) pp. 11 ff.

compositions differ in many important ways: in melodic style, rhythmic organization, harmonic idiom, texture and instrumental timbre. But they are alike in one fundamental respect. In this music, tones are related to and imply one another. Think, for instance, of the 'Liebestod' of Wagner's *Tristan*, rising in cumulative sequences towards its powerful moment of climax; or of the kinetic intensity with which the slow introduction of Bartók's *Sonata for Two Pianos and Percussion* surges toward the Allegro which follows; or of the way in which the rondo-finale of a Haydn symphony plays with our expectations that the main theme will return – failing to appear just when everything seems ready for its return or arriving just when it is least expected.

Because of its marked, though not necessarily obvious, structure and pattern, as well as because of our past experience with its grammar and syntax, such music is perceived as having a purposeful direction and goal. As we listen, we make predictions – albeit unconscious ones – as to where the music is going and how it will get there. Of course, our predictions may not be correct. What we expect may not occur or may do so at an unexpected time or in an unexpected way. But whether expected or not, what actually does take place is colored by the fact that predictions were made. That is, musical events are felt to be normal and regular, surprising, amusing, or even shocking, as they conform to, or deviate from, our predictions. Such goal-oriented music I shall call *teleological*. (Similarly, the converging lines of perspective in a painting by Raphael or David, the swirling kinetic curves in a Delacroix or Van Gogh, the directional 'arrows' in a Tintoretto or Picasso, all focus the viewer's attention upon particular points of structural culmination – upon visual goals. And in literature the normal syntax of language, the delineation of human motivation, the explication of causal relationships among the sequential events of a narrative, and the presentation of dialectically structured thought processes – all combine to create a purposeful, goal-oriented art.)

But the music of the avant-garde directs us toward no points of culmination – establishes no goals toward which to move. It arouses no expectations, except presumably that it will stop. It is neither surprising nor, once you get used to its sounds, is it particularly startling. It is simply *there*. And this is the way it is supposed to be. Such directionless, unkinetic art, whether carefully contrived or created by chance, I shall call *anti-teleological* art. Here is what one young composer, Christian Wolfe, has to say about this music:

> The music has a static character. It goes in no particular direction. There is no necessary concern with time as a measure of distance from a point in the past to a point in the future. It is not a question of getting anywhere, of making progress, or having come from anywhere in particular . . .[1]

What is involved here is not simply a new technique or method for realizing similar ends – as in the music of Haydn, Wagner, or Bartók where different means of creating goal-directed motion were employed. What is involved is a radically different set of ends, whether these ends be achieved by careful calculation as in the music of Stockhausen, the paintings of Tobey or Rothko, and the writings of Beckett and Alain Robbe-Grillet, or by random operations as in the music of Cage, the paintings of Mathieu, or the chance theatre of MacLow's *The Marrying Maiden*. And underlying this new aesthetic is a conception of man and the universe, which is almost the opposite of the view that has dominated Western thought since its beginnings.

In spirit, practice, and general aesthetic outlook anti-teleological art has much in common with that inspired by existentialism. Nevertheless, on the philosophical level at least, these positions can be distinguished. Because the differences between these facets of avant-garde art may be important in the future, I shall, where it seems useful, attempt to describe them. However, since both positions continue to change and evolve, the distinctions must be taken as only suggestive and provisional. The relationship of anti-teleological aesthetic to Oriental philosophy – and particularly to Zen Buddhism – is more direct and obvious. For many of these artists have read and been influenced by both Eastern and Western

[1] Quoted in Cage, *Silence*, p. 54.

writings on Oriental philosophy. However, it is important to remember that 'influence' is not a one-way reaction. The artists' thinking and his creative attitudes must be *ready* to be influenced. It is said, for instance, that Debussy was 'enthralled by the Javanese *gamelang* at the Exposition Universelle' of 1889.[1] He was able to be 'enthralled' because the art of music, and his attitude towards it, had developed to a point where such an experience was possible. Had Beethoven heard the same music a hundred years earlier, he would probably have walked away muttering: 'Barbarians!' It is because Western art had already developed ways of perception, modes of organization, and philosophical attitudes approximating those of the Orient that the avant-garde could be influenced by them.

III

In his book, *Silence*, John Cage urges the composer to 'give up the desire to control sound, clear his mind of music (in the ordinary sense), and set about discovering means to let sounds be themselves rather than vehicles for man-made theories or expressions of human sentiments'.

Several important facets of the aesthetic of anti-teleological art are implicit in this quotation. In the first place, one is not listening to the relationships among the sounds presented, but just to the sounds as sounds – as individual, discrete, objective sensations. A syntax or grammar, which would order these sounds and relate them to one another — creating goals, expectations, or a basis for prediction – is to be avoided at all costs. (And one way to make sure that you establish no syntactical-grammatical relationships is to employ the systematic use of chance as a technique of composition.)

Just as composers have sought, by chance or calculation, to destroy musical syntax by avoiding tonal relationships, repetitions, regular rhythmic patterns and the like, so painters have avoided symmetry, perspective, and the presence of recognizable objects or

[1] Edward Lockspeiser, *Debussy* (1936) p. 240.

patterns because these tend to structure visual experience, creating goals and points of focus. Similarly in literature the elements of syntactical organization – plot, character and conventions of grammar – have been progressively weakened until almost only words remain.

Why must one avoid the structured syntax of pattern and form? Can't sounds be heard as sounds, or colors be seen as colors, and still be, so to speak, embedded in an order which relates the sounds or colors to each other? Perhaps. But it seems clear that the more one perceives the relationships among things, the less one tends to be aware of their existence as things in themselves – as pure sensation. You may, at some time, have had a radio or TV go haywire so that the sound was completely distorted. If so, you may recall that when the syntax and grammar became obscured and meaning was lost, you became very aware of sound *qua* sound – you became conscious of the bleeps, bloops and squeaks. Or, if a color slide is so out of focus that the objects depicted cannot be recognized, one becomes intensely aware of the experience of color as color.

It is to the naïve and primitive enjoyment of sensations and things for their own sakes that these artists seek to return. We must rediscover the reality and excitement of a sound as such, a color as such, and existence itself as such. But our habits of perception and apprehension – the accumulation of traditional preconceptions which we bring to aesthetic experience – prevent us from seeing and hearing what is really *there* to be perceived. The avant-garde novel aims, writes Bruce Morrissette, at

> an art which creates a basically true and real image of man's situation among men and in the universe of neutral objects, without metaphysics, and scraped clean of the 'crust' of obsolete ideas.[1]

Traditions, theories, systems are obstacles to be overcome by the artist as well as the writer. 'As examples of such obstacles', the painter, Mark Rothko, cites '(among others) memory, history or

[1] 'The New Novel in France', in *Chicago Review*, XV 19.

geometry, which are swamps of generalization from which one might pull out parodies of ideas (which are ghosts) but never an idea in itself.'[1]

The existentialists, too, seek to destroy our habitual modes of perception and thought. But for somewhat different reasons. The anti-teleological position holds that traditions, systems, and the like are evil because they limit our freedom of thought and action, deaden our sensitivity to sensation and feeling and, in the end, alienate man from nature of which he should be a part. Art should, in Cage's words, be

> an affirmation of life – not an attempt to bring order out of chaos nor to suggest improvements in creation, but simply a way of waking up to the very life we're living, which is so excellent once one gets one's mind and one's desires out of its way and lets it act of its own accord.

For the existentialists, on the other hand, man's alienation is part of the very nature of things. Nor is the revitalization of sensitivity of paramount importance. For them the accretion of traditional patterns of behavior and modes of thought must be stripped away not only because they limit human freedom, but because, as noted later, they limit the individual's responsibility for the choices he makes.

Particularly when contrasted with the more somber outlook of existentialism, the anti-teleological position with its emphasis upon the value of naïve, direct experience and upon the natural goodness of man, seems characteristically American. This, despite clear overtones of romanticism à la Rousseau. Cage's words, quoted above, remind us of Thoreau's:

> If men would steadily observe the realities only, and not allow themselves to be deluded, life, to compare it with such things as we know, would be like a fairy tale and the Arabian Nights' Entertainments . . . (However) by closing the eyes and slumbering, and consenting to be deceived by shows, men establish and confirm their daily life of routine and habit everywhere, which is still built on purely illusory foundations.

[1] *15 Americans*, ed. Dorothy C. Miller (New York, 1952) p. 18.

On a somewhat less romantic level, the grammar and syntax of art – and their counterparts in the world of affairs: custom, law, and philosophy – are to be avoided because they continue to act as the vehicles for social and personal teleology. The anti-novel in which nothing happens because no event follows from any other, the directionless painting in which lines and colors lead to no points of culmination, and the anti-kinetic musical composition in which tones are without implications are perhaps at least in part a reaction to the mess that goals, purposes, and strivings have got us into.

The language of science, so full of words like force, tendency, and natural selection which imply purposes and goals, is, according to this viewpoint, misleading. Rightly understood these are purely descriptive terms. Nature has, in fact, no purpose or goal. It simply is. And like nature, art should simply present. Thus Rauschenberg contends that 'painting is always strongest when . . . it appears as a fact or an inevitability, as opposed to a souvenir or arrangement.[1]' Alain Robbe-Grillet makes a similar point when he says of Beckett's *Waiting for Godot* that 'the theatrical character is on *stage*, this is his primary quality – he is there'. Or, put negatively, the scenes in Robbe-Grillet's novel, *Jealousy*, are, Morrissette tells us, presented 'without a word of analysis or commentary, in the pure domain of phenomenological semantics'. Similarly Cage, as we have seen, emphasizes that sounds should simply 'be themselves rather than vehicles for man-made theories or expressions of human sentiments'.

Our relationship to art, like our relationship to nature, ought to be one of acceptance. This is true for both the artist and the audience. The artist, whether employing chance methods of composition or applying a predetermined arbitrary formula, should accept the unanticipated result without seeking to impose his personal will on the materials or making them conform to some syntactical preconception of what ought to take place. Similarly the audience should entertain no preconceptions, make no predictions as to what will occur, and force no organization upon the

[1] *Sixteen Americans*, ed. Dorothy C. Miller (New York, 1959) p. 58.

series of individual sounds, colors or words presented to it. A composer whose graphs are realized or whose notated fragments are ordered by a performer must accept what happens – and so should the audience, just as one accepts the sounds of a thunderstorm, a crying baby, a busy office, or silence.

Here another difference between the anti-teleological position and that of existentialism becomes apparent. In the anti-teleological view, existence is *one*. Being and non-being are not opposites, but merely different states which may happen to something. Death is a change in existence, not the negation of it. (Again one is struck by the kinship with a sort of pantheistic romanticism and thinks, perhaps, of Wordsworth's poem, 'A slumber did my spirit seal'.) Silence is just as real, just as much a part of existence as sound. As Rauschenberg has said: 'A canvas is never empty.' For the existentialists, however, being and non-being are categorical opposites. Death is a horrible stupidity, making life absurd, yet at the same time making the human responsibility for individual choice the crucial fact of existence and the basis for whatever human dignity there is.

IV

The denial of the reality of relationships and the relevance of purpose, the belief that only individual sensations and not the connections between them are real, and the assertion that predictions and goals depend not upon an order existing in nature, but upon the accumulated habits and preconceptions of man – all these rest upon a less explicit but even more fundamental denial: a denial of the reality of cause and effect. Once this is seen, the aesthetic of the avant-garde begins to make sense. For this is a position of uncompromising positivism[1] – or what I shall hereafter call *radical empiricism*.[2]

[1] After writing the first draft of this article, I discovered that George Rochberg had also used the word 'positivism' to characterize the tendency towards indeterminacy in contemporary music. See *Score* (Jan. 1961) p. 11.

[2] I have decided to call the particular facet of avant-garde art with which I shall be concerned 'radical empiricism' rather than using the more usual designation of

It may, at first blush, seem ridiculous to deny the reality of cause and effect – the existence of necessary connections between events. However, we should remember the contentions of such philosophers as David Hume. And in the world of contemporary science – particularly in quantum mechanics where events are not fully determined or predictable, but only probable – the concept of cause and effect has again become problematical. After quoting from the second edition of Kant's *Critique of Pure Reason* to the effect that 'all changes happen in accordance with the law of the connection of cause and effect', Henry Margenau states that 'physics knows of no such law; as a matter of fact there is no plausible way of defining cause and effect'.[1]

Actually this point requires some qualification. What is denied in quantum mechanics and in the aesthetic of radical empiricism is not the theoretical possibility of a principle of causation, but the theoretical possibility of isolating any particular event as being the cause of another particular event. This is the case because, since the world is seen as a single interrelated field or continuum in which everything interacts with – is the 'cause' of – everything else, there are no separable causes and effects. Thus, discussing the emission of alpha-particles, Heisenberg writes that:

> We know the forces in the atomic nucleus that are responsible for the emission of the α-particle. But this knowledge contains the uncertainty which is brought about by the interaction

'Abstract Expressionism' for several reasons: First, the term abstract expressionism has generally been used to apply to painting, but I shall be talking about a movement in all the arts; second, the term has been employed to designate several different tendencies in contemporary painting and consequently lacks precision; third, and more important, applied to the art and aesthetic with which I am concerned, the term is inaccurate and misleading. For the art we are discussing is not abstract in the sense of 'being derived from' or a 'distillation of'. Quite the contrary. It is concrete in the extreme. Nor is it an 'expression' of the artists' will or mind. Intention and communication are not involved. However, I did not want to use the term 'positivism' because today, at least, that philosophical movement has been engaged in the construction of abstract, logical systems – a concern alien to many of the artists I am discussing.

[1] 'Meaning and Scientific Status of Causality', in *Philosophy of Science* (New York, 1960) p. 437.

between the nucleus and the rest of the world. If we wanted to know why the α-particle was emitted at that particular time we would have to know the microscopic structure of the whole world including ourselves, and that is impossible.[1]

This viewpoint, developed in connection with the *micro*scopic world of electromagnetic phenomena and quantum mechanics, has been applied with varying degrees of precision by the radical empiricists to *macro*scopic events.[2] Cage, for instance, writes that 'there are an incalculable infinity of causes and effects . . . in fact each and every thing in all of time and space is related to each and every other thing in all of time and space'. Doré Ashton seems to echo this point when he tells us that Mark Tobey's paintings symbolize 'his Heraclitan conviction that all things come out of one and one out of all things'.[3] In a similar vein Robbe-Grillet asserts that chronological time distorts our experience because it 'forces events into a pattern of causality and imposes an unjustifiable logic upon them'.[4]

To deny causality is to deny the possibility of prediction. All notions of 'if this occurs, then that must, or will probably, follow' disappear. Consequently (if I may be permitted so teleological a word), the music, art and literature of the avant-garde is characteristically unkinetic and unfocused. In a novel by Robbe-Grillet, a composition by Cage, or a painting by Guston one does not, and should not, feel that one event follows *from* (is the result of) what went before. It simply 'comes after'. And since no event or

[1] Werner Heisenberg, *Physics and Philosophy* (New York, 1962) pp. 89–90.

[2] Paradoxically, the aesthetic of the avant-garde at one and the same time accepts and rejects contemporary science. On the one hand, it employs the concepts and terminology of modern physics – indeterminacy, field theory, and the relativity of space-time – with freedom, if not always with accuracy, to rationalize and support its position. On the other hand, it represents a revolt against the world which science has revealed – a world which is an abstract, man-made construct of unseen particles governed by unknown forces. And the radical empiricists, reacting against the artificiality of this unreal world (as well as its fruits), have sought to reaffirm the existence, the poignancy, and the value of directly experienced sensation.

[3] 'Mark Tobey', in *Evergreen Review*, IV 31.

[4] Quoted in Richard Gilman, 'Total Revolution in the Novel', in *Horizon*, IV 99.

action refers to or leads us to expect any other event or action, the sequence of events is, in any ordinary sense of the term, meaningless.

Again there is a difference in emphasis, if not in practice, between the existentialist wing of the avant-garde and the radical empiricist wing. For the radical empiricist, the isolated object freshly experienced is the chief source of value. The existentialist position, on the other hand, is apparently paradoxical: the meaning of the art work lies in its objectification of the meaninglessness of life itself. 'What Sartre calls the "anti-novels" of Nathalie Sarraute', writes Norman Podhoretz, 'seem . . . to represent a total submission to the meaninglessness of existence.'[1]

The denial of causality and the correlative denial of predictability have important consequences. In the first place, rational choice, which depends upon the possibility of envisaging the results of alternative courses of action, becomes a senseless fiction. (This being so, it makes no difference whether an art work is produced by the consistent use of chance, by a purely gratuitous act, or by the rigid application of a predetermined formula.) And attending to such a work of art, we, the audience, should not attempt to choose, even unconsciously, among alternative possibilities for continuation. We ought to remain detached: seeing, hearing, and observing the objective series of empirical events.

In their attitude toward choice the existentialists differ fundamentally from the radical empiricists. In the existentialist view, one performs a gratuitous act not because choice is meaningless, but because only by such an act can the individual become fully responsible for his actions. In all other actions, responsibility can, in part at least, be attributed to the social order, traditional modes of thought and behavior, habit, and the like. Seen in this light, existentialism seems closer to the tradition of western culture than does radical empiricism. For existentialism still seeks to solve the problems of the human condition – of man's despair in the face of death and his alienation from the world – within the basic

[1] 'The New Nihilism and the Novel', in *Partisan Review*, XXV 585. [Since reprinted in Podhoretz, *Doings and Undoings* (New York and London, 1964). *Ed.*]

framework of humanism, in which man is morally responsible for his own acts.

If predictability and choice are impossible, art cannot be a form of communication. For communication requires that the artist imagine or predict how others – the audience – will interpret and respond to the words, sounds, or visual designs he produces. As I write or speak, I choose my words by acting as my own audience; and I presume that you will respond to my words as I do. If I can't imagine what your responses will be – and the systematic use of chance, for instance, precludes this possibility – then there can be no communication. Furthermore, in literature and music at least, communication depends to a considerable extent upon the use of a traditionally established, shared syntax and grammar. When these are destroyed, communication is substantially weakened. The artists and composers of radical empiricism are well aware of this. The painter, Clyfford Still, for instance, asserts that: 'Demands for communication are both presumptuous and irrelevant. The observer usually sees what his fears and hopes and learning teach him to see.'

Furthermore, because aesthetic experience involves no predictions, no meanings, and no communication, the value of the work of art cannot be judged – any more than one can judge nature or natural objects in themselves. 'Value judgments', writes Cage, 'are not in the nature of this work as regards either composition, performance, or listening. The idea of relation being absent anything . . . may happen. A "mistake" is beside the point, for once anything happens it authentically is.' Since error depends upon having a preconceived idea of what should occur, this is indeed an art without error. As the painter, Georges Mathieu, has said: 'if we reduce the part played by conscious control in favor of spontaneity, we find ourselves in the position where *the very notion of error* . . . disappears'.[1]

To deny the existence of causality is to deny the possibility of *form*. For implicit in relational concepts such as beginning, middle and end, antecedent-consequent, or periodicity, is the belief that

[1] *From the Abstract to the Possible* (Paris, 1960) p. 21.

the events in question are causally connected. An end, or conclusion, is something *caused* by what went before. However, in order to follow the form of a painting by Jackson Pollock, writes Allan Kaprow, 'it is necessary to get rid of the usual idea of "Form", i.e. a beginning, middle, and end, or any variant of this principle – such as fragmentation'.[1] Or, as Robert Goldwater has said: 'In Mark Rothko's pictures the apparent end lies close to the apparent beginning – so close in fact, or in apparent fact, that they are almost indistinguishable.'[2] In a similar vein the composer, Stockhausen, has spoken of 'creating in each piece an individual, self-contained world like a crystal, which, when one turns it, is always different, but always the same. It should not matter whether the music is played from the beginning, middle, or end, so long as it goes full circle.'[3] In literature, too, syntactical form has disappeared. Because the human mind – and the world as seen through it – is considered to be an unorganized conglomeration of sensations, thoughts, memories, and effects whose relationships (if such exist) we can never really know, the words and phrases describing the mind's activity have been divested of syntactical significance. The functional relationships among parts of speech tend to disappear. Similarly, sentences and paragraphs do not follow from one another. On the highest architectonic level — that of the succession of described events — expressed motivation and 'all rhetorical analysis of psychology' are rejected.[4] 'Character and plot having disappeared from the novel,' writes Jean Bloch-Michel, 'what is left? The object, replies Robbe-Grillet. And an object without meaning.'[5]

Because it presents a succession rather than a progression of events, this art is essentially static. There are no points of culmination or of focus. All events are equally important and time, as we ordinarily conceive of it, dissolves. There is only duration. For

[1] 'The Legacy of Jackson Pollock', in *Art News*, LVII 26.
[2] 'Reflections on the Rothko Exhibition', in *Arts*, XXXV 43.
[3] Quoted in Francis Burt, 'An Antithesis', in *Score* (March 1957) p. 69.
[4] Morrissette, 'The New Novel in France', in *Chicago Review*, XV 19.
[5] 'The Avant-Garde in French Fiction', in *Partisan Review*, XXV 469.

ordered time depends upon the existence and recognition of the beginnings and terminations of separable events or patterns. Stockhausen's image of music as a turning crystal which is always the same, yet always different, suggests Alfonso Ossario's description of a painting by Jackson Pollock:

> The picture surface, with no depth of recognizable space or sequence of known time, gives us the never-ending present. We are presented with a visualization of that remorseless consolation – in the end is the beginning.[1]

And writing of Samuel Beckett's novel, *Malone*, Robert Hatch says that we 'cannot possibly tell whether we are with him (Malone) twenty minutes, two months, or ten years'.[2]

These remarks suggest why radical empiricism probably finds its most idiosyncratic and convincing expression in the plastic arts. Since meaningful visual experience is, so to speak, directly and naturally presentational and objective, painting and sculpture can excite our interest and contemplation in the absence of explicit representation and an established vocabulary, grammar and syntax. We can, that is, respond sensitively to fortuitous coincidences of line, color, space and texture, delighting in the patterns and relationships which we discover, even as we do in looking at nature.

Even more important, the plastic arts are *de facto* static and timeless. Motions, goals, time and syntax are not explicitly stated, but must be inferred by the viewer. Hence the order in which events are perceived is never fully determined in painting or sculpture. Even a teleological work in which our attention is directed toward definite focal points, can be viewed in many different orders. Similarly it is possible to experience the structure of the visual world, whether ordered or disordered, without presuming that it communicates, has purposes, or even involves cause and effect.

In music and literature, on the other hand, a *de facto* chronology is *necessarily* established – even in a work whose order is the pro-

[1] *15 Americans*, p. 15. [2] 'Laughter at Your Own Risk', in *Horizon*, III 113.

duct of pure chance. And we tend, whether by nature or learning, to infer causal relationships from such a sequence of events. We attempt, that is, to relate earlier events to later ones, discovering implications and attributing a causal order to the series of stimuli. These tendencies are enforced by the fact that the sounds to which we attend most carefully are man-made, conventional events in which teleology and communication are almost invariably presumed. However, though both music and literature are by nature syntactical, temporal arts, they differ in that literature necessarily represents events in the external world of objects, actions, passions and the like, while music does not.

If this analysis is correct, is it not possible that the arts will move in the coming years *not* toward a common, monolithic aesthetic as they seem to be doing today, but toward a plurality of aesthetics, each appropriate to its particular art? The aesthetics of the visual arts might, for instance, continue to develop the tendencies implicit in radical empiricism, reflecting the culture's conceptualization of the natural order of the material universe. And, since language is man's means of relating himself to the external world and to other men, literature might continue to be primarily concerned with the relationships of men to each other and to the universe – with the social-moral order or, if you will, disorder. And music, operating in the realm of pure syntax without reference to external objects or events would, then, develop an order reflecting and paralleling the structure and patterns of human mental processes.

V

Whatever one may think of the art of radical empiricism, the philosophical position of which it is the expression is, as I have tried to indicate, a consistent and tenable one. That this is the case was pointed out by Alfred North Whitehead:

> Suppose that two occurrences may be in fact detached so that one of them is comprehensible without reference to the other. Then all notion of causation between them, or of conditioning,

> becomes unintelligible. There is – with this supposition – no reason why the possession of any quality by one of them should in any way influence the possession of that quality, or of any other quality, by the other. With such a doctrine the play and inter-play of qualitative succession in the world becomes a blank fact from which no conclusions can be drawn as to past, present, or future, beyond the range of direct observation. Such a positivistic belief is quite self-consistent, provided that we do not include in it any hopes for the future or regrets for the past. Science is then without any importance. Also effort is foolish, because it determines nothing.[1]

New art has always been difficult to understand because it has always sought to replace old habits of thought and perception, old preconceptions and prejudices with new ways of looking at the world and fresh startling insights. But however drastically they may have modified the means of expression, the content, or the form of art, composers, artists and writers of the West have, until now, had the same essential ends – the same essential philosophical orientation – as their predecessors. There is a clear line of development from Aeschylus to Shakespeare to Joyce, from Phidias to Michelangelo to Picasso, and from Monteverdi to Beethoven to Stravinsky.

Radical empiricism is not, however, an attempt to redefine goals and values within the long tradition of western art and thought. Rather it seeks to break decisively with the most basic tenets of that tradition. 'This new literature', says Robbe-Grillet, '. . . is going to represent – in its fulfillment – a revolution more total than those from which such movements as romanticism and naturalism were born.'[2] And Cage, criticizing Edgar Varèse, the patron saint of experimental music, for injecting his personality – his teleology – into the music he writes, says that Varèse 'is an artist of the past. Rather than dealing with sounds as sounds, he deals with them as Varèse.'

Man is no longer to be the measure of all things, the center of

[1] *Modes of Thought* (New York, 1938) p. 226.
[2] Quoted in Gilman, in *Horizon*, IV 96.

the universe. He has been measured and found to be an undistinguished bit of matter different in no essential way from bacteria, stones and trees. His goals and purposes; his egocentric notions of past, present and future; his faith in his power to predict and, through prediction, to control his destiny – all these are called into question, considered irrelevant, or deemed trivial. For these artists, writers and composers – and, however influential they may be, it must be remembered that they represent only a small segment of the world of contemporary art – for these radical empiricists, *the Renaissance is over.*

Here is Georges Mathieu's description of the present situation:

> Our whole culture has allowed itself to be permeated, since the end of the Middle Ages, by Hellenistic thought patterns which aimed at bringing the cosmos down to human proportions and limited the means of access to an understanding of the Universe to those provided by reason and the senses. . . . For the past ten years, painting . . . has been freeing itself from the yoke of this burdensome inheritance. After twenty-five centuries of a culture we had made our own, we are witnessing in certain aspects of lyrical non-configuration a new phenomenon in painting – and, one might add, in the arts in general – which calls into question the very foundations of 40,000 years of aesthetic activity.[1]

Whether the Renaissance is over for the rest of us – for our culture generally, only the future will tell. But whether it is over or not, the merit of considering the art and aesthetic of radical empiricism seriously is that it challenges us to discover and make explicit the grounds for beliefs and values which we unconsciously take for granted. If we are to defend our beliefs – our faith in a world of purpose and causality, time and prediction, choice and control, communication and morality, we must ask the most fundamental questions that can be asked: questions about the nature of man, his relationships to other men, and his place in the universe. Can we do more than simply assert our beliefs? Can we give empirically verifiable reasons for them?

[1] Op. cit., p. 9.

Frank Kermode Modernisms

I

A few weeks ago there was an advertisement in the *New York Review of Books* for a novel – an 'ardent novel available only by mail' – described by its publishers as 'the story of a *modern* American marriage'. A favourable review is cited; this explains that 'the painfully significant enigma' of modern marriage is the ambition and aggressiveness of woman. The husband in Meredith's sequence, lying there in tragic parody of a knight on a tomb, thought it was her infidelity. To both novelist and poet, 'modern' seems to mean something not altogether agreeable and disturbingly at odds with the way things used to be. If pressed, they might talk about radical changes in sensibility, as they affect love. Pressed harder, they might have to admit that ambition, aggression, infidelity, are no newer in women than refined or perverse sensibility in men.

The fact is that we all use the word in this unexamined way, and nobody notices how nearly meaningless it is until called to order by some pronouncement about The Modern. The context will usually be aesthetic, but even this limitation is not enough to ensure accurate definition. In 1894 John Lane announced that his *Yellow Book* 'would seek always to preserve a delicate, decorous and reticent mien and conduct' but 'at the same time have the courage of its modernness'; that it would be 'charming', 'daring' and 'distinguished'. The first number included a poem by Gosse, Saintsbury on wine, and a very good story by James, but only Beerbohm's 'Defence of Cosmetics' could be called 'daring' or, in its fashion, courageously modern. Later this might be said of the realism of Crackanthorpe; for modernism was not only the dangerous line of Beardsley, the clever excess of Wilde and Beerbohm; it was also the French cult of things as they now are. These two modernist strains were well distinguished by Arthur Waugh, in his attack on the magazine; he found on the one hand 'a want of restraint which starts from enervated sensations', and on the other an 'excess which results from a certain brutal virility', itself the consequence of 'coarse familiarity with indulgence'. Or you might say, exquisite sensibility and realism. The new sensibility required formal experiment, which was therefore associated with 'decadence'; squatness and ugliness of presentation, a prudent lack of enterprise in content, could now confer upon publishers who declined the financial and social risks of modernity a certain adventitious virtue. 'Modernness', in its Flaubertian alliance of formal experiment and realism, took over the old role of shock and protest, and its practitioners dissociated themselves from many concerns that seemed characteristically bourgeois, such as politics.

Politics returned in a later phase of modernism, and has now gone away again; on the whole one would want to say that politics has no essential part in the Movement. If there is a persistent world-view it is one we should have to call apocalyptic; the modernism of the nineties has a recognisable touch of this, if decadence, hope of renovation, the sense of transition, the sense of an ending or the trembling of the veil, are accepted as its signs. At such times there is a notable urgency in the proclamation of a break with the immediate past, a stimulating sense of crisis, of an historical licence for the New. And there appears to be a genuine continuity here, for all modernist art and literature between the nineties and now is associated with similar assumptions in some form or other. Naturally the contents of *The Yellow Book* have long ceased to look modernist; its cosmetic avant-gardism is archaic, as neurasthenia is archaic; its artists were not only Beardsley and Conder but Puvis de Chavannes and Moreau. The radical changes that were *implied*, somehow, by what they were doing – revolutions in architecture, music, painting and poetry of which the historical sources were already available – were of a kind that shocked such a survivor as Beerbohm and forced Yeats to accept the necessity to 'remake' himself. The difference between *The Yellow Book* and, say, *Blast*, indicates that however persistent the apocalyptic background may have been, some pretty radical changes of manner had occurred. The nineties were certainly precursors, but anybody who thinks about what modernism now means will rightly look more closely at the period between 1907 and, say, 1925; this is true despite the fact that the 'aestheticist' element in later modernism is often underplayed, and still accounts for that disregard of politics in relation to literature characteristic of so much modern criticism, so that Conor Cruise O'Brien justly but hopelessly complains that even intelligent critics are 'acute on small matters and absent-minded on very large ones'.[1]

There is at present much interest in this question of the modern. Professors Ellmann and Feidelson published a huge 'case-book' on the subject;[2] it was a work of which Professor O'Brien might well complain in the same terms, but it was also a serious attempt to get into one volume most of the radical documents of modernism, to explain the parts of Kant and Blake, Nietzsche and Darwin, Wilde and Pater, as well as Apollinaire and Tzara, Werner Heisenberg and Karl Jaspers. Now Mr Cyril Connolly, by way of choosing and describing its '100 Key Books', has undertaken to characterise what he calls *The Modern Movement*.[3] He limits himself to the years between 1880 and 1950, and to works in English and French. The American book is vast, solemn, and not easy to get on with; Mr Connolly's is light, bright, superficially stylish; but the Americans offer much useful and reliable information. Mr Connolly's book does not.

It seems a pity that Mr Connolly, so well equipped by temperament and experience, should have settled for *sprezzatura* and forsworn accuracy and sometimes thought itself. He sneers at professional students not for their real faults but because they get

[1] *Writers and Politics* (1965).

[2] *The Modern Tradition* (*Backgrounds of Modern Literature*), ed. Richard Ellmann and Charles Feidelson, Jr (London and New York, 1965).

[3] *The Modern Movement. 100 Key Books from England, France and America, 1880–1950* (1965).

things right, and at 'theses' because they begin when 'the Titans depart'; yet after all he is a professional student, and this is a thesis, written, on the author's view, when the Titans have departed, arguing a view of a literary period, and complete with a bibliography (admittedly by another professional hand, and not in any case very useful). Whether we call it a thesis or not, it too often lapses into its own kind of nonsense and bad writing: 'As all objectives were gained and the complacent hypocrisy of the nineteenth century punctured, its materialism exposed, the Movement ground to a halt.' It is hard to say whether a good supervisor would be more depressed by the historical generalisation or by the prose.

However, Mr Connolly is not wholly serious. That books are written in German or Russian will not prevent some of them from being 'Key Books', and he also omits all books he does not like (Claudel, Stein); all books that are not both good and rebellious, as well as historically important; and all books that are simply think-books (Bergson, Freud, Russell, Wittgenstein, etc.). With what is left he is pleasantly dogmatic. The Modernists inherited 'critical intelligence' from the Enlightenment, and 'exploring sensibility' from the Romantics. As near as it can be dated, the union of these qualities occurred around 1880; the Journals of Baudelaire and the *Bouvard et Pécuchet* of Flaubert ('our two fallen fathers') appeared posthumously in the following year. Mr Connolly's comment on Baudelaire can only reinforce the strong sense we may already have of slapdash unexamined history; he claims that this poet, 'after being for many years the private literary property of Arthur Symons . . . has emerged to be re-interpreted by Sartre and magnificently translated by Robert Lowell'. After 1880 modernism came on in waves: the generation of James, Mallarmé, Villiers de l'Isle Adam, Huysmans, is followed by that of Debussy, Yeats, Proust, Jarry, Valéry, and that by the generation of Eliot, Pound, Lawrence and Joyce; and so on. Admittedly such lists don't lend themselves to fine distinctions and discriminations, but this one makes the subject sound unintelligibly weird.

It is true that there was a sort of *translatio studii moderni* from France to England and America, and that the peak period of the Movement must be placed somewhere around 1910–25, as Connolly says. But it is begging many questions to argue that after the death of Virginia Woolf and Yeats the Movement became 'degenerate'. He avoids some difficulties by saying that Beckett, together with Robbe-Grillet and Butor, 'falls just outside my dateline' (*whoroscope*, 1930, *Proust*, 1931, *More Pricks than Kicks*, 1934, above all *Murphy*, 1938). The 'frustrated forties' saw the end of the Movement. Burroughs and the Beats represent a continuing rebelliousness here attributed merely to the prevalence in America of 'unrevised attitudes to drug-addiction and homosexuality'. The best Mr Connolly can say about the future is that the Movement's 'twin features', described arbitrarily as 'faith in the intellect' and 'belief in the validity of the imagination', together with 'the enlargement of sensibility', will again 'inspire a masterpiece'.

It all sounds much too simple, and it is – labels are doing the work, announced as a labour of historical enquiry; words such as 'imagination' and 'sensibility' are being left to get on with it while the author chats brightly. Why did the Movement peter out? Because there were so many defectors from Humanism: 'some followed Huysmans into the religious fold (Eliot, Edith Sitwell, Waugh, Auden), some became fascists (Pound, Lewis) etc.' Subsequently modernism flourishes best in the theatre, where there is more to rebel against (Artaud, Ionesco, Pinter). If anybody would have been more surprised than Wyndham Lewis to be called a humanist or a defector from humanism, it might perhaps have been Artaud. Malraux defected from humanism by becoming a politician. What can 'humanism' mean in this discussion where 'dehumanisation' is more commonly regarded as a symptom of the modern? Well, Gide and Forster perhaps; but when one speaks of their humanism one is simply in a different context from that appropriate to a discussion of modernism. By his abuse of this word, and in an entirely different way, of 'sensibility', Mr Connolly simply obscures this interesting issue;

his book will add confusion where there is enough already.

Since there is so much talk about these and related matters at the moment, it might be useful to look about for recent writing that has something to say. With this in mind, and perhaps somewhat naïvely, I turn to a very large new *Encyclopedia of Poetry and Poetics*[1] and look up 'modernism'. This volume is the work of very learned contributors and editors. If you want to look up *meiosis* or *meiurus, payada* or *penthemimer*; if you need a quick run through Albanian, Byelorussian, Danish, Persian, Romansh or Yiddish poetry; if you are disturbed by the problems of belief, meaning, intention, or by the relationship of poetry with science or religion; if more modern critical terms baffle you, and you are interested in *tenor and vehicle, symbol, pseudo-statement, tension, ambiguity, aesthetic distance*; or in the vexed problems associated with *baroque, mannerist, conceit*, then on all this and more you will as a rule be amply supplied. But if you look up 'modernism' you will be told that it was 'the movement in Hispanic letters which began in the 1880s in Sp. America, blending Sp., Fr., and other foreign influences. . . .' Hard by, however, there is a long entry on *Modern Poetics*; it begins at 1750, which is justifiable, and begins to cater for our present interest when it reaches, after much scholarly explanation, our fallen father Baudelaire and his accursed sons the Symbolists. They were in favour of music and against logic (of course; and for all Mr Connolly says anti-intellectualism is a characteristic of the modern) – and they gave rise to a newly orientated poetry, arcane even when colloquial, interested in mental states below consciousness ('extended sensibility') and prolific of very difficult notions, such as Rilke's *Dinge* and Imagism and the vorticised or classicised Symbolism of Hulme, Pound, and Eliot. Hence 'the theoretical banishment from poetry (we might add the visual arts) of much that has been generally thought to give it seriousness'; and hence also a number of baffling ambiguities in the terminology, still troublesome; for it is hard to say what, for example, 'imagist' means, and even harder to be clear about 'abstraction' (good in, say,

[1] ed. Alex Preminger (Princeton and London, 1965).

Worringer and Stevens, bad, generally, in the literary critics)[1] or even 'intellect', an anti-poetic instrument which poets are always blamed for not using.

There is some use in the *Encyclopedia* article; it ends with a very cautious statement of one of the major issues in later modernism, warning us that if we think poetry 'the completest mode of utterance' we should not be too anxious to separate it from other forms of discourse. Can 'art' and 'life' really be as discontinuous as the early modernists implied? More of that later, when it will emerge, I think, that poetry is not the best point of departure here. The theory behind very modern poems (like, for example, the enchanting 'Message Clear' of Edwin Morgan, in the *TLS*, 13 Jan. 1966) seems to derive from the thinking of artists and musicians, and finally we shall have to turn to them. The poetry encyclopaedia has, not surprisingly, no entry under avant-garde or New, though there are the Neoterici of Cicero to prove how old the New really is, as well as the New Criticism, now worn out, and the New Humanism, another historical description. It does not help us much with the modern Modern, the new New.

Professors Ellmann and Feidelson find the concept of the modern 'intimate and elusive' but are quite sure it does not refer, as some now argue, only to what was happening almost half a century back; according to them, it 'designates a distinctive kind of imagination, themes and forms, conditions and modes of creation, that are interrelated, and comprise an imaginative whole'. This suggests a sort of imaginative mutation, ways of looking and making virtually unrelated to older ones; and that is another frequent claim one should look into. But it also suggests, and rightly, that we will agree to call a great many different things modern – not only the novel I mentioned at the start, or *Who's Afraid of Virginia Woolf?* ('strange love talk, is it not?' as Meredith remarked), but all manner of superficially incompatible things: *Howl* and *The Waste Land*, Cubism and Pop Art, Stravinsky and Stockhausen, Gaudier-Brzeska and Tinguely. Other things we

[1] The *Encyclopedia*, I have just confirmed, provides a good brief account, under 'Concrete and Abstract', of the way they use such words.

shall most of us agree not to call modern: Meredith, for instance, Verlaine; and some we're not sure about: Freud, for example. We might even agree, at any rate so far as the arts are concerned, to a useful rough distinction between two phases of modernism, and call them palaeo- and neo-modernism; they are equally devoted to the theme of crisis, equally apocalyptic; but although they have this and other things in common, they have differences which might, with some research, be defined, and found not to be of a degree that prevents our calling both 'modernist'.

Before these or any other phenomena are called 'modern' there must, presumably, be a general sense of escaping from an older state of affairs, an *ancient* state of affairs. *Devotio moderna* was not only a movement for a new morality and a new piety, but a movement against pilgrimages and excessive ornament. The Moderns of the seventeenth century had a programme with a similar double aspect. Their enemies would call it a preference for grubs and darkness over sweetness and light, but in its positive aspect it was a programme calling for new knowledge and assuming such knowledge could be made relevant to human concerns; while in its negative aspect it contested the view that the culture of their time necessarily imitated and must always be a derivative of ancient culture. This was perhaps the decisive confrontation, involving as it did the overthrow of ideologies both ecclesiastical and secular: the revision of the theologian's *curiositas*, which limited the bounds of intellectual enquiry in one way, and of the secular ideologies, imperial or sentimental-republican, which insisted upon classical norms and tended to equate change with decay. This was the Modernism that created a climate in which hypothesis and fiction replace myth, in which the nature of ideologies is to undergo rapid alteration and fragmentation, as ours do. Imperialism, republicanism, and classicism survive, of course, but much fragmented and modified, and usually in a posture of resistance. In short, the great seventeenth-century Modernism involved getting out from under something, and modernist programmes have the habit of claiming that this is what they always have to undertake.

What we got out from under is one of those questions that set up, it seems, an infinite recession. Certainly it wasn't Victorian complacency, as Mr Connolly is satisfied to say; and the reason why the American scholars find themselves reprinting Goethe and Kant is quite simply that the historical study of modernism will certainly take you back there, and beyond, to the seventeenth century obviously, and less obviously beyond that. This was long ago recognised, but stated in a distorted way, by those who sought parallels between the two periods as each exhibiting the catastrophes that come from too much brain and too 'abstract' sensibility. It is now much more fashionable to regard our plight as without parallel, and the past as irrelevant – an equally misleading error, and one which is responsible for further ideological muddle, as well as for certain false oppositions between palaeo- and neo-modernisms.

Nothing can so muddle argument as the claim that there exist no standards by which an argument can be judged, or even no language in which it can be opposed; this claim is now supported by several influential epoch-makers, notably Marshall McLuhan, an admirable and fertile enquirer who has brought science fiction to history and sociology. There are other theorists who overdevelop the metaphor of a cultural *mutation* and say that this renders the old 'humanism' powerless to judge or communicate, since the mutants speak an anti-language and aim at anti-art, anti-ethics, anti-sex; and instead of merely revising the concept of form – as the Romantics and the palaeo-modernists did – have abolished it. Indeed, if we want to understand the similarities and differences between the modernisms we shall have to look at this question of form more closely, and one way to do it is to introduce into the discussion some books and articles which seem to have a more direct view of the problem than any I have cited so far.

II

Do we have a 'rage for order'? It has long been thought so, and the arts have long been thought ways of appeasing it. But there is a difference between 'order' and 'an order'; and what looked like the first can become simply the second: the conventional literary epic, or pastoral poetry, or the heroic couplet, or history-painting, or sonata form. In the older modernism, order grew mysterious. Following the organicist view of the Romantics, and the sophisticated gloss put on it by the Symbolists, poets treated it as the property of works purged of personality and emotion, new shapes out there and independent, perceptible by an *élite* which had transcended bourgeois literacy and could operate a logic of imagination divinely void of intellect. Thus the highly original forms of Mallarmé and, later, Eliot have only a tenuous relation to more vulgar notions of form; and in the novel, for instance, the kind of extreme deviation from prevailing norms which had formerly occurred only now and again became a regular feature. The great experimental novels of early modernism – Kafka, Proust, Joyce, Musil, for instance – are all characterised by a kind of formal desperation.

Yet such forms continue to assume that there was an inescapable relationship between art and order. Admittedly when the forms of the past grew 'rigid and a bit absurd' you undertook a new research and produced modern forms. They might indeed be extremely researched, as Wallace Stevens suggests when he says we can't have the old 'romantic tenements' and that what will now suffice may be much less palpable: merely, perhaps

> a woman dancing, a woman
> Combing. The poem of the act of the mind –

but the act of the mind is still a form-creating act, and the form it creates provides satisfactions of the rage for order that cannot be had in life not so organised, so that art is different from life at least in this respect. And this view of the matter is still in many ways standard. Its various implications – 'autonomy', anti-didacticism, everything that attracts, both for the arts and the criticism that attends them, the epithet 'formalist' – are, whether we like it or not, still in the minds of most of us when we consider a work of art. The first thing we think about is that this is a poem or a painting, and if it were not we should find another way of speaking than the one we choose. 'Art is not life and cannot be/A midwife to society', as Mr Auden pedagogically explained. It may be somewhat illiberal, even untruthful, and reactionary by its very nature, as Mr Trilling thinks; he is supported in his opinion by the theorist of the formal *nouveau roman*,[1] and also, as we will see, by the Apollinaire of the New York renaissance, Harold Rosenberg.

The fact that we have inherited the set of aesthetic assumptions I have very roughly sketched above makes it all the more difficult for most of us to understand the new men, who claim to be destroying the barrier between life and art, asserting their indifference to the question 'Is this a picture?' and professing contempt for ideas of order, especially when they can be associated with the art of the past. Nevertheless we shall certainly understand the older modernism better if we come to terms with the newer.

There seems to be much agreement that the new rejection of order and the past is not quite the same thing as older rejections of one's elders and their assumptions. It is also agreed that this neo-modernist anti-traditionalism and anti-formalism, though anticipated by Apollinaire, begins with Dada. Whether for the reason that its programme was literally impossible, or because their nihilism lacked ruthlessness, it is undoubtedly true, as

[1] Robbe-Grillet's collection of essays, *Pour un nouveau roman* (1963), has now been translated, together with the short pieces called *Instantanes* of the same year, by Barbara Wright (*Snapshots & Towards a New Novel*).

Robbe-Grillet comes out strongly for the view that art is gratuitous, and from the revolutionary point of view 'useless, if not frankly reactionary'; the fact that it will be on the good side at the barricades must not be allowed to interfere with our freedom to pursue 'art for art's sake'. This book, obviously one of the really important contributions to the theory of the novel, deserves much more discussion than it has yet had in England or the U.S., and the translation is welcome. Incidentally, there is some justice in his claim that it is other people who have *theories* of the novel; his is an anti-theory, so to speak, and for all his 'formalism' that is modern enough.

I should also mention here Anthony Cronin's *A Question of Modernity* (1966), which is somewhat commonplace in the title essay, and often simply bad-tempered, but as to the matter of art and life there are some fine things, including a brilliant long essay on *Ulysses* and one about the novel which is full of original ideas.

Harold Rosenberg has observed, that Dada had many of the characteristics of a new art movement, and that its devotees treated it as such, so in some measure defeating its theoretical anti-art programme. Raoul Haussmann only recently attacked the 'Neo-Dadaists' because what they were doing was ignorantly imitative, but also because it wasn't 'art'. If what we want is to understand anti-art I suppose our best plan is to follow the signs back to Duchamp, whose importance in this context is that he expressly and intelligently sought ways of 'no longer thinking the thing in question is a picture'.

The point is simply this: whereas such a poem as *The Waste Land* draws upon a tradition which imposes the necessity of form, though it may have none that can be apprehended without a disciplined act of faith, a new modernism prefers and professes to do without the tradition and the illusion. At this point there begin to proliferate those manifold theoretical difficulties associated with neo-modernist art. They are usually discussed in terms of the visual arts and music, probably because they are palpably even greater in the case of literature. Duchamp could pick something up and sign it, as he did with his 'ready-mades', and this raises problems, but at least it does not move from 'the plane of the feasible'.[1] In poetry one can of course use chunks of economic history and the collage of allusion, but usually for some formal irony, or to get a special effect by juxtaposition; simply to sign a passage ready-made by somebody else is not to change it but to plagiarise it. It would not matter if the borrowed passage were in most ways as commonplace as a mass-produced artefact; it would only be a more obvious case of plagiarism. A legal argument about a Duchamp ready-made might be interesting, but one would not expect a plausible defence in a case on literary ready-mades. The closest poetry can get is to cultivate impersonality and objectivity – Williams' wheel-barrow and Robbe-Grillet's

[1] The phrase is Beckett's. His 'Three Dialogues with George Duthuit' (on Tal Coat, Masson, and Bram von Velde) have been published, together with the early Proust essay, as *Proust and Three Dialogues* (1965). They are excellent examples of Beckett's philosophico-farcical manner in the discussion of the arts.

out-there coffee-pot. The things made are not wheel-barrows and coffee-pots; but similar theoretical assumptions are involved.

Duchamp used to speak of 'Dada blankness' – a way of making or naming things which has no relation to humanity or nature, no 'responsibility'; 'alien objects of the outer world', as Lawrence D. Steefel puts it, 'are reduced to instruments of the artist's transcendence of them'.[1] Blankness and indifference, like the 'impersonality' of Eliot, become, from one angle, a kind of egoism, indeed dehumanisation has always been, from this angle, the apotheosis of the *culte du moi*. Dada, at its most apocalyptic, had it both ways, and proclaimed that after the present phase of quasi-Oriental 'indifference' there was to follow an era of purged personality, 'the cleanliness of the individual' (according to Tzara). The extreme and, on the face of it, paradoxical individualism of, say, Eliot, Lewis, and Pound, is the parallel case.

There is, in short, a family resemblance between the modernisms. 'Indifference' and the abrogation of 'responsibility' are the wilder cousins of the more literary 'impersonality' and 'objectivity'. The palaeo-modernist conspiracy which made a cult of occult forms is not unrelated to the extremist denial that there are any. These are the self-reconciling opposites of modernism.

Duchamp, like some of the older poets, is a man whose intelligence has been dedicated to anti-intellectualist ends. The paradoxical pursuit of randomness in the arts – a consequence of doctrinaire anti-formalism – is now carried on with every resource of ingenuity by very intelligent men. To early modernists the subjection of personality and the attack on false orders were one and the same process; the logicians of neo-modernism have not only accepted the position but developed it into an attack on order, perhaps not successfully, but with energy. Viewed in this light, the new theory bristles with paradoxes as, for instance, in Rauschenberg's remark: 'I consider myself successful only when I do something that resembles the lack of order I sense.'

The theoretical situation is in detail puzzling, but it must be

1 'The Art of Marcel Duchamp', in *Art Journal*, XXII (Winter 1962–3).

admitted that in its practical and personal manifestations it is often pleasing, and indeed funny. For this reason Calvin Tomkins' book, which is not only a set of 'profiles' but an intelligent presentation of ideas, is as amusing as it is informative.[1] His four subjects are Duchamp, Cage, Tinguely, and Rauschenberg. They are all, as he says, very different – Duchamp more detached, Tinguely more destructive, Cage more programmatic, and Rauschenberg more anti-art than the others – but they have many interests in common. For instance, all of them say that *art is much less interesting than life*, and not generically different from it. *All* seek impersonality (though strong personalities are vividly present in their work) and therefore *experiment with chance. All accept that art is characteristically impermanent*, being made up of things without transcendence. And *all* rejoice to *work on the borders of farce.* They make random and unpredictable things in a world consisting of random and unpredictable things, an activity that is anyway absurd; the purposeless is pursued with fanatic purpose, and this is farcical in itself. One difference between a Tinguely machine and a Heath Robinson is that Tinguely takes it past the drawing-board stage, but another is that Robinson aimed to amuse, whereas Tinguely, though he doesn't mind amusing, has no affective purpose at all; and there is a somewhat similar distinction to be drawn between a Hoffnung concert and a Cage recital.

These propositions and attitudes are characteristic of neo-modernism, and the literary man should learn what he can from them. The view that art is not distinct from life, to which (in Cage's words) it is 'inferior in complexity and unpredictability', is of course 'anti-formalist'. In the past we have simply been wrong in supposing that order is a differentia of art; hence the new doctrine, propounded by Cage and given an elaborate philosophical defence in Morse Peckham's recent book, *Man's Rage for Chaos*, that 'a work of art is what the perceiver observes in what has been culturally established as a perceiver's space. This can be anything. . . .' In Cage's *4′ 33″* the pianist sits before a closed

[1] *The Bride and the Bachelors* (1965).

piano for four minutes and thirty-three seconds, and the only sound is what floats in randomly from outside – bird songs, buses – or what the spectators make themselves. So long as there is a concert-situation there is a concert, although the content of the concert is random and minimal. This is a logical step forward from Satie's musical collage, and is perhaps more like Kurt Schwitters simply planting bits of things before the observer in a 'perceiver's space'. It pushes the protest against 'retinal' art, and its musical equivalent, to the point where it is a protest against the seriousness of palaeo-modernist protest, and where the difference between art and joke is as obscure as that between art and non-art. A point to remember, though, is that the development can be seen as following from palaeo-modernist premises without any violent revolutionary stage.

I myself believe that there is a difference between art and joke, while admitting that it has sometimes been a difficult one to establish; and I would want to call *4′ 33″* and Tinguely's famous self-destroying machine ('Homage to New York') jokes, if only because however satisfying they may be, they do not seem sufficient in respect of the needs which what is called art has usually sufficed. But this is to use very inadequate criteria; and having supposed vaguely that neo-modernism was heavily dependent on the extension of modernist *theory*, I was glad to find a philosopher, Arthur Danto,[1] saying this very thing in a sharper way. Danto says the difficulties begin when one forsakes the old mimetic assumptions and says, for example, that a painting of a table is as real as a table. If this seems hard to take when the painting is Post-Impressionist, it becomes easier when the objects painted are strictly inimitable – the numeral 3, for example. Any copy of that simply *is* the numeral 3. What kind of mistake would you be making if you tried to sleep in Rauschenberg's famous *Bed*, which is a bed? You cannot mistake reality for reality. Danto suggests that we use *is* in two distinct senses. We say a spot of white paint 'is' Icarus, and also that 'this is a bed'. These two usages are presumably both present when we say that

[1] 'The Artworld', in *Journal of Philosophy*, LXI (1964) p. 571.

Bed is a bed; but if it has paint on it and is in a 'perceiver's space' then the Icarus *is* is dominant.

Actually for Danto the physical location is less important than a sort of intellectual or theoretical space – call it the atmosphere of intellectual assumptions breathed alike by the artist and the game spectator. 'To see something as art requires something the eye cannot descry – an atmosphere of artistic theory, a knowledge of art: an artworld.' But it all comes to the same thing. If Brillo made their boxes out of plywood they would still not be Warhols, and if Andy Warhol made his out of cardboard they would not be Brillo boxes. Provided the 'space' and the aesthetic convention were right he could simply sign a real Brillo box ready-made. We know what it is by where it is, and by our being induced to make the necessary theoretical dispositions (or not, as the case may be). As Jasper Johns puts it, 'What makes an object into art is its introduction into the art context.' Examination question: what is a signed Warhol Brillo box, found among a stack of Brillo boxes in a supermarket? Assuming, of course, that the customer knows the name, and what Mr Warhol does for a living. Another related question is, 'What makes an object into a joke?'

The theory so far is, then, that art is whatever you provide when the place in which you provide it is associated with the idea, and contains people who are prepared to accept this and perhaps other assumptions. Mr Peckham would argue that our failure to have noticed this earlier resulted from persistent brainwashing of the kind that stuck us with the notion that we have a 'rage for order' – that we seek the consolations of form amid natural chaos inhospitable to humans. This on his view is entirely false. We have, on the contrary, a natural rage for *chaos*, and that is why, truth prevailing, the concept of form is dead. With it, of course, dies the notion that the artist has to do with establishing and controlling a formal order in his work (what Keats in ignorance called 'information') and, also, the notion that this order has a high degree of permanence. Of course these notions have at one time or another been challenged before, though perhaps not in their totality. Artists have always known that there was an element of luck in good work ('grace', if you like) and that they rarely knew what they meant till they'd seen what they said; and there are milder traces of a doctrine of impermanence in palaeo-modernism, even in poetry, where Stevens articulates it clearly. But once again neo-modernism presses the point, and gives it practical application.

The most notable instance of this seems to be the neo-modernist *interest in chance*, a long way on from what Pope called 'a grace beyond the reach of art'. Although 'indeterminacy' has affected literature, it has had more importance so far in music and painting, and these are the areas of theoretical enquiry. There is obviously room for teleological differences between artists who employ random methods. Duchamp argued that 'your chance is not the same as my chance', and when he wrote random music insisted on regarding it as personal to himself and also funny. His dislike of order (perhaps as betraying him) emerges in his publishing the notes on *La Mariée mise à nu par ses célibataires, même* in random order, so anticipating the cut-up-fold-in Burroughs techniques as he had anticipated the methods of aleatory music. Duchamp, incidentally, for all that he anticipated so many innovations, was always aware of a tradition, which he saw himself at the end of; he is a very sophisticated figure, and his critical superiority over some of his imitators is demonstrated by his immediate dismissal of the idea that there could be any relation at all between indeterminacy in the arts and indeterminacy in physics - this covert bid for prestige promotes nothing but confusion, of which (*pace* Peckham) there is quite enough already.

The layman who wants to know what Cage is up to has to confront the whole problem of chance. Without being at all solemn, Cage employs his considerable intellectual resources on constantly changing experiments of which the object is to ensure that his art shall be 'purposeless play'. Not for the first time in musical history, harmony (ideologically associated with ideas of order) had to go; it is replaced by 'duration', as percussion replaces melody. Music now deals in every kind of natural sound (the extreme naturalism of Cage is attributed by Tomkins to the influence of Coomaraswamy) but every other kind of sound too, except what might be made by conventional instruments. The piano has bolts between the strings to make it simply percussive. As to indeterminacy, Cage achieves it by many methods, including the use of the Chinese *I Ching*, coin-tossing, and yarrow-sticks. In one piece every note required 18 tosses of the coin. He has now found speedier methods, using, like Rossini before him, the imperfections in paper as a suggestion for notes.

On this view of the matter there can be no question of judging a particular work. 'There are no catastrophes', he says. But audiences can of course be affected in different ways, and Cage has experienced wildly various reactions from his auditors. Certainly he sometimes makes it seem that aleatory art is, in a manner as yet unexplored, close to humour, as in the view of some tragedy is close to farce. Tomkins quotes Virgil Thomson's account of a concert given in New York's Town Hall in 1958, which was

> a jolly good row and a good show. What with the same man playing two tubas at once, a trombone player using only his instrument's mouthpiece, a violinist sawing away across his knees, and the soloist David Tudor crawling around on the floor and thumping the piano from below, for all the world like a 1905 motorist, the Town Hall spectacle, as you can imagine, was one of cartoon comedy . . . it is doubtful whether any orchestra ever before had so much fun or gave such joyful hilarity to its listeners.

This is very sympathetic, but Cage believes that 'everything is music', and if, out of all the possibilities, he often chooses what makes for hilarity, this is evidence that such an assumption tends to confuse art and joke. There is a current of apocalyptism in all neo-modernism, and it is no bad thing that the Last Days should occasionally be good for a giggle, as they are in Beckett and in Tinguely. 'When seeing a Tinguely mechanism for the first time,' says Mr Tomkins, 'most people burst out laughing.' Peter Selz, the Curator of Painting and Sculpture at the Museum of Modern Art, was delighted with the famous *Homage*, which destroyed itself successfully, though not quite in the manner planned by the artist, before a distinguished audience. 'Art hasn't been fun for a long time', he said. Duchamp congratulated Tinguely on being funny, and said that humour was a thing of great dignity.

It is, no doubt, part of the picture that all this would have been less funny had it gone according to plan. The humour is a matter of chance, of 'aleation'. Aleation in the arts, I suggested, pushes into absurdity a theory based on observation, that chance or grace plays a role in composition. In so far as palaeo-modernism pretended to be classical, it played this down; but between it and neo-modernism stands surrealism, and other manifestations of irrationalism. On the new theory, which has a wild logic, you leave everything to chance, and the result will make its mark either as very natural or as providing the material from which the spectators in the right place will make whatever they need for their own satisfaction. Anything random has some kind of an order, for example a bag of marbles emptied on to a table. Or, as Monroe Beardsley puts it in that interesting section of his *Aesthetics* from which I have already borrowed, 'they are in an order but not in order'. The difference between aleatory art and the art which appealed to 'the logic of imagination' (if for a moment we imagine them both as doctrinally pure) is simply this: the first in theory seeks only to produce an order (and in this it cannot fail) whereas the palaeo-modernists had not reduced grace to chance, and sought to make order.

So far as I can see this would be disastrous to aleatory art were it absolutely true, because the reason why we speak of 'an order' as against 'order' is that we drop the article as a sign of our wish to dignify what interests us more. We have discovered, in the process of getting by amid what Cage thinks of as the wonderful complexities of life, that order is more *useful* than an order: for example, the telephone book would be harder to use if the names were printed haphazardly. In a way, the alphabetical arrangement is perfectly arbitrary, but it happens to be something that the people who compose it and the people who use it agree upon. It might, of course, be said to give a very imperfect impression of the chaos and absurdity of metropolitan life, or life at large, and the consolation of knowing you can find your way about in it is in some ways on some very strict views perhaps somewhat fraudulent. It is not quite 'order', anyway, though it is not merely *an* order. And this in-between order is what most of us mean when we talk about 'order' in aesthetic contexts. One can avoid a divorce between art and life without going to the extremes recommended by Cage. When Cage grew interested in mushrooms, Mr Tomkins tells us, he quickly discovered that some knowledge of their botanical classifications was a necessary modification to the practice of eating them at random. Also, that when somebody arranged a happening in his honour, which required that he should be physically assaulted, he had to say that whereas his view was still that 'anything goes', this was so only on condition that one could manage to be free without being foolish. The implied criteria can only derive from the sort of education which distinguishes between an order and order. Order turns out to be more comfortable and useful. If our orientation towards it is not biological, then it is cultural or educational; and the reason why an order posing as order sometimes seems funny is that it is always presupposing orderly criteria by which its randomness can be measured; so, having reduced tradition to absurdity, one makes allusions to tradition by which the absurdity can be enjoyed as such. Thus silent music and Void or all-black painting presuppose music which employs conventional sounds and paintings with colour and shapes. They are piquant allusions to what fundamentally interests us more than they do, and they could not exist without it.

Aleatory art is accordingly, for all its novelty, an extension of past art, indeed the hypertrophy of one aspect of that art. Virgil Thomson, who has been very sympathetic to Cage, allows that his random music is not really a matter of pure chance but a game of which the rules are established by Cage himself. No matter how much he tries to eliminate his own choices, it is always a Cage-game, and it involves calculation and personal choice. Admirers of William Burroughs' *Nova Express* admit that the randomness of the composition pays off only when the text looks as if it had been composed straightforwardly, with calculated inspiration. The argument is too obvious to labour. Even Duchamp didn't pick up *anything* and sign it. What seems clear is that a gross overdevelopment of the aleatory element in art tends to make it approximate to humour; thus the seventeenth-century conceit, over-extended, became a joke, and Jan Kott can turn *King Lear* into an Absurd farce. The transformation would be impossible without the theory and practice of predecessors. Its nihilism is meaningless without an assumption of the plenitude of the past. Thus neo-modernists tend to make the mistake they often scold other people for, which is to attribute too much importance to the art of the period between the Renaissance and Modernism. By constantly alluding to this as a norm they despise, they are stealthy classicists, as the palaeo-modernists, who constantly alluded to Byzantine and archaic art, were stealthy romantics.

The point that in theory there is nothing very new about the New, that it is in this respect little more than a reverie concerning the more important and self-conscious theoretical developments of an earlier modernism, was made by Harold Rosenberg himself, when he observed that an Oldenburg plastic pie is not so much art, and not so much a pie, as 'a demonstration model in an unspoken lecture on the history of illusionism', adding that this kind of thing represents the union of many different tendencies in the art of the past half-century. As to why modernism should tend in this way towards pure farce, he cites Marx's observation that farce is the final form of action in a situation which has become untenable. Like Beckett's hero we can't and must go on, so that going on is bound to look absurd, a very old-fashioned thing to be doing in a situation you have shown to be absolutely new. On rather similar grounds he attacks the fashionable 'aesthetics of impermanence', saying that the time-philosophy involved is evidently wrong, and that 'art cannot transform the conditions of its existence'.

Such comment amounts to a radical criticism of the theoretical bases of extreme neo-modernism, and it prepares one for the impact of one of Rosenberg's best essays, so far uncollected, which appeared five years ago in *Partisan Review* under the title 'Literary Form and Social Hallucination'.[1] When the subject is literary, this critic seems to see with great clarity truths which become obscure when the topic is painting. He argues that the form of a literary work militates against its ability to 'tell the truth'; that part of its function is in fact to 'tease us out of thought' (an argument employed, though with differences, by Iris Murdoch). From the political point of view this makes form suspect, anti-liberal; for by inducing us to descend into 'outlived areas of the psyche' it takes our eye off the actual demands and complexities of the world, arms us against the fact. It could perhaps be said that here the criticism is of Form when it ought to be of forms; that the constant researches of the arts into form have as a principal motive the fear that obsolescent *fictions of form* will cause them to be untruthful, or at any rate less truthful than they might be. Thus it is in the popular arts, where the question of fidelity to the world as the clerisy understands it does not arise, that conventions have the longest life. While the highbrows are pondering the *nouveau roman*, the great mass of fiction, which satisfies readers who would never dream of asking that it do more than a token amount of truth-telling, continues to use the old stereotypes.[2] It would probably not occur to the readers of such fiction that truth required the abolition of form, and if it did they might think the point too obvious to mention. Fiction, they know, is different from fact because it is made up. Yet it is precisely this point that, as Rosenberg sees, we need to be reminded of. Theoretical contempt for form in the arts is a fraud:

> Formlessness is simply another look and a temporary one at that. In time, organisation begins to show through the most

[1] *Partisan Review*, XXVII (1960) pp. 638–51.

[2] It is obviously in order to meet this situation head-on that Robbe-Grillet makes his fantastic claim to have at last found a novel-form acceptable to the man-in-the-street.

> chaotic surface . . . the subversion of literary form cannot be established except by literary means, that is, through an effort essentially formal.

This must be true, despite all the recent anti-formalist researches, aleatory, schismatic, and destructive. In neo-, as in paleo-modernism, research into form is the true means of discovery, even when form is denied existence. So it becomes a real question whether it helps to introduce indeterminacy into the research, even if it is agreed that this is possible to any significant degree (and it is not). With Danto's remarks in mind we can at least ask ourselves whether dependence on an erroneous or distorted theory cannot be in some measure incapacitating. We need not expect a simple answer, since a great deal that is done in the arts is founded on theoretical positions which are later found to be leaky. We should need to reflect that there is a certain prestige to be had in minorities by professing to concur with what appear to be revolutionary advances in thinking about the arts, so that to find an audience claiming proficiency in a 'new' language is at present by no means difficult.

This is not a problem one can discuss now. What one can do is to say of the theoretical bases of neo-modernism, in so far as they show themselves in relation to form, chance, humour, that they are not 'revolutionary'. They are marginal developments of older modernism. It can be added that disparagement and nihilist rejection of the past are founded partly on ignorance and partly on a development of the earlier modernist doctrine which spoke of retrieving rather than of abolishing tradition, just as the abolition of form is a programme founded on the palaeo-modernist programme to give form a new researched look. A certain extremism is characteristic of both phases. Early modernism tended towards fascism, later modernism towards anarchism. What Cyril Connolly calls the evolution of sensibility is a matter of changing theory, Romantic egotism becoming 'impersonality' and this later turning into 'indifference'. In the same way chance replaces the quasi-fortuitous collocation of images characteristic of earlier modernism. The anti-humanism – if Mr Connolly will allow the expression – the anti-humanism of early modernism (anti-intellectualist, authoritarian, eugenicist) gives way to the anti-humanism (hipsterish, free-sexed, anti-intellectualist) of later modernism. As to the past, history continues to be the means by which we recognise what is new as well as what is not. What subverts form is 'an effort essentially formal'; and the sense of standing at an end of time, which is so often invoked as an explanation of difference, is in fact evidence of similarity. The earlier humanism went in a good deal for the capitalisation of what Mr Rosenberg calls 'outlived areas of the psyche', and so does the new modernism. For a 'movement' united by a detestation of logic, Modernism has generated an immense amount of theory; this was admittedly much more coherently expressed in the earlier phase. Later it has been scrambled by the babble of smaller voices, and in some aspects has been heavily over-developed, as I have tried to show. In both periods there was a natural tendency (inescapable from the Modern at any period and easier to justify half a century back) to exaggerate the differences between what one was doing and what had been done by the old guard, and this has helped to conceal the truth that there has been only one Modernist Revolution, and that it happened a long time ago. So far as I can see there has been little radical change in modernist thinking since then. More muddle, certainly, and almost certainly more jokes, but no revolution, and much less talent.

That is why, on the one hand, one cannot accept Cyril Connolly's assurance that it is virtually all over, and on the other Leslie Fiedler's claim that we have a new art which reflects a social revolution so radical that he can call it a 'mutation' and its proponents 'The New Mutants'. Henceforth, he thinks, literature and criticism will forget their traditional observance of the past, and observe the future instead. Pop fiction demonstrates 'a growing sense of the irrelevance of the past' and Top writers ('post-Modernists') are catching on. The new subject will be 'the end of man' and the transformation of the human life into something else (curious echoes of Mr Connolly, who also thinks of modern writers as post-Modernist in sensibility, and anti-humanist). Mr Fiedler explains that he means by humanism the cult of reason, from Socrates to Freud. This is what is being annihilated, and the Berkeley students were protesting against universities as the transmitters and continuators of the unwanted rationalist tradition. The protest systematically *anti*-s everything: a Teach-in is an *anti*-class, banners inscribed FUCK are *anti*-language, and so on. Actually a teach-in is only an especially interesting class, because the teachers are volunteers and just as engaged with the subject as you are. There is the oddity that this class really works as a 'dialogue' and goes on and on. The banners are no more anti-language than collage is anti-painting; and the absolutely blank banners which succeeded the 'dirty' ones were certainly a very good joke in the new manner, like Rauschenberg erasing a De Kooning, or a Klein Void.

Fiedler's observations on the new life-style of his 'mutants' are more interesting. He stresses a post-Humanist contempt for ideology; a post-Humanist sexuality which has discounted masculinity and developed characteristic patterns of homosexuality, usurpation of female attitudes, polymorphous perversity; and a new range of post-Humanist stimulants (LSD, airplane glue, etc.). This amounts, he argues, to 'a radical metamorphosis of the Western male', a real revolt, unlike our ritual contentions with father. These young people have made the breakthrough into new psychic possibilities, and recognise in Burroughs the laureate of their conquest.[1]

Whether this is nonsense, and whether it is dangerous, is not in my brief. I will only say that the whole argument about 'mutation' is supererogatory; the phenomena should be explained more economically. If the prole has replaced the shepherd, the

[1] It may be worth pointing out that Burroughs himself is far from thinking that drugs will bring this about. His recent *Paris Review* interviewer (Fall 1965) asked: 'The visions of drugs and the visions of art don't mix?' and he said, 'Never. . . . They are absolutely contraindicated for creative work, and I include in the lot alcohol, morphine, barbiturates, tranquillisers.'

savage, and the child as pastoral hero, it isn't surprising that those who seek to imitate him should imitate his indifference to ideology and history and sexual orthodoxies. This is not the first recorded instance of libertinage among the well-heeled. Drugs and four-letter words are not new, even among poets, even among the young. The display may seem unusually ostentatious, but it is worth remembering that Fiedler's prime example derives from that highly abnormal institution, the University of California, the unbelievably well-endowed organ of the educational aspirations of a state which is not only very rich but is famous for the unique predominance of the young in its population. In so far as the protest was 'pure' protest, protesting against nothing whatever, it was surely luxurious attitudinising on a familiar undergraduate model but hypertrophied by sociological causes well within the purview of old-style analysis. A thirst for the unique and unprecedented can lead to the exaggeration of triviality or to claims which the record refutes. Thus Fiedler finds in Ken Kesey's (very good) novel *One Flew Over the Cuckoo's Nest* evidence that for the mutants the schizophrenic has replaced the sage as culture hero, whereas by narrating this madhouse fiction from the point of view of an inmate of limited and varying perceptiveness Kesey is using a now time-honoured technique. So with his sociological observations. Even the male behaviour to be observed after midnight on 32nd and 43rd Streets hardly needs to be explained in terms of 'mutation'. To treat such symptoms as unique, as signs that the Last Days are at hand, is to fall headlong into a very naïve – and historically very well-known – apocalyptism.

It is the constant presence of more or less subtle varieties of apocalyptism that makes possible the repetitive claims for uniqueness and privilege in modernist theorising about the arts. So far as I can see these claims are unjustified. The price to be paid for old-style talk about 'evolving sensibility' is new-style talk about 'mutation'. It is only rarely that one can say there is nothing to worry about, but in this limited respect there appears not to be. Mr Fiedler professes alarm at the prospect of being a stranded humanist, wandering among unreadable books in a totally new world. But when sensibility has evolved that far there will be no language and no concept of form, so no books. Its possessors will be idiots. However, it will take more than jokes, dice, random shuffling, and smoking pot to achieve this, and in fact very few people seem to be trying. Neo-modernists have examined, in many different ways (many more than I have talked about), various implications in traditional modernism. As a consequence we have, not unusually, some good things, many trivial things, many jokes, much nonsense. Among other things they enable us to see more clearly that certain aspects of earlier modernism really were so revolutionary that we ought not to expect – even with everything so speeded up – to have the pains and pleasures of another comparable movement quite so soon. And by exaggerating the drawing, the neo-modernist does help us to understand rather better what the Modern now is, and has been during this century.

On the whole the older modernists understood all this better. Eliot in his last book, tired and unadventurous as it is, said it once again, and said it right:[1]

> A new kind of writing appears, to be greeted at first with disdain and derision; we hear that the tradition has been flouted, and that chaos has come. After a time it appears that the new way of writing is not destructive but re-creative. It is not that we have repudiated the past, as the obstinate enemies – and also the stupidest supporters – of any new movement like to believe; but that we have enlarged our conception of the past; and that in the light of what is new we see the past in a new pattern.

This does not allow for the possibility that chaos and destruction could be introduced into the programme, except by its 'stupidest supporters'; but it does seem to make sense in terms of a quest for 'what will suffice'. In the end what Simone Weil called 'decreation' (easy to confuse with destruction) is the true modernist process in respect of form and the past. Or if it is not we really shall destroy ourselves at some farcical apocalypse.

[1] *To Criticise the Critic* (1965).

Ihab Hassan The Literature of Silence

O lovely green dragon of the new day, the undawned day, come, come *in touch, and release us from the horrid grip of the evil-smelling old Logos! Come in silence, and say nothing.*

D. H. LAWRENCE, *Apocalypse*

Nowadays, the idea of an avant-garde in literature seems unduly naïve. Inured to crisis, we have also lost the confident sense of direction. Which way is forward? Literature, turning against itself, aspires to silence, leaving us with uneasy intimations of outrage and apocalypse. If there is an avant-garde in our time, it is probably bent on discovery through suicide. Thus the term anti-literature, like anti-matter, comes to symbolise not merely an inversion of forms but will and energy turned inside out. Is the future, then, all vagrancy and disaster for all who profess the Word?

Though I cannot believe that the Word exhausts the possibilities of spirit, I know enough to admit that disaster comes and goes in cunning rhythms. Mystics have always maintained that the way down is always the way out, and that the end of things heralds a new beginning. Negative transcendence, as we nowadays say, is transcendence nevertheless. And therefore silence in literature does not necessarily augur the death of spirit.

The point to be made about the new literature is different: whatever is truly new in it evades the social, historical, and aesthetic criteria which defined the identity of the avant-garde in other periods. The force of evasion (or absence) in the new literature is radical indeed; it strikes at the roots and induces a great silence. But the same force, moving in trunk and foliage, bursts into a great babel of noises. The most audible of these is the cry of outrage, the voice of apocalypse. Henry Miller and Samuel Beckett, both intimates of silence, are both such obsessive babblers; between them, they sound all the notes of the new hollow speech. Their conjunction is therefore no mere conceit. Standing as mirror images of the contemporary imagination, they end by reflecting its peculiar assumptions. In old-fashioned parlance, they are the two masters of the avant-garde today.

But my discourse on Miller and Beckett may become inaudible without some clarification of the terms of silence. Let me begin with outrage.

'Is art always an outrage – must it by its very nature be an outrage?' Lawrence Durrell, who had Miller in mind, once asked. We can grant that art contains an element of danger and even subversion without conceding that all art is outrage. A particular genre of modern literature, however, seems to vindicate Durrell's view; it constantly touches on the experience which awes him. That experience is one of metaphysical revolt: Ahab striking the sun if it insulted him, or Ivan Karamazov returning his life-ticket to God. It is metaphysical revolt and at the same time metaphysical surrender, which is the desire for nothingness: 'the cry of the mind exhausted by its own rebellion', as Camus put it. In outrage, then, the very being of man is put on trial. What ensues is a dialectic of violence, demonic action and demonic reaction compressed into a terrible unity which becomes finally a naught.

The violence I associate with the new literature is obviously of a special kind. It presupposes Dachau and Hiroshima but is not necessarily limited by them. It is absurd in the sense that no meaning or value can be assigned to it. Its function is to turn men into things. Under its pressure, the metamorphosis of the human form is downward, towards the worms of Beckett, the insect people and sentient ooze of Burroughs. It is not temporal but spatial, not historical but ontological, an inescapable part of the landscape. Indeed, as Frederick Hoffman argues in *The Mortal No*, this landscape of violence suggests a 'total withdrawal of the humanly familiar from both assailant and victim. Moreover, the assailant and the victim are both part of the landscape'. This metaphor of violence as landscape or inscape is an extreme definition of outrage which my discussion assumes. We can begin to see such a landscape take shape in the surreal Broadway scenes of Miller's *Tropic* books, and we can see what is left of it, as violence recedes into death, in the empty spaces of Beckett's *Endgame* or *How It Is*. Over these scenes there always hangs a frightful stillness.

Precisely at this point, a reversal of motive may take place in the literature of silence; a new term may come into play. For if outrage is a metaphor of the void, may it not also serve as an appeal to being, and thus beget its opposite, which is a metaphor of apocalypse?

The transformation is easy to see in Negro literature where old-fashioned protest yields to modern outrage and outrage becomes apocalypse. Thus James Baldwin derives the title of his threatening book from a Biblical epigraph: 'God gave Noah the rainbow sign: No more water, *the fire next time*.' Apocalyptic violence, as D. H. Lawrence knew, can be conceived by the oppressed as retribution rather than reward, and even the Millennium can be understood by them as an idea of power rather than of love. In other types of recent literature, however, the feelings behind apocalyptic metaphors are more complex. Implied in them is something close to a total rejection of Western history and civilisation. Implied in them, too, is a rejection of human identity, the image of man as the measure of all things. 'I want to be a machine,' says Andy Warhol, and whether he speaks in earnest or in jest, he speaks for the cripples of Beckett, the satyrs of Miller, and the junkies of Burroughs. Indeed, revulsion against the Western self strikes deeper than the repudiation of history and civilisation. When such loathing fails to find consummation in orgiastic destruction, it may spend itself in Zen Buddhism, Pataphysics, or even Camp.

Revulsion against the self serves as a link between the destructive and visionary impulses of modern apocalypse; it prepares for rebirth. Thus D. H. Lawrence believes: 'Start with the sun, and the rest will slowly, slowly happen.' The sun, however distant, is within view of the eye. Whitman, who is in some ways more prophetic of our mood, locates millennial perfection in the everlasting present:

> There was never more inception than there is now,
> Nor any more youth or age than there is now,
> And will never be any more perfection than there is now.

Apocalpyse is *now!* The term recovers its original sense, which is literally revelation; vision penetrates the perplexities of the moment to the heart of light. In current parlance, this antinomian belief is sometimes called the alteration of consciousness, and traces of it may be recognised in the psychedelic experiments of Alpert and Leary, in the poetry of Ginsberg, in the Reichian view of orgasm advertised by Norman Mailer, and in the psychomystic revelations of Norman O. Brown. The alteration of consciousness is also the constant hope of Miller throughout his apocalyptic harangues, and the object of parody in Beckett's Cartesian monologues, both of which project antithetical states of wordless perfection. Revelation, however, is not confined to shamanistic frenzy or unearthly trance. As Leslie Fiedler put it in *Waiting for the End* (1963): 'We can *see* a different world without firing a shot or framing a syllogism, merely by altering our consciousness; and the ways to alter it are at hand. . . .' This is the dream of a revolution to end all revolutions – and perhaps all dreams.

Outrage and apocalypse, then, provide mirror images of the contemporary imagination, images that contain something vital and dangerous in our experience. They are also mirror images in the sense that Miller and Beckett reflect inverse worlds. For Beckett leaves us with a world so depleted of life that nothing short of a cataclysm can renew it; we are close to the absence of outrage. And Miller presents us with a chaotic world constantly on the verge of transformation; we are witness to the rage of apocalypse. What both worlds share is the decree of silence. For the human tongue is speechless in fright and ecstasy.

Yet if the new literature can be delimited by the extreme metaphors of outrage and apocalypse, other ideas help to maintain the silence at its centre. Foremost among these, perhaps, is the idea of absurd creation which compels the author to deprecate and even to spurn his activity. 'Creating or not creating changes nothing', Camus said. 'The absurd creator does not prize his work. He could repudiate it.' Thus the imagination renounces its ancient authority, finding its apotheosis not in the romantic idea of the damned poet but in the ironic attitude of the wordless author binding a sheaf of blank pages.

When the writer deigns to put words to paper, he is apt to conceive anti-literature either as pure action or futile play. The view that art is action, we know, finds sanction in Sartre's *What is Literature?* To speak is to act, Sartre claims, and everything we name loses its innocence, becoming part of the world we live in. If art has value, it is because art declares itself as a public appeal. Likewise, Camus extolled (in *The Myth of Sisyphus*) *savoir-vivre* over *savoir-faire*. This view finds a strange and defiant conclusion in the action paintings of Jackson Pollock who saw art not as a public appeal but as the process of creating art. This process is individual if not entirely private; its value redounds to the author more than to his audience. Miller's view is unexpectedly similar. For him writing is autobiography, and autobiography is therapy which is a form of action upon the self. 'We should look to the diary . . .' Miller says, 'not for the truth about things but as an expression of this struggle to be free of the obsession for truth.' The struggle belongs mainly to the diarist, or, when the action is directed outward, to the poet; for Miller also says: 'I do not call poets those who make verses, rhymed or unrhymed. I call that man poet who is capable of profoundly altering the world.'

Writing for Beckett, however, is absurd play. In a certain sense, all his works may be thought of as a parody of Wittgenstein's notion that language is a set of games, akin to the arithmetic of primitive tribes. Beckett's parodies, which are full of self-spite, designate a general tendency in anti-literature. Hugh Kenner brilliantly describes this tendency when he states: 'The dominant intellectual analogy of the present age is drawn not from biology, not from psychology (though these are sciences we are knowing about), but from general number theory.' Art in a closed field thus becomes an absurd game of permutations, like Molloy sucking stones at the beach; and 'the retreat from the word' (the phrase is George Steiner's) reduces language to pure ratio.

The conceptions of literature as game and as action merge in another form of silence: literary obscenity. The term is notoriously difficult to define except by court action; I use it here to refer mainly to works which connect obscenity with protest. It is easy to understand that in a culture given to sexual repression, protest may possess the motive and ring of obscenity. The literature which exposes this motive is thus a literature of revolt. Obscenity, however, is cruelly reductive; its terms, counters, and clichés are sharply limited. When the anger behind it is chilled, obscenity appears as a game of permutations, relying on few words and fewer actions. Surely this is the double impression we take from the writings of the Marquis de Sade: that his protest is monstrous and his game is finally numbing. Sade, whom it is fashionable nowadays to consider the first avant-gardist, projects a curious stillness; his obscene and repetitious violence muffles language. In bequeathing porno-aesthetics to literature, he also made it possible for Mailer, say, or for Burroughs, to develop parodies of sexual violence. The sexual heroics of Miller are still too naïve to realise their full potential for self-parody, while the excremental obsessions of Beckett parody themselves and deny all love. In the game of parody as in the act of obscenity, anti-languages rule; and Miller and Beckett, standing again in contrast, suggest the manner of genital and anal pornography.

But the literature of silence manages to deny the time-honoured functions of literature in yet another way: it aspires to an impossible concreteness. The new literalism emerges in the *musique concrète* of Stockhausen, in the collages of found objects of Cornell and Robert Rauschenberg, in the environmental sculpture of Kurt Schwitters, and, under the combined influence of Schwitters and Apollinaire, in that hybrid form of verbal and visual effects, concrete poetry, which relies on the alphabet to make pictures. A less obvious aspiration to concreteness may be sensed in Truman Capote's *In Cold Blood.* Declining the appeal of Fantasy, Capote pretends to adhere meticulously to Fact, and writes, as he claims, the first 'non-fiction novel'. In recent European literature, neo-literalism is sometimes linked with the phenomenology of Husserl. A difficult thinker who exerted considerable influence on men as different as Sartre and Heidegger, Husserl cannot be summarised without gross distortions. Yet it is fair to say that the result of Husserl's philosophy is to define a pure form of subjective consciousness which has no components and which can never become an object of experience. This form of consciousness, isolated by a series of 'reductions', is not part of the common world of objects, feelings, or sensations. What we usually accept as the inmost self, the ego, must itself be 'bracketed', or set aside, as an empirical unity subject to the final 'transcendental reduction' which yields pure consciousness. Stated crudely, then, the true self is unknowable and, perhaps like Beckett's anti-hero, unnamable.

How does this conclusion affect the novel?

The old principles of causality, psychological analysis, and symbolic relations, principles on which the bourgeois novel once comfortably rested, begin to crumble. Beckett's *Molloy* may have been the first novel to be written in the new manner though Sartre's *La Nausée* attracted wide attention. In Roquentin, we see a character convinced of universal irrelevance; things have broken loose from words, and no connection between subject and object can be made. It remains for Robbe-Grillet to reject the humanism of Sartre by rejecting his pananthropism. If man desires to be alone, declining communion with the universe, if man proves, after all, not to be the answer to the eternal riddle of the Sphinx, then his fate can be neither tragic nor absurd. 'Things are things, and man is only man', Robbe-Grillet argues happily. 'Henceforth, we refuse all complicity with objects. . . . We must refuse, that is, any idea of pre-established order.' It follows that the novelist can be only a literalist, naming the names, or entertaining pure images. Without character, plot, metaphor, or meaning, without any pretence of 'interiorness', the French anti-novels of Sarraute, Butor, and Robbe-Grillet aim, like the new cinema, at the effect of a silent reel. What Harold Rosenberg says seems equally apposite to literature as to the visual arts: 'All the French alchemists are after the same thing, the actuality which is always new – and which will come only forth out of silencing the existing rhetoric.'

Silence in the new literature is also attained through radical irony, a term I apply to any statement which contains its own ironic denial. The Cretan who claimed all Cretans were liars may serve as an example; the machine of Tinguely, which has no function but to destroy itself, serves as another. Radical irony, in other words, requires not a collage of found objects, but an empty canvas. Its modern origins may be traced back to some of the major figures of our century, notably Kafka and Thomas Mann. Kafka, we know, came close to rendering the experience of blank and frozen spaces. And Mann prized the voice of consummate irony, rising only to cancel itself in self-parody which, as Mann came to believe, held the only hope of art. Erich Heller is right in noting: 'Art tragically laments the loss of its own mystery in *Doctor Faustus*, and gaily reports it to the cosmic police in *Felix Krull*.' This trend finds still earlier precedents among the German Romantics and the French Symbolists. In recent times, however, radical irony has increased in sophistication. Heidegger's idea of 'the mystery of oblivion' and Blanchot's view of literature as a form of 'forgetfulness' suggest a theoretical development of irony. More concretely, Mailer's *An American Dream* (1964) frankly burlesques, and actually denies, the novel form by transforming it into pop art. Nathalie Sarraute's *The Golden Fruits* (1963) is a novel about a novel called *The Golden Fruits* which cancels itself by drifting into oblivion, during the act of reading. This reflexive technique was probably developed by Beckett; it was certainly perfected by him. The conclusion of his latest novel, *How It Is* (1964), is that the book is really about 'How It Wasn't'. Such legerdemain is not frivolous; for the paradox of art employing art to deny itself is rooted in the power of human consciousness to view itself both as subject and object. Within the mind is the Archimedean point: when the world becomes intolerable, the mind lifts itself to nirvana or drops into madness. Or it may resort to radical irony in order to reveal art at the end of its tether. Thus in Beckett, literature rigorously unmakes itself, and in Miller, literature pretends, erratically, to be life. What is harder to discern in radical irony is that it disguises genuine aggressions against art. Through it, the artist makes his last devotions to the Muse, and through it he desecrates her too. This ambivalence is obvious in both Miller and Beckett.

Finally, literature strives for silence by accepting chance and improvisation; its principle becomes indeterminacy. By refusing order, order imposed or discovered, this kind of literature refuses purpose. Its forms are therefore non-telic; its world is the eternal present. We are invited to regain our original innocence; error and revision, now irrelevant, are forever banished. Like the stepping stones in a Zen garden, random literature seems to celebrate things as they are. This impression is confirmed by the writings of a man as much a composer as a poet: John Cage, who, more than Mathieu or Satie, has shocked his public into a sacramental awareness of random composition. This is what Cage says in *Silence*:

> Our intention is to affirm this life, not to bring order out of a chaos nor to suggest improvements in creation, but simply to wake up to the very life we're living, which is so excellent once one gets one's mind and one's desires out of its way and lets it act of its own accord.

Traces of this attitude may be found throughout the works of Henry Miller, and in the poetry of Ginsberg, the novels of Jack Kerouac, and the later stories of J. D. Salinger. Unlike Cage, however, these authors seem superficial in adapting their spiritual life to the practice of literature. Miller, for instance, likes to pose as a garrulous *raconteur* despite all his affection for Tao and Milarepa. Whatever appears random in his work can be ascribed less to design than to disposition. Many years ago, Dadaists and Surrealists came close to the dismemberment of literary forms with less spiritual *chic*. Perhaps this is also true, in our time, of random authors like Marc Saporta and William Burroughs. In *Number 1*, Saporta invites the reader to create his own book each time he sits down to a set of inscribed cards. His 'shuffle novel' is a stratagem which proposes chance as a legitimate part of the literary experience. And Burroughs, who believes that to speak is to lie, attempts to evade mendacity through 'The Cut Up Method of Brion Gysin.' Harking back to the Dadaist antics of Tristan Tzara, Burroughs explains:

> Method is simple: take a page or more or less of your own writing or from any writer living or dead. And written or spoken words. Cut into sections with scissors or switch blade as preferred and rearrange the sections. Looking away. Now write out the result. . . .
>
> Applications of cut up method are literally unlimited cut out from time limits. Old word lines keep you in old word slots. Cut your way out. Cut paper cut film cut tape. Scissors or switch blade as preferred. Take it to cut city.

Dadaist collage, Zen Buddhism, or even Johann von Neumann's theory of games seem equally valid in freeing man from the word habit. Burroughs, who has something in common with Beckett, ends by sharing with the latter the jerky rhythms of a subtracting machine. The machine has one purpose: to operate on language, and subtract thereof all meaning.

Clearly, the silence at the centre of anti-literature is loud and various. Whether it is created by the shock of outrage or of apocalypse, whether it is enhanced by the conception of literature as pure action or pure play, and of the literary work itself as a concrete object, a blank page, or a random array, is perhaps finally irrelevant. The point is this: silence develops as the metaphor of a new attitude that literature has chosen to adopt towards itself. This attitude puts to question the peculiar power, the ancient excellence, of literary discourse – and challenges the assumptions of our civilisation.

It is rather puzzling that this attitude has failed, on the whole, to make an impression on English and American critics. The sensible, practical outlook of the former, and the laborious formalism which still engages the latter may partially account for their antipathy. Moreover, anti-literature tends to unsettle critics with a firm humanistic bent, and to repel others, Marxists or Socialists, who are committed to a certain idea of realism.

French critics, who can be as doctrinaire or provincial as any others, manage to remain the exception. Sartre, we know, reflected at length, in *What Is Literature?*, on the Dadaist and Surrealist crisis of language at the beginning of our century; a decade later, he wrote the introduction to Nathalie Sarraute's *Portrait d'un Inconnu* and spoke 'of works, lively yet entirely negative, which might be called anti-novels'. Thus a new term was given to the vocabulary of mid-century. In *Le Livre à Venir*, Maurice Blanchot identified Rousseau as the first culprit in the tradition of silence, 'raging to write against writing'; and saw literature approaching 'the era of wordlessness' which, like some works of Miller and Beckett, can be understood only as incessant sound. Thus, according to Blanchot, literature moves towards its essence, which is disappearance. Likewise, the theme of Roland Barthes' *Le Degré Zéro de L'Ecriture* is absence. 'Modernism begins with the search for a literature of impossibility', Barthes proposes; the conclusion to this search is the Orphic dream: 'an author without Literature'. And Claude Mauriac, who was perhaps the first to include Miller and Beckett in the same critical study, notes in *The New Literature*:

> After the silence of Rimbaud, the blank page of Mallarmé, the inarticulate joy of Artaud, a literature finally dissolves in alliteration with Joyce.... For Beckett... words all say the same thing.

Obviously, the spirit of French lucidity cannot bring itself to rail at silence in literature.

But I suspect that lucidity may no longer be wholly adequate to the ambitions of criticism. We increasingly feel that criticism should do more than clarify; it should also possess wisdom of the senses and of the spirit. We want it to endanger itself, as literature does, and to testify to our condition. We even hope that it can sustain the burden of revelation. This hope has led me to suggest that criticism may have to become apocalyptic before it can compel our sense of relevance. It will have, at the very least, to entertain some sympathy for the metaphors of apocalypse in order to test the intuitions of anti-literature. This is evident in a rare piece of American criticism which attempts precisely this task. In 'The New Mutants', Leslie Fiedler shows that he understands the complex alliances which the literary imagination now makes with silence, with obscenity, with madness, and even with those post-sexual states akin to mystical trance. He also knows that crucial for our time is

> the sense in which literature first conceived the possibility of the future . . . and then furnished that future in joyous or terrified anticipation, thus preparing all of us to inhabit it.

Anti-literature should finally be seen in the light of particular examples. The examples which seem to me most pertinent to the development of that literature are, once again, those of Miller and Beckett, and perhaps of Burroughs who stands between the two. The contrasts of Miller and Beckett often are obvious. But lest my choice of paradigms may appear curious, let me add a few words about each.

Next to Ezra Pound, Henry Miller is the oldest major American author still living. Unlike Pound, however, Miller sees himself as a patagonian, a literary gangster; and the great modern movement represented by Eliot, Joyce, and Proust remains alien to him. '*Art as the substitute for life*', he snorts. 'The literature of flight, of escape, of a neurosis so brilliant that it almost makes one doubt the efficacy of health'; instead, Miller turns to the hellions of our age: 'I owe much to the Dadaists and Surrealists. I prefer the French writers who are un-French.' If it is not obvious what Miller owes to the Dadaists, it is clear that he was one of the first writers – Lawrence may be another – to make a break with the tradition of the modern, and to establish an outlook more 'schismatic'[1] than any adopted by the literary masters of his day. Every subject Miller touches – art, history, civilisation, religion – is fired by his sense of outrage and transfigured by his hope of apocalypse. 'Crime begins with God', Miller says in *The Air-Conditioned Nightmare*. 'It will end with man, when he finds God again.' And in *The Wisdom of the Heart*, he notes:

> All art, I firmly believe, will one day disappear . . . . The artist who becomes thoroughly aware consequently ceases to be one. And the trend is towards awareness, towards that blinding consciousness in which no present forms of life can possibly flourish, not even art.

Miller, that American transcendentalist of foreign city streets, demands an end to history and hails a transformation of consciousness. His work marks the end of the French Symbolist tradition which made art its religion and therefore contained within itself – witness the example of Rimbaud – the death of art. Miller turns literature into autobiography of a special kind; for his work is less an effort to record and comprehend his life than it is an attempt to *live* it, live it over and over again. Loose patterns of recall to which he delivers himself follow the flux of human experience and respond to its random compulsions. Unable to redeem his life in art, he calls for a transcendence of both. In this sense, Henry Miller may be considered the first author of anti-literature.

Samuel Beckett, on the other hand, tries bravely to be its last. Knowing that art cannot be art nowadays unless it is wrested from impossibility, he comes close to reducing literature to a mathematical tautology. The syllogism of Beckett assumes that history has spent itself; we are merely playing an end game. The syllogism can be relentless. Language has become void; therefore words can only demonstrate their emptiness. Certainty in knowledge is no longer possible; therefore epistemology must become parody. Religion and metaphysics have lost their authority; therefore we

[1] The term is Frank Kermode's, who takes a different view of modernism.

shall wait for Godot in vain. Human relations are at bottom cruel; therefore love is a disguise of power and power a disguise of solitude. Decaying matter remains forever alien to the mind; therefore mind and crippled body can have no union.

In this Cartesian nightmare, Beckett leaves only one thing intact; the capacity of human consciousness to reflect upon itself and to entertain its own end. Thus literature becomes the inaudible game of a solipsist. No wonder that Beckett believes art to be the apotheosis of solitude. In this rigorous fidelity to failure, he also reveals the secret tendency of literature to contract into silence. Despite the monstrous endurance of his characters and the deadly skill of his words, Samuel Beckett may be considered the author who wants to seal the lips of the muse. Yet his silence, despite its grim, satiric note, has something in common with the silence of holy men who, after knowing pain and outrage, reach for a peace beyond human understanding. Pronko is probably right when he claims: 'Beckett's view of life is basically a religious one: it is the view of a man who seeks some meaning beyond the trivial happenings of everyday life, a purpose beyond the physical needs of a specific time and place.'

Miller and Beckett are both comedians of our darkest hopes. Their comic spirit distorts literature in different ways. Miller stretches literature beyond its usual limit and Beckett shrinks it to naught; but expansion and contraction end by serving the same purpose, which is to alter the function of words within any given literary form. This alteration tends towards a state that I have metaphorically called silence. Put another way, silence is the new attitude that literature has chosen to adopt towards itself. Is this attitude really new?

We can recall that Elizabeth Sewell said of Rimbaud and Mallarmé something very close to what I have said of Miller and Beckett: that Rimbaud's language moves towards the disorder of dream and Mallarmé's towards the perfection of number. We cannot be very sure nowadays of what is new. But of this we can be more certain: whether the literature of silence proves a passing fashion or a phase of literary history, it is a judgment of the

Western conscience, and of its consciousness, upon ourselves. Lionel Trilling sensed this judgment, somewhat faintly, when he said: 'It is possible to say that – whether for good or for bad – we confront a mutation in culture by which an old established proportion between the pleasure-seeking instincts and the ego instinct is being altered in favour of the latter.' Trilling's point is that modern literature allies itself increasingly with the death rather than with the pleasure principle. The alliance, as Trilling fails to see, may be in the interests of a new life. Perhaps Durrell is right, after all, when he says in *Balthazar*: 'The object of writing is to grow a personality which in the end enables man to transcend art.' Perhaps this is the function of silence.

The function of silence in Burroughs' work is clear. In the opening pages of his latest book, *Nova Express*, Burroughs nastily asks: 'What scared you all into time? Into body? Into shit? I will tell you: "*the word*". Alien Word "*the*". "*The word*" of Alien Enemy imprisons "*thee*" in Time. In Body. In Shit. Prisoner, come out.' The framework of his 'trilogy', *Naked Lunch*, *Soft Machine*, and *Nova Express* (another version of this was published in Paris under the title of *The Ticket That Exploded*, 1962), is science fiction, the new map of our hell, the nightmare that our machines dream when they dream of history. A galactic war, spearheaded by Inspector J. Lee (an alias Burroughs once used in writing *Junkie*), is waged to exterminate all Nova Criminals. The latter are controllers or deceivers of life, and their most powerful weapon of all is language, for language *is* deceit and control.

The myth of technology also provides Burroughs with the opportunity to express both outrage and apocalypse. The outrage is expressed grossly, fantastically, through 'Insect People' and 'Vegetable People' who collaborate with death, who invite the void. The apocalypse can be icy (whole planets approaching the Absolute Zero) or explosive (the refrain is always, 'Minutes to go'). Obscene idealist, satiric and visionary, lacing scientific jargon with poetic hallucination and cutting up and folding his pages cannily, William Burroughs is finally led to deny not only the

Word but also the Flesh. His aim is to make man bodiless and language silent. Utopian or nihilist, he demonstrates the passions that feed both in a form which compels literature to move beyond its accepted limits. If his work does not help to create a new human personality, it forces us to reconsider the traditional terms of literature.

In Burroughs, in Beckett, even in Miller, the destructive capabilities are clear; all three authors serve to hasten the end, and silence is a metaphor of their complex rage. We are tempted to ask, what do they offer when all is unsaid and undone? The question assumes polarities of creation and destruction, affirmation and denial, which the modern experience tends to render obsolete. Camus, and Nietzsche before him – and who else before? – knew that the act of negation is an assertion of value. Men have learned to refuse with honour ever since refusal has required from them, in this era of terror, a monstrous price. The polarities of creation and destruction no longer exclude one another; they exclude the middle. For if silence is holy, and if it brings with it intimations of a whole, new life, silence is also demonic, and it permits old terrors. Outrage and apocalypse are two faces of the same reality; this has been all along my point.

Admitting this final peril, how then can men of good will discern value in the silence which the new literature whispers into our inner ears? The answer depends on whether we can still afford anything but radical solutions. The statement, I know, has sickening echoes; we have heard of radical solutions before which have brought only radical dissolutions. I offer no way out of this perplexity though I claim it is the perplexity we must somehow meet. My hope is that Silence and Love may recover their ancient connection. This is what Norman O. Brown says in *Love's Body*: 'The true meanings of words are bodily meanings, carnal knowledge; and the bodily meanings are the unspoken meanings. What is always speaking silently is the body.' And again: 'The matrix in which the word is sown is silence. Silence is the mother tongue.'

E. H. Gombrich Art at the End of its Tether

'*Etonnez moi*' – the famous words which Diaghilev is said to have spoken to the young Cocteau conveniently sum up the theory of art proposed in this book [Morse Peckham, *Man's Rage for Chaos: Biology, Behavior and the Arts* (New York, 1966)]. Stripped of its involvement with transactionist psychology and translated from a rather polysyllabic terminology into simple language, Professor Peckham's hypothesis amounts to the assertion that art is an institution to which we turn when we want to feel a shock of surprise. We feel this want because we sense that it is good for us once in a while to receive a healthy jolt. Otherwise we would so easily get stuck in a rut and could no longer adapt to the new demands life is apt to make on us. The biological function of art, in other words, is that of a rehearsal, a training in mental gymnastics which increases our tolerance for the unexpected. In the author's words: 'There must . . . be some human activity which serves to break up orientations . . . to prepare the individual to observe what the orientation tells him is irrelevant, but what very well may be highly relevant' (p. xi); '. . . art is the reinforcement of the capacity to endure disorientation so that a real and significant problem may emerge' (p. 314).

It is clear from the whole tenor of the book that it was his encounter with contemporary avant-garde art that gave the author this shock of disorientation that set him in search of a new and significant problem. To accommodate it, he had indeed to break up the aesthetic orientations on which he had been brought up. 'The artist', he came to conclude, 'is the challenger; his role requires him to create unpredicted situations' (p. 76). As an example of what he calls 'the inarticulate insight into exactly this way of defining art', he quotes John Cage's notorious concert-item entitled *3½*, which consists of so many minutes of non-performance at the piano. Any decision that governs the artist's choice of the surprises he wishes to offer the public, the author infers, 'is determined by the values, both implicit and explicit, of his cultural environment. If he is a New York artist of the 1960s, those values tell him that, to be a successful artist, he must make a great innovative leap; if he can, he must start a whole new artistic fashion. If that is beyond him, he must make as much of a discontinuity as he can in the current fashion' (p. 262).

It has often happened that the innovations of contemporary artists have helped critics and historians to look at the past with fresh eyes and to discover new values in previously neglected styles. True, these rediscoveries were often accompanied by certain distortions of the historical truth, but even when these were corrected and adjusted by subsequent generations enough remained to justify such an exercise in projection. I was therefore very ready to go along with the author of this book and to test with him how far his generalizations may take us in that revision of aesthetic orthodoxy that he demands. It is indeed a radical revision. His emphasis on surprise makes him contemptuous of the traditional idea that art should be in any way concerned with order. He has a point when he insists that order is something we impose on any perception and that the picture of a chaotic world of experience is untrue to biology and psychology. 'Whatever the world of an amoeba or an earthworm may be like' – I myself once argued against Malraux – 'it certainly is not chaotic but structured. Where there is life there is order.' I also gladly hailed the author as an ally when I found him attacking and dissecting the approach to period styles, popular with survey courses, which looks for a common structure in the poetry, the music, the paintings and architecture of a given period. His insistence, mentioned above, that art is not a peculiar kind of structure but rather an institution demanding a type of behavior also strikes me as fruitful. Moreover it is always fun watching a gifted critic demolishing tired old orthodoxies. Like the artists from whom he takes his cue Professor Peckham is out to astonish by innovatory behavior, and in his first chapters he succeeds remarkably well. I particularly liked his pages on the dramatic metaphor (pp. 49–59), in which the sociological concept of role playing is vividly presented and illuminated. Altogether I would not hesitate to recommend his opening chapters as a subject for any seminar in criticism and the arts for, whether one agrees or not, they contain many excellent debating points.

It is all the more disappointing to have to confess to a feeling of let-down as soon as the author attempts in the subsequent chapters to build up a theory of his own that could be successfully applied to the arts and styles of all times. Stimulated, as he says, by the experiments of abstract art, notably by the theories of Kandinsky and Malevich, he first goes in search of what he calls 'primary signs' in the arts, those aspects, that is, of sensory experience like loudness and softness in music to which we can respond physiognomically. Strangely enough he believes that 'little study has been devoted to them' (p. 101). He is quite unaware of the tradition that reaches back from Kandinsky to the Romantic painter Humbert de Superville's *Essai sur les signes inconditionels dans l'art* (1827), the content of which Charles Blanc had passed on to Seurat.

With his characteristic verve Professor Peckham seeks to disarm criticism by telling us that 'if the reader feels annoyed and disgusted I will not blame him in the least'. But what if he feels bored and dispirited? What else can be the result of reading that 'in painting and architecture verticality is a sign of demand, horizontality of acceptance' (p. 161)? Those, for instance, who entered Mussolini's notorious audience chambers, in which the dictator sat at the the distant end from the door, did not report that they experienced the vast horizontal expanse they had to cross till they reached the presence as 'a sign of acceptance'. Here as always it has been shown long ago that there is no generalization of this kind to which a counter-example cannot easily be found. This does not prove that the quest is entirely useless, but it is useless on this level. The author is quick in accusing critics of what he calls ethnocentricity, the tendency to look at all art in the light of their own national tradition, but the ethnocentricity of his treatment of 'primary signs' in poetry really takes one's breath away. 'In English poetry', he observes, 'comic verse is invariably rhymed, while double and triple rhymes are so thoroughly identified with comic verse that they are entirely excluded from serious verse' (p. 140). Rhyme, he therefore concludes, is a primary sign of 'adequacy' and thus 'rhymed tragedy flourished only briefly'. This may be true of England, but obviously not of France. His conclusion that this sense of adequacy belonging to comedy is achieved by short lines rather than long ones is equally refuted by Aristophanes. Goethe also often experimented with short lines and even with repeated rhymes in dramatic context of high seriousness.

It must be admitted, though, that the weakness of this chapter, of which the author is aware, is not fatally damaging to his fundamental thesis, which identifies art with the upsetting rather than with the creation of order. But the subsequent chapter on the formal aspects reveals, to my mind, such a fatal misunderstanding that little, if anything, can be rescued of his original hypothesis.

His starting point here is the correct observation that works of art do not generally exhibit mathematical order and that the form postulated as a rule would feel lifeless and mechanical if it were not broken and transgressed in a thousand ways. Great poems do not scan with relentless regularity. Renaissance Madonnas are not really arranged in triangles, and Bach's fugues are not merely exercises in musical patternmaking. Here too the author may overrate the novelty of his emphasis. The Bergsonian philosopher Ludwig Klages stressed more than a generation ago that the hallmark of real music is not the monotonous beat (*Takt*) but the living flow of rhythm – not identical units in identical intervals of time but similar units in similar intervals. Nearer to our time Dr Anton Ehrenzweig in his book on *The Psychoanalysis of Artistic Vision and Hearing* has drawn attention to the many elements of 'disorder' that play hide-and-seek in art behind the facade of measured regularity. All this is true and important, but it does not suffice to establish Mr Peckham's central thesis that the work of art comes into being by what he calls 'discontinuity', the violation of form or more exactly of the receiver's expectation. If this were all, Cage's *3½* would really be the supreme piece of music and the best stories ever told would be 'shaggy dog' stories.

Obviously the surprise which great art offers us is of a very different character. What we experience is not only unexpected, it is better than we ever managed to expect, a thrilling masterstroke which yet triumphantly meets and exceeds the perceiver's expectation. It is true, of course, that the entirely expected move in art strikes us as trivial, boring, and lifeless. After a time it may even fail to register altogether and becomes mere background. Simple music moving regularly between tonic and dominant can have this effect. But if a deviation from the expected were all that was required to relieve the situation, any false note would do the trick. It may indeed wake us up, it may even train us painfully to face the imperfections of life in general, but it is not art. When we listen to great music of the classic period, every move arouses indeed expectations, we know of familiar paths by which the tension might be relieved. But we find to our delight that the master knows of a better, more unexpected and yet more convincing way to take us home to the tonic on an adventurous road. The same is true of literature. The rigid conventions of certain genres do not exclude surprise, they arouse it. Even where we know that in the end the lovers will fall into each other's arms we may still admire the surprising way in which the author reaches and presents this expected consummation. Even our response to performance on the stage or in music depends not only on our being surprised but on our being convinced. It would be easy enough to stage Hamlet as a comedy or to open his monologue with a yawn. It would not be convincing. When we say that a performance has restored the freshness of the work of art we do not mean that it has upset the expected order, but that it has shown us much more of it than we ever knew.

Granted that order may be something we impose. There are

limits, both logical and psychological, to this relativism. It is not meaningless to say – as Professor Peckham seems to think – that an order can be discovered. There is an objective difference between crystals and clouds. It is true that our ability to see order differs and that it can be trained and extended to take in greater complexities. Nobody has ever denied this. But the introduction of greater complexity, which has indeed been traditionally connected with stylistic developments, surely differs from that discontinuity Professor Peckham sees as the dynamism behind any change in art.

If he were entirely right that the sole function of art is to teach us how to cope with unsettling experiences, there would be no point in ever returning to a work of art we have encountered before. This may be true of Cage's trick, for it loses its point once we know what he is up to. Mozart is more durable. Indeed one of the psychological mysteries of artistic surprise is that it does not wear off. A thriller may not be worth re-reading once we know who dun it. But we can read the Odyssey any number of times and look forward to the vicarious surprise Penelope will feel when the hero reveals himself at last. We can even wait with keen anticipation to a certain modulation in Schubert which we know by heart.

A theory of stylistic change based on such insecure foundations is bound to disappoint. Professor Peckham's idea that the dynamics of change are all-pervasive in art and apply to the styles of all cultures is fundamentally mistaken. He emphasizes (p. 261) that the immutability of Egyptian art is a myth because Egyptologists are able to date Egyptian artifacts with some confidence. Yet the discussions concerning the dates to be assigned to some famous products of conservative cultures – Chinese scrolls, Byzantine ivories, or Russian ikons – certainly show that such confidence is not unlimited. Moreover – and this is decisive – there is a vital difference between stylistic drift and a desire for change. Language too changes with time but vowel shifts do not occur to perform the biological function of disorientation. Where art is bound up with ritual, as it is in the majority of cultures, its social function is preservation rather than change. Ritual, religious or secular, should reinforce expectations, not disappoint them. Its consoling and edifying character lies precisely in its relative immunity to change. Even in times of stress and disintegration people will try to hold fast to ritual, to celebrate Christmas and to sing the old songs which give them the reassurance of stability. Historians may discover that the Christmas tree is a comparatively recent innovation, but surely it was not introduced to provide a shock of novelty. Change in social institutions is not always due to the search for originality.

Professor Peckham chides academic critics who believe in the rules inherent in certain forms and who debate, for instance, whether Tschaikowsky's Sixth Symphony deserves to be called a symphony. In calling it so, the author argues (p. 237) that the composer intended the listener to relate his work to the tradition of the symphony from which he departed. The point is well taken where the arts of the last hundred years are concerned, but it would be unintelligible to members of more ritualistic cultures. It would be senseless to say that any poem one chooses to call a haiku thereby becomes a haiku. The form demands the arrangement of words in a certain order just as it demands the competition in haiku to follow certain ceremonial rules. These rules may drift but they are not revolutionized.

It may be argued, even, that the subtlety and refinement that develop in the arts of a stable élite, where connoisseurship learns to appreciate the slightest nuance, are unattainable in rapidly changing styles. Compared to Chinese bamboo paintings, European art may always be coarse-grained. Be that as it may, the author's proposal for the explanation of the relationship of the arts rests entirely on combining his ideas about primary signs with his interpretation of discontinuity. In other words, what the various arts of an individual period have in common is not a particular structure, but a certain preference for primary signs of adequacy or the reverse coupled with a given tolerance for rule-breaking and for change. It is clear that this solution is also derived from a contemplation of the contemporary scene. The attempt to apply it to the traditional sequence of Baroque, Enlightenment, and Romanticism lands the author unfortunately in the same kind of vague generalization about periods he had promised to banish. Even his verve and wit almost desert him in a chapter that recalls the worst sins of Spenglerian historicism. Thanks to the emergence of science (we are told), 'Baroque artists were governed by an orientation that gave a high value to problem exposure . . . their art showed an unusually high level of discontinuity' (p. 265).

The direct influence of science is also seen in the emergence of a lucid prose style (again a very ethnocentric observation); the fugue emerged from the *ricercare* which means 'research' and the 'plunge into depth of the Baroque landscape . . . is exposure without the defenses of recession in planes and successive reduction of color iconicity . . .'; 'the essence of Baroque architecture is spatial disorientation and the dissolution of solids and screens' (p. 269). We are thus back with our old friend the 'essence'. In contrast to the 'cognitive tension' experienced on the top of the cultural pyramid during the period of the Baroque, the pleasures of cognitive harmony descended on the intellectual leaders of the Enlightenment leading to a reduction of tension. Thus while 'the melodies of Bach in the 1740s are jagged . . . those of Mozart ripple up and down the scale of the triad' (p. 283), in Tiepolo's ceiling frescoes 'the proportion of figures to sky becomes steadily smaller' (p. 283), and English poetry declines into prose. It is only too easy to recognize in these characterizations the old clichés about the shallowness of the Age of Reason.

But it would be unfair to concentrate too much on this attempt to apply the author's theory to the history of the arts. For even here, as I have said, this somewhat misguided exercise springs from his wish to generalize on what he has found true of the contemporary scene. There must be something that unites the arts, his argument runs, for the same break that is visible in painting with the rise of Cubism is noticeable in music with the emergence of atonality, and in literature with its various forms of experimentalisms. If all these exhibit these discontinuities, if all these, moreover, show the same preference for primary signs of tension and inadequacy, the same unity must be observable in previous stylistic breaks. The argument looks plausible, but it overlooks an important novel element in the twentieth-century situation that was absent from earlier epochs. This element is the degree of historical self-consciousness that governs the behavior of both the producers and the perceivers of art. It was the philosophy of Hegelian historicism (to use Popper's term) which reacted back on the arts to an ever increasing extent and led to that self-fulfilling prophecy of a 'new art for a new age' which the various forms of futurism had postulated. The historiography of art history had its share in this self-consciousness that aimed at continuing the sequence of styles which had allegedly expressed the changing essence of past ages. If this experience is any guide, Professor Peckham's book in its turn will speed up the Rage for Chaos and the craving for novelty 'at the top of the cultural pyramid'. It would be a pity if this happened. For the author himself is shocked by what he considers the 'arrogance and indifference . . . of artist and perceiver . . . so perplexing, so monstrous'; his human compassion is outraged by what he sees as the '*cruelty* of art' (p. 307).

The sentiment does him credit. But instead of trying therefore to justify the ways of art to man by inventing a new theory that fits the contemporary scene, he could also have looked at it with more critical detachment. It may be true (as I myself have recently suggested) that 'today the conviction is almost universal that those who stick to obsolete beliefs and who refuse to change will go to the wall . . . that we must adapt or die'. Hence the eagerness of those who want to stay on that 'top of the pyramid' to jump on the bandwagon (for which there always seems to be room on the top). But to equate this strenuous exercise with art is really an illicit extrapolation.

Quite near the opening of his Preface the author tells us how he sat in a concert some ten years ago and found it increasingly astonishing 'that a couple of thousand people should sit quietly in a darkened auditorium while another hundred people made carefully predetermined sounds'. It was right that he wondered, but he would not have done so in a ritualistic culture, nor – dare one guess? – in a concert that everybody really enjoyed. If today those thousands are ready to submit to the cruelty of art in a ritualistic celebration of progress, a painful initiation ceremony into the priesthood of change, this is indeed an interesting phenomenon. Whether it is also as healthy as Professor Peckham thinks is a different matter.

Morse Peckham A Reply

Nothing could be more pleasing to an author than to have as reviewer so distinguished a scholar as E. H. Gombrich, and to receive from him so intelligent, sympathetic, and generous a review of a contentious book. To be sure, Professor Gombrich makes a few errors in his account of what I say. It is not true that my 'search of what he calls "primary signs" ' was 'stimulated . . . by the experiments of abstract art'. I am not 'unaware of the tradition that reaches back from Kandinsky to the Romantic painter[s]'. (It is always unwise to accuse an author of ignorance of something he has not mentioned.) I cannot be attacked by the assertion that 'Moreover – and this is decisive – there is a vital difference between stylistic drift and a desire for change', since this is the point at which I begin and which is the basis for all that follows. It is not true that my theory cannot account for 'ritualistic' cultures in which stylistic change is slow; it can, and does; ritual belongs to the semantic aspect of art, and from my theory one would predict that in a ritualistic culture stylistic change would be slow, as Professor Gombrich says.

The source of these errors, and of my reviewer's failure to understand me, seems to come first from his belief in the correctness of his statement, 'If he were entirely right that the sole function of art is to teach us how to cope with unsettling experiences, there would be no point in ever returning to a work of art we have encountered before.' I do not say that that is the sole function of art. I say that the *defining* attribute (*not* the *sole* attribute) of artistic experience is exposure to perceptual disorder. After all, more than a third of the book is devoted to the meaning of art, which is not a defining attribute; any semantic function in art can be found outside of art. Further, if Professor Gombrich had fully grasped my position he would never have drawn his conclusion 'that there is no point,' etc. Works of art do, however, wear out for us, and my theory can explain both how and why, and how and why we can renew them.

His failure to understand me appears to arise from his making an assumption for which there is no basis in the book. He says, 'It is clear from the whole tenor of the book that it was his encounter with contemporary avant-garde art that gave the author this shock of disorientation that set him in search of a new and significant problem', and later, '[he tries] to justify the ways of art to man by inventing a new theory that fits the contemporary scene'. Actually the theory, for whatever it is worth, started from utter dissatisfaction with the *traditional* descriptions and explanations of English prosody for the phenomenon of stress in *traditional* English poetry, and with the traditional discussions of 'form' and 'style' in painting and music *before* 1900. Anyone who understands my theory, including my undergraduates, realizes that from it one would arrive at the conclusion that contemporary art probably will lack durability because it offers too little perceptual disorder, not because it offers too much. Indeed, it could be argued that my reviewer's error supports my position, for it suggests that the theory on offer can explain contemporary art in a way that traditional theories cannot.

This error about my intention is responsible, I think, or at least immediately responsible, for Professor Gombrich's failure to grasp the real nature of my argument; whether or not it is capable of standing up under criticism, anyone who wishes to demolish it – most critics and aestheticians – must first understand it. But perhaps an ultimate difficulty for Professor Gombrich is that he is interested in art. I am not; I am interested in behavior. My real hope is to enable people to play the role of art-perceiver so well that they do not have to play it so often.

But in spite of all this, I am grateful to Professor Gombrich for his courtesy and for his praise of what he felt he could praise, as well as for his own admirable book, *Art and Illusion*, which is one of the rocks on which I have built my wilderness chapel.

E. H. Gombrich replies:

I am grateful to Professor Peckham for his courteous letter. I think my very fully annotated copy of his book would at least convince him that I have tried hard to understand it. If I have nevertheless failed to grasp some of his arguments I can only express the hope that this failure will help him to formulate his hypothesis more clearly in a subsequent book.

Marshall McLuhan **The Relation of Environment to Anti-Environment**

Under the heading that 'What exists is likely to be misallocated' Peter Drucker in *Managing for Results* discusses the structure of social situations. 'Business enterprise is not a phenomenon of nature but one of society. In a social situation, however, events are not distributed according to the "normal distribution" of a natural universe (that is, they are not distributed according to the bell-shaped Gaussian curve). In a social situation a very small number of events *at one extreme* – the first 10 per cent to 20 per cent at most – account for 90 per cent of all results; whereas the great majority of events accounts for 10 per cent or so of the results.' What Drucker is presenting here is the environment as it presents itself for human attention and action. He is confronting the phenomenon of the imperceptibility of the environment as such. It is this factor that Edward T. Hall also tackles in *The Silent Language*. The ground rules, the pervasive structure, the overall pattern eludes perception except in so far as there is an anti-environment or a counter-situation constructed to provide a means of direct attention. Paradoxically, the 10 per cent of the typical situation that Drucker designates as the area of effective cause and as the area of opportunity, this small factor is the environment. The 90 per cent area is the area of problems generated by the active power of the 10 per cent environment. For the environment is an active process pervading and impinging upon all the components of the situation. It is easy to illustrate this.

Any new technology, any extension or amplification of human faculties when given material embodiment, tends to create a new environment. This is as true of clothing as of speech, or script, or wheel. This process is more easily observed in our own time when several new environments have been created. To take only the latest one, TV, we find a handful of engineers and technicians in the 10 per cent area, as it were, creating a set of radical changes in the 90 per cent area of daily life. The new TV environment is an electric circuit that takes as its content the earlier environment, the photograph and the movie in particular. It is in the interplay between the old and the new environments that there is generated an innumerable series of problems and confusions. They extend all the way from how to allocate the time of children and adults to the problem of pay-TV and TV in the classroom. The new medium of TV as an environment creates new occupations. As an environment, it is imperceptible except in terms of its content. That is, all that is seen or noticed is the old environment, the movie. But even the effects of TV on the movie go unnoticed, and the effects of the TV environment in altering the entire character of human sensibility and sensory ratios is completely ignored.

The content of any system or organization naturally consists of the preceding system or organization, and in that degree acts as a control on the new environment. It is useful to notice all of the arts and sciences as acting in the role of anti-environments that enable us to perceive the environment. In a business civilization we have long considered liberal study as providing necessary means of orientation and perception. When the arts and sciences themselves become environments under conditions of electric circuitry, conventional liberal studies whether in the arts or sciences will no longer serve as an anti-environment. When we live in a museum without walls, or have music as a structural part of our sensory environment, new strategies of attention and perception have to be created. When the highest scientific knowledge creates the environment of the atom bomb, new controls for the scientific environment have to be discovered, if only in the interest of survival.

The structural examples of the relation of environment to anti-environment need to be multiplied as a means of understanding the principles of perception and activity involved. The Balinese say: 'We have no art – we do everything as well as possible.' This is not an ironic but a merely factual remark. In a pre-literate society art serves as a means of merging the individual and the environment, not as a means of training perception upon the environment. Archaic or primitive art looks to us like a magical control built into the environment. Thus to put the artefacts from such a culture into a museum or anti-environment is an act of nullification rather than of revelation. Today what is called 'Pop Art' is the use of some object in our own daily environment as if it were anti-environmental. Pop Art serves to remind us, however, that we have fashioned for ourselves a world of artefacts and images that are intended not to train perception or awareness but to insist that we merge with them as the primitive man merges with his environment. The world of modern advertising is a magical environment constructed to produce effects for the total economy but not designed to increase human awareness. We have designed schools as anti-environments to develop the perception and judgment of the printed word. There are no means of training provided to develop similar perception and judgment of any of the new environments created by electric circuitry. This is not accidental. From the development of phonetic script until the invention of the electric telegraph human technology had tended strongly towards the furtherance of detachment and objectivity, detribalization and individuality. Electric circuitry has quite the contrary effect. It involves in depth. It merges the individual and the mass environment. To create an anti-environment for such electric technology would seem to require a technological extension of consciousness itself. The awareness and opposition of the individual are in these circumstances as irrelevant as they are futile.

The structural features of environment and anti-environment appear in the age-old clash between professionalism and amateurism, whether in sport or in studies. Professional sport is environmental and amateur sport is anti-environmental. Professional sport fosters the merging of the individual in the mass and in the patterns of the total environment. Amateur sport seeks rather the development of critical awareness of the individual and most of all, critical awareness of the ground rules of the society as such. The same contrast exists for studies. The professional tends to specialize and to merge his being uncritically in the mass. The ground rules provided by the mass response of his colleagues serve as a pervasive environment of which he is uncritical and unaware.

The party system of government affords a familiar image of the relations of environment and anti-environment. The government as environment needs the opposition as anti-environment in order to be aware of itself. The role of the opposition would seem to be that of the arts and sciences in creating perception. As the government environment becomes more cohesively involved in a world of instant information, opposition would seem to become increasingly necessary but also intolerable. Opposition begins to assume the rancorous and hostile character of a Dew Line, or a Distant Early Warning System. It is important, however, to consider the role of the arts and sciences as Early Warning Systems in the social environment. The models of perception provided in the arts and sciences alike can serve as indispensable means of orientation to future problems well before they become troublesome.

The legend of Humpty-Dumpty would seem to suggest a parallel to the 10–90 per cent distribution of causes and effects. The impact that resulted in his fall brought into play a massive response from the social bureaucracy. But all the King's horses and all the King's men could not put Humpty-Dumpty back together again. They could not recreate the old environment, they could only create a new one. Our typical response to a disrupting new technology is to recreate the old environment instead of heeding the new opportunities of the new environment. Failure to notice the new opportunities is also failure to understand the new powers. This means that we fail to develop the necessary controls or anti-environments for the new environment. This failure leaves us in the role of automata merely.

W. T. Easterbrook has done extensive exploration of the relations of bureaucracy and enterprise, discovering that as soon as one becomes the environment, the other becomes an anti-environment. They seem to bicycle along through history alternating their roles with all the dash and vigor of tweedle-dum and tweedle-dee. In the 18th century when *realism* became a new method in literature, what happened was that the external environment was put in the place of anti-environment. The ordinary world was given the role of art object by Daniel Defoe and others. The environment began to be used as a perceptual probe. It became self-conscious. It became an 'anxious object' instead of being an unperceived and pervasive pattern. Environment used as probe or art object is satirical because it draws attention to itself. The romantic poets extended this technique to external nature transforming nature into an art object. Beginning with Baudelaire and Rimbaud and continuing in Hopkins and Eliot and James Joyce, the poets turned their attention to language as a probe. Long used as an environment, language became an instrument of exploration and research. It became an anti-environment. It became Pop Art.

The artist as a maker of anti-environments permits us to perceive that much is newly environmental and therefore most active in transforming situations. This would seem to be why the artist has in many circles in the past century been called the enemy, the criminal. It helps to explain why news has a natural bias toward crime and bad news. It is this kind of news that enables us to perceive our world. The detective since Poe's Dupin has tended to be a probe, an artist of the big town, an artist-enemy, as it were. Conventionally, society is always one phase back, is never environmental. Paradoxically, it is the antecedent environment that is always being upgraded for our attention. The new environment always uses the old environment as its material.

In the Spring 1965 issue of the *Varsity Grad* Glenn Gould discusses the effects of recorded music on performance and composition. One of his main points is that as recorded music creates a new environment the audience in effect becomes participant both in performance and in composition. This is a reversal or chiasmus of form that occurs in any situation where an environment is pushed up into high intensity or high definition by technological change. A reversal of characteristics occurs as in the case with bureaucracy and enterprise. An environment is naturally of low intensity or low definition. That is why it escapes observation. Anything that raises the environment to high intensity, whether it be a storm in nature or violent change resulting from a new technology, such high intensity turns the environment into an object of attention. When an environment becomes an object of attention it assumes the character of an anti-environment or an art object. When the social environment is stirred up to exceptional intensity by technological change and becomes a focus of much attention, we apply the terms 'war' and 'revolution'. All the components of 'war' are present in any environment whatever. The recognition of war depends upon their being stepped up to high definition.

Under electric conditions of instant information movement both the concept and the reality of war become manifest in many of the situations of daily life. We have long been accustomed to war as that which goes on between publics or nations. Publics and nations were the creation of print technology. With electric circuitry the publics and nations became the content of the new technology: 'The mass audience is not a public as environment but a public as content of a new electric environment.' And whereas 'the public' as an environment created by print technology consisted of separate individuals with varying points of view, the mass audience consists of the same individuals involved in depth in one another and involved in the creative process of the art or educational situation that is presented to them. Art and education were presented to the *public* as consumer packages for their instruction and edification. The new mass audience is involved immediately in art and education as participants and co-creators rather than as consumers. Art and education become new forms of experience, new environments, rather than new anti-environments. Pre-electric art and education were anti-environments in the sense that they were the content of various environments. Under electric conditions the content tends however towards becoming environmental itself. This was the paradox that Malraux found in *The Museum Without Walls*, and that Glenn Gould finds in recorded music. Music in the concert hall had been an anti-environment. The same music when recorded is *music without halls*, as it were.

Another paradoxical aspect of this change is that when music becomes environmental by electric means, it becomes more and more the concern of the private individual. By the same token and complementary to the same paradox the pre-electric music of the concert hall (the music when there was a public instead of a mass audience) was a corporate ritual for the group rather than the individual. This paradox extends to all electrical technology whatever. The same means which permit, for example, a universal and centralized thermostat do in effect encourage a private thermostat for individual manipulation. The age of the mass audience is thus far more individualistic than the preceding age of the *public*. It is this paradoxical dynamic that confuses every issue about 'conformity' today and 'separatism' and 'integration'. Profoundly contradictory actions and directions prevail in all of these situations. This is not surprising in an age of circuitry succeeding the age of the wheel. The feedback loop plays all sorts of tricks to confound the single plane and one-way direction of thought and action as they had been constituted in the pre-electric age of the machine.

Applying the above to the Negro question, one could say that the agrarian South has long tended to regard the Negro as environmental. As such, the Negro is a challenge, a threat, a burden. The very phrase 'white supremacy' quite as much as the phrase 'white trash' registers this environmental attitude. The environment is the enemy that must be subdued. To the rural man the conquest of Nature is an unceasing challenge. It is the Southerner who contributed the cowboy to the frontier. The Virginian, the archetypal cowboy as it were, confronts the environment as a hostile, natural force. To man on the frontier, other men are environmental and hostile. By contrast, to the townsmen, men appear not as environmental, but as content of the urban environment.

Parallel to the Negro question is the French Canada problem. The English Canadians have been the environment of French Canada since the railway and Confederation. However, since the telegraph and radio and television, French Canada and English Canada alike have become the content of this new technology. Electric technology is totally environmental for all human communities today. Hence the great confusion arising from the transformation environments into anti-environments, as it were. All the earlier groupings that had constituted separate environments before electricity have now become anti-environments or the content of the new technology. As such, the old unconscious environments tend to become increasingly centres of acute awareness. The content of any new environment is just as unperceived as the old one had been initially. As a merely automatic sequence, the succession of environments and of the dramatics thereto appertaining, tend to be rather tiresome, if only because the audience is very prone to participate in the dramatics with an enthusiasm proportioned to its unawareness. In the electric age all former environments whatever become anti-environments. As such the old environments are transformed into areas of self-awareness and self-assertion, guaranteeing a very lively interplay of forces.

Eric Havelock in his book *Preface to Plato* has clarified the stages by which the written word served to detribalize the Greek world. After the tribal encyclopedia of oral and memorized wisdom, writing enabled man to organize knowledge by categories and classifications; what Plato called the *ideas*. With the origin of classified data, or visual organization of knowledge, there came also representation in the arts. Representation is itself a form of matching or classifying, unknown to preliterate or native artists. Today we return to non-objective art, non-representational art, because in the electric age we are leaving the world of visual organization of experience.

The visual sense, alone of our senses, creates the forms of space and time that are uniform, continuous and connected. Euclidean space is the prerogative of visual and literate man. With the advent of electric circuitry and the instant movement of information, Euclidean space recedes and the non-Euclidean geometries emerge. Lewis Carroll, the Oxford mathematician, was perfectly aware of this change in our world when he took Alice through the looking glass into the world where each object creates its own space and conditions. To the visual or Euclidean man, objects do not create time and space. They are merely fitted into time and space. The idea of the world as an environment that is more or less fixed, is very much the product of literacy and visual assumptions. In his book *The Philosophical Impact of Modern Physics* Milic Capek explains some of the strange confusions in the scientific mind that result from the encounter of the old non-Euclidean spaces of preliterate man with the Euclidean and Newtonian spaces of literate man. The scientists of our time are just as confused as the philosophers, or the teachers, and it is for the reason that Whitehead assigned; they still have the illusion that the new developments are to be fitted into the old space or environment.

One of the most obvious areas of change in the arts of our time has not only been the dropping of representation, but the dropping of the story line. In poetry, in the novel, in the movie, narrative continuity has yielded to thematic variation. Such variation in place of story line or melodic line has always been the norm in native societies. It is now becoming the norm in our own society and for the same reason, namely that we are becoming a non-visual society.

In the age of circuitry, or feedback, fragmentation and specialism tend to yield to integral forms of organization. Humpty-Dumpty tends to go back together again. The bureaucratic efforts of all the King's horses and all the King's men were naturally calculated to keep Humpty-Dumpty from ever getting together again. The Neolithic age, the age of the planter after the age of the hunter, was an age of specialism and division of labour. It has reached a somewhat startling terminus with the advent of electric circuitry. Circuitry is a profoundly decentralizing process. Paradoxically, it was the wheel and mechanical innovation that created centralism. The circuit reverses the characteristics of the wheel, just as Xerography reverses the characteristics of the printing press. Before printing, the scribe, the author, and the reader tended to merge. With printing, author and publisher became highly specialized and centralized forms of action. With Xerography, author, and publisher, and reader tend to merge once more. Whereas the printed book had been the first mass-produced product, creating uniform prices and markets, Xerography tends to restore the custom-made book. Writing and publishing tend to become services of a corporate and inclusive kind. The printed word created the Public. The Public consists of separate individuals, each with his own point of view. Electric circuitry does not create a Public. It creates the Mass. The Mass does not consist of separate individuals, but of individuals profoundly involved in one another. This involvement is a function, not of numbers, but of speed. The daily newspaper is an interesting example of this fact. The items in the daily press are totally discontinuous and totally unconnected. The only unifying feature of the press is the date line. Through that date line the reader must go, as Alice went, 'through the looking glass'. If it is not today's date line, he cannot get in. Once he goes through the date line, he is involved in a world of items for which he, the reader, must write a story line. He makes the news, as the reader of a detective story makes the plot.

Just as the printed press created the Public as a new environment, so does each new technology or extension of our physical powers tend to create new environments. In the age of information, it is information itself that becomes environmental. The satellites and antennae projected from our planet, for example, have transformed the planet from being an environment into being a probe. This is a transformation which the artists of the past century have been explaining to us in their endless experimental models. Modern art, whether in painting, or poetry, or music, began as a probe and not as a package. The Symbolists literally broke up the old packages and put them into our hands as probes. And whereas the package belongs to a consumer age, the probe belongs to an age of experimenters.

One of the peculiarities of art is to serve as an anti-environment, a probe that makes the environment visible. It is a form of symbolic, or parabolic, action. Parable means literally 'to throw against', just as symbol means 'to throw together'. As we equip the planet with satellites and antennae, we tend to create new environments of which the planet is itself the content. It is peculiar to environments that they are complex processes which transform their content into archetypal forms. As the planet becomes the content of a new information environment, it also tends to become a work of art. Where railway and machine created a new environment for agrarian man, the old agrarian world became an art form. Nature became a work of art. The Romantic movement was born. When the electric circuit went around the mechanical environment, the machine itself became a work of art. Abstract art was born.

As information becomes our environment, it becomes mandatory to program the environment itself as a work of art. The parallel to this appears in Jacques Ellul's *Propaganda* where he sees propaganda, not as an ideology or content of any medium, but as the operation of all the media at once. The mother tongue is propaganda because it exercises an effect on all the senses at once. It shapes our entire outlook and our ways of feeling. Like any other environment, its operation is imperceptible. When an environment is new, we perceive the old one for the first time. What we see on the late show is not TV, but old movies. When the Emperor appeared in his new clothes, his courtiers did not see his nudity, they saw his old clothes. Only the small child and the artist have that immediacy of approach that permits perception of the environmental. The artist provides us with anti-environments that enable us to see the environment. Such anti-environmental means of perception must constantly be renewed in order to be efficacious. That basic aspect of the human condition by which we are rendered incapable of perceiving the environment is one to which psychologists have not even referred. In an age of accelerated change, the need to perceive the environment becomes urgent. Acceleration also makes such perception of the environment more possible. Was it not Bertrand Russell who said that if the bath water got only half a degree warmer every hour, we would never know when to scream? New environments reset our sensory thresholds. These, in turn, alter our outlook and expectations.

The need of our time is for the means of measuring sensory thresholds and of discovering exactly what changes occur in these thresholds as a result of the advent of any particular technology. With such knowledge in hand it would be possible to program a reasonable and orderly future for any human community. Such knowledge would be the equivalent of a thermostatic control for room temperatures. It would seem only reasonable to extend such controls to all the sensory thresholds of our being. We have no reason to be grateful to those who juggle the thresholds in the name of haphazard innovation.

Richard Kostelanetz
Marshall McLuhan

One tends to be content to attribute importance to what is measurable merely because it happens to be measurable. KARL MANNHEIM

Marshall McLuhan's two recent books are an intellectual necessity, but hardly a critic's delight. They repel the impatient reader. Their sentences are generally clumsy, despite scattered passages of high grace and true wit; the paragraphs are carelessly constructed; his thoughts are so diffusely organized that the book's pages need not be read chronologically. Moreover, the ideas are so original that they often evade immediate comprehension; and McLuhan's presentation of his insights at first seems arbitrary in manner and excessively dogmatic in tone. To make matters more difficult still, *Understanding Media* often inspires an animus (unjustified, I believe) in people excessively committed to the culture of print. Still, since these are books that must be assimilated, it is nothing but scandalous that between the few short reviews and the numerous profiles in the popular press, the anxious puffs and the ill-considered demolitions, truly open and discriminating criticism of McLuhan's hypotheses has been sparse.

In his first work, *The Mechanical Bride* (1951), needlessly out-of-print and exorbitantly expensive on the used-book markets, McLuhan explains his 'method' as adapting the analytical techniques of modern art criticism to the study of both popular culture and society itself; and like the best art criticism, his original insights are most adept at illuminating forms other eyes have missed – when they literally render the invisible visible.

In the opening pages of *The Mechanical Bride*, McLuhan perceives, 'It is on its technical and mechanical side that the front page [of newspapers] is linked to the techniques of modern science and art. Discontinuity is in different ways a basic concept of both quantum and relativity physics. It is the way in which a Toynbee looks at civilization, or a Margaret Mead at human cultures. Notoriously, it is the visual technique of a Picasso, the literary technique of James Joyce.' In addition to being indubitably true in its individual perceptions, this passage, as it incorporates a wide range of examples, succeeds in identifying a central overarching characteristic of the contemporary sensibility. I would place it among the most illuminating passages in all modern criticism.

In *The Gutenberg Galaxy*, perhaps McLuhan's most coherently realized book, he offers the following broad insight into the impact of print on the culture of Western man: 'The visual [the perceptual mode of the man raised on print] makes for the explicit, the uniform, and the sequential in painting, in poetry, in logic, in history. The non-literate modes are implicit, simultaneous, and discontinuous whether in the primitive past or in the electronic present.' Here McLuhan transcends his earlier insight by explaining why contemporary culture should find discontinuity a more congenial organizing principle than causality.

Unlike *The Mechanical Bride*, realized as just a series of explanatory glosses, the two more recent books embody significant theses about the major causes of historical change and the radical character of contemporary civilization. Adopting a mode of explanation I can only christen, against his objections, 'technological determinism', McLuhan suggests that the invention of a certain, crucially relevant tool or machine initiates huge transformations in the physical environment, man's social relations, and his perception of experience. For instance, McLuhan surmises that the railroad, in centralizing commerce and transportation around depots, historically shaped the structure of the cities, the character of urban social life, and the peculiar sensibilities of city people; however, the automobile initiated similarly widespread changes in developing the suburbs where houses are accessible largely, if not entirely, through private transportation.

With the crossing of the new technology with the old environment – when the automobile enters the city – the result is chaos.

Pursuing this principle of technological determinism, McLuhan develops a more specific scheme of historical explanation, which I would call 'informational technological determinism'. Here he suggests that a radical change in the dominant technology of communication is the prime initiating force behind human change. By weaving a mosaic of examples (which offer a theme), rather than developing an argument (which would offer a thesis), he suggests in *The Gutenberg Galaxy* that the invention of movable type, which made the printing press possible, radically transformed the culture of Western man, producing phenomena as various as the predominantly visual orientation of the man who prefers print, the linear structure that superseded the repetitious forms of medieval art, a kind of music abstractly divorced from the art's origins in speech, a Protestant religion made possible by the book's capacity to induce individual revelation, the psychological mode of inner-direction, the epistemology of causal explanations, and the mechanical technology that created man's sense of alienation from his environment.

As an interpretation of cultural history, McLuhan's scheme contributes to the contemporary quarrel with those traditional methods of historiography which emphasize, for example, politicians or 'great men' as the prime movers, economic factors as predominantly determining, and the mind as a stronger force than matter. The theme of technological determinism is hardly McLuhan's invention. What is original is McLuhan's outrageous comprehensiveness – his willingness to interpret so many aspects of experience as shaped by technologies of communication – as he weaves the diverse observations of others (extensively quoted and credited) into a moderately coherent whole.

In *Understanding Media*, very much the sequel to *The Gutenberg Galaxy*, McLuhan's theme is that the new electronic communications technologies of the twentieth century are the determining force in shaping modern culture. Telegraph, telephone, radio, television, automation have radically transformed all experience ranging from social organization to human perception of space and time; for just as the telephone significantly speeds the flow of business, so television makes all news current. Whereas the predominant organizing principle of print culture was linear – introduction, development, and conclusion – contemporary culture is characterized by repetition, juxtaposition, overlap and disjunction. 'Electricity', writes McLuhan, 'ended sequence by making things instant; it is the new mosaic form of the TV image that has replaced the Gutenberg structural assumptions.' Electronic media also downgrade the visual capacity by requiring multi-sensory comprehensions – aural and kinetic as well as visual – as in the movies, and now television.

Unlike intellectuals who condemn the mass media completely – the larger the mass the more vehement the condemnation – or look at them only as an occasion to damn them again, McLuhan was among the first North American intellectuals to investigate precisely what the new media implied and how their forms would affect people. Essentially, McLuhan recognizes that the new media represent 'extensions of man'; as such, they embody both opportunity and threat. First, they increase the range of man's control and impact over his environment – the telephone extends the voice and ear; all switches and dials extend the power of thought. Yet they also increase the environment's potential power over him.

Most of *Understanding Media* is devoted to McLuhan's examination of the major electronic media to define the peculiar character of each, which is to say its limitations and possibilities in communication, as well as the ways it characteristically handles experience. Here the techniques of art criticism are crucially useful, because they illuminate forms that might otherwise remain unperceived.

To define, first, the nature of the medium's expression and, second, the interaction of a medium with human attention, McLuhan posits the descriptive terms of 'hot' and 'cool'. The former word identifies media (or experiences or people) with highly defined contents – a considerable amount of detailed information. Instances include a movie screen or a page of print. Low-definition or 'cool' media offer only outlines; examples include cartoons and television. Secondly, where a hot medium fosters detachment and skepticism, a cool medium requires that its audience mentally participate to complete the communication. Watching television, for instance, requires more concentration than mere looking, because the dots of the screen offer only outlines of figures; thus our brain literally learns to flesh in the characters on the screen. Similarly, conversation has a low definition – it is 'cool'; a lecture is definitely hot.

Although most hot media create hot responses, a hot medium can be used to stimulate the cool, participational quality of television and *vice versa*. Alain Resnais' *Last Year at Marienbad* (1961) offers a cool experience in a hot medium; a play presented on radio has a cooler impact than it would in a theatrical performance (because it forces us to visualize the characters); a face-to-face argument creates a hot experience in the cool medium of human talk. Applying this distinction, McLuhan illuminates phenomena that others perceive but cannot explain, such as why the contents and effects of television are so different from those of either radio or movies. Whereas radio requires, for example, a performance of high definition – announcers attempt to develop a distinctive voice that is instantly recognizable – television favors performers of a definition so low they appear almost bland, like Jack Paar, Johnny Carson and Ed Sullivan.

Indeed, perhaps the most extraordinary quality of McLuhan's mind is that it discerns significances where others see only data or nothing; he tells us how to measure, in the Mannheim sense, phenomena previously unmeasurable. 'What Parkinson hides from himself and his readers is simply the fact that [clerical staff always increases because] the main "work to be done" is actually the movement of information.' '"Mass media", "mass entertainment" [are] useless phrases obscuring the fact that English itself is a mass medium.' Most of his most perspicacious insights stem from considering how differences in the sensory ratios of a culture affect its cultural materials. One can imagine a Ph.D. thesis (if not several) slogged out of the following off-hand remark: 'In [contemporary] literature only people from backward oral areas had any resonance to inject into the language – the Yeatses, the Synges, the Joyces, Faulkners and Dylan Thomases.' 'The printed book will naturally tend to become a work of reference rather than a speaking wisdom.' Conversely, the advertising jingle contributes to the return to oral (and aural) guidance. 'The unique character of our alphabet [is that, unlike idiograms or hieroglyphs, it] separates all meaning from the sounds of letters.' These remarks resemble McLuhan's books; for they are more valuable for their stimulating insights that complement our understanding than for any final definitions of formative forces.

Because his perceptions penetrate beneath the surface of observations, McLuhan's ideas also have much in common with other radical tendencies in contemporary American thought. Like Buckminster Fuller and Herbert Marcuse, McLuhan recognizes that cybernation (the automation of work processes), as it eliminates work and increases leisure, promises to give nearly every man the opportunity to devote all his energies to the cultivation of his powers; and not only does McLuhan favor a guaranteed income (in Robert Theobald's anthology of that title), but he also envisions that continuous education will become the prime business of a future society.

Also, like Paul Goodman and Edgar Z. Friedenberg, McLuhan argues that today's conventional education hardly engages the interest of young people, largely because it insufficiently equips them for coping with the actualities of their world. 'Our classrooms and our curricula', he writes in Charles R. Dechert's (ed.) *The Social Impact of Cybernetics*, 'are still modeled on the old industrial environment. What is indicated for the new learning procedures is not the absorption of classified and fragmented data, but pattern recognition with all that that implies of grasping interrelationships.' Like Herman Kahn and Norman O. Brown, McLuhan believes in thinking which is exploratory and speculative, rather than substantive and definitive; and the books of all three are products of men who do not necessarily believe in their thoughts. Just as Norman O. Brown insists in *Life Against Death* that he tries 'merely to introduce some new possibilities and new problems into the public consciousness', by offering a series of unashamedly outrageous speculations, so Herman Kahn imagines 'scenarios' to conjecture about future possibilities; and so McLuhan speculates about the impact of media. Finally, all three men are similar in that they offer not theses but themes.

Particularly in their grasp of the development of civilization, McLuhan and Brown posit similar ideas. In *Life Against Death*, Brown reinterprets the later thought of Sigmund Freud to suggest not only that the repressiveness of civilized society is the prime cause of neurosis but also that mankind, in the course of human history, is slowly eliminating instinctual repressions for a more fully libidinal existence. McLuhan parallels Brown by arguing that while mechanized society, derived in principle from print, alienates man from his environment, electronic media usher in the end of alienation, first, by extending man's senses into his surroundings; secondly, by favoring more participational, low-definition experiences; and, thirdly, by recreating that oral bond that tied primitive society together. In short, by locating the prime source of mental distress not in man but in his environment, both men predict that as changing society becomes more sympathetic to the human essence, most anxiety and neurosis will disappear.

Similarly, both thinkers predict the end of man's slavery to segmented time; for future man will have less awareness of past and future. 'Both time (as measured visually and segmentally) and space (as uniform, pictorial, and enclosed) disappear in the electronic age of instant information', McLuhan writes; and Brown identifies the connection between timed existence and civilization's repression. 'Only repressed life is in time, and unrepressed life would be timeless or in eternity.' It follows that as man loses his sense of quantified time (and, thus, his conception of life as a series of stages), he develops a different attitude toward death. 'Eternity', Brown writes, 'is therefore a way of envisaging mankind's liberation from the neurotic obsession with the past and the future.' McLuhan conjectures that the electronic media will return man to the pre-print perspective that views death as not a termination of existence but an extension of life into a different realm – literally, a life after life. (Indicatively, only non-print cultures can accept the idea of reincarnation.)

Most conspicuously absent from *Media* is any discussion of the future of sexual activity; but on this subject, I believe, McLuhan's implications correspond with Brown's ideas. The latter thinker envisions the decline of sexuality focused upon genital contact and a return to the 'polymorphously perverse', unfocused, purely libidinal pleasure characteristic of the baby; McLuhan's thoughts suggest, by extension, that the focus upon genital pleasure, particularly upon the genital orgasm, is related to print; for not only does genital sexuality resemble reading in requiring a concentration of attention, but also its conception of pleasure is analogous to the reading of a traditional novel – a progressive heightening of tension to a total release. In contrast, polymorphous, omniattentive sensuality is formally analogous to the constant pleasures afforded by the electronic media, with their diffusion of attention and absence of climax; and just as the child's sexuality is 'cool' and unfocused until society teaches him a 'hot' genital orientation, so a baby's attention is unfocused until he learns to read print.

Indicatively, the sexual manuals of pre-print cultures, such as the *Kama Sutra*, espouse a notion of sexual pleasure considerably different from the predominantly genital (and orgasmic) preoccupations of Alfred Kinsey and Wilhelm Reich. Sex in the future, both Brown and McLuhan suggest, will be more continuous or constant in time and more diffuse in its multiple erotogenic range. In these respects – the proliferation of pleasure, the disintegration of linear time, the increase in diverse libidinal pleasure – both Brown and McLuhan imagine a future similar to, as its participants describe it, the hallucinogen experience on a grand scale; and all together, these radical thinkers and actors suggest a future utopia on earth not unlike our traditional conceptions of heaven.

Not everything in McLuhan's books is true or perceptive; for McLuhan's methods for achieving insights frequently inspire incredible, if not inscrutable, leaps from reality. Some problems stem from his major theme that 'the medium is the message', which is to say several things: first, the ultimate content of the medium is the medium itself; that is, people watch movies primarily for pleasures offered by a kinetic screen accompanied by relevant sound, just as people like reading for the joy of watching print pass before their eyes. Second, 'it is the medium that shapes and controls the scale and form of human association and action'; that is, communications media are the primary force in shaping a society. Third, the 'message' of the medium is its impact upon society – the idea of informational technological determinism; that is, 'the message of the movie medium is that of transition from lineal connection to configuration'.

In the first sense, I believe McLuhan is largely wrong; for he completely discounts the question of what appears on the screen and speaker. As anyone who has ever watched movies knows, some of them are more interesting – more engaging and stimulating – than others (just as some are more soporific); and much of the difference depends upon the quality of what we traditionally call the program's 'content'. However, McLuhan is correct in implying that we are more tolerant of bad content in the media we favor; as a writer I can read most anything, whereas a bad movie either puts me to sleep or drives me out of the theater.

The second dimension of 'The medium is the message' has considerably more truth. What McLuhan says here is that the medium determines the kinds of experience and information it can most propitiously present and, thus, what kinds of impact it can have. For philosophical exposition, for instance, the book is quite obviously the most viable medium; for it allows each reader to pursue the thought at his own pace as well as to recheck on earlier statement. Moreover, the second corollary says that as media shape the modes and situations of response – continuity or discontinuity; by oneself, or in a group – they influence ('shape' more than 'control') human social life. Thus, he conjectures that TV and movies, where large numbers watch the same thing all at once, will institute retribalization; however, since media are often observed alone and since not everyone watches the same program, retribalization through TV alone would be unlikely. In short, then, where McLuhan's thesis of the medium and the message runs false is precisely in its exclusionary determinism. *The medium is not the entire message, just as it does not totally control the message.* What McLuhan does, here and elsewhere, is escalate a real insight into a fantastic iron-clad generalization; so that only if one takes these grandiose statements with skepticism will one grasp the truths they have to offer.

McLuhan's mind is, by nature, more admissive than exclusionary; not only is it open to experience that other intellectuals either dismiss or neglect, but he also exhibits the tendency to admit all his own thoughts to print. Just as some of them are more comprehensible than others, so some are considerably more perceptive. What I fear is that many people impressed with the brilliance of so much will suspect that everything McLuhan says is true – even worse, true in precisely the way he says it.

Since even the author regards his insights as 'exploratory probes', the reader must, of necessity, subject these perceptions to the most rigorous critical scrutiny. McLuhan is deeply indebted to James Joyce – indeed, floating around in *Media* is the nucleus of a brilliant critical book on Joyce's work (a task, I understand, he has passed on to his eldest son); and McLuhan has said, 'Much of what I talk about is in *Finnegans Wake*.' The trouble is that in addition to taking his love of punning from Joyce, McLuhan adopts Joyce's most indulgent habits of thought. The organizing principle of the *Wake*, one remembers, is that one story is all stories – to put it differently, at the base of the novel's major actions is the tale of familial conflict. Thus, on the same page, Joyce writes about a range of filial relationships – England and Ireland, Eliot and Yeats, Romulus and Remus, Mutt and Jeff, Shem and Shaun, Greece and Rome, etc.

What Joyce did, then, was transcend the metaphoric relation – that one story is like another – for associations that, as they eliminate the metaphoric dimension completely, transform analogies into identities. McLuhan performs similar leaps, as he writes in *Media* that 'The electric light is pure information.' By this gnomic sentence, he intends a metaphoric meaning – that the electric light resembles an information medium in that it tells us about something else; without the light, we would not recognize the content it illuminates. However, such an elliptical statement obfuscates meaning, and such an inclusive intelligence loses its sense of discrimination – if they are so much like each other, then there would be no discernible difference between them.

This process of converting correspondences into identities (which, indicatively, also informs Norman O. Brown's *Love's Body*) accomplishes, metaphorically, a transubstantiation, a doctrine which generally separates the post-print Protestant intelligence from the pre-print Catholic; where the former says the bread *represents* the body of Christ, the latter rules that, at a certain point in the Mass, it *is* the body of Christ. What may rationalize McLuhan's inclusive logic, perhaps, is his notion that differentiation and classification are modes typical of the age of print; he quotes, for example, Philippe Ariès' observation that the idea of 'childhood' as a distinct stage did not arise until the seventeenth century.

In contrast, the contemporary modes, McLuhan feels, are inclusion and unification; and just as the avant-garde in each modern art overlaps into another – theatre into dance with *The Brig* and Happenings and music into theatre with John Cage – so newspapers and mass magazines deny traditional difference by homogenizing all experience. Similarly, where uniformity in grammar and definitions is a product of print, the new writing, like much new art (and McLuhan's new scholarship), is less committed to traditional precision; and McLuhan's use of certain abstract words such as 'myth' and 'archetype' is highly idiosyncratic – perhaps more metaphoric than accurate. ('Printed grammars since the eighteenth century', writes McLuhan, 'created a fog based on the concept of correctness.')

The major trouble with, say, the transformations of analogies into identities are, first, that they betray the experience we know – the light bulb is simply not an informational medium in the way televison is – and, second, that such statements, as they defy precise analysis, corrupt the language of explanation. Until man ceases to recognize such crucial differences, perhaps (and only perhaps) an inevitable result of the electronic revolution, McLuhan errs in neglecting them. 'You can prove nothing by analogy', Ezra Pound says in *ABC of Reading*, incidentally one of McLuhan's favorite books. 'The analogy is either range-finding or fumble. Written down as a lurch toward proof... it leads mainly to useless argument.' Alas, Pound, too, exaggerates his perception.

Likewise Joycean is the circular structure of all McLuhan's books; for the principle he announces in *The Mechanical Bride* – 'No need for it to be read in any special order' – is more or less applicable to his other books. McLuhan's rationale for such a procedure is buried in an extraordinary passage on page 26 of *Media*:

> The Hebrew and Eastern mode of thought tackles problem and resolution, at the outset of a discussion, in a way typical of oral societies in general. The entire message is then traced and retraced, again and again, on the rounds of a concentric spiral with seeming redundancy. One can stop anywhere after the first few sentences and have the full message, if one is prepared to 'dig' it. [This] redundant form [is] inevitable to the electric age, in which the concentric pattern is imposed by the instant quality, and overlay in depth, of electric speed. But the concentric with its endless intersection of planes is necessary for insight. In fact, it is the technique of insight, and as such is necessary for media study, since no medium has its meaning or existence alone, but only in constant interplay with other media.

This I consider among McLuhan's most disturbing ideas; and although I recognize that presentation and arguments are rhetorically tied to the linear form, I am not sure, as McLuhan is, that insight is instantaneous. A full understanding of any process, whether of complicated mechanisms or complex ideas, requires some form of successive thought; and if the process is to be effectively communicated, the writer (or speaker) should use developmental syntax.

The most obvious criticism of McLuhan's interpretations is his rampaging tendency to over-explain. Not only are his ideas too deterministic, not only does he facilely transform analogies into identities, not only does he tend to encompass all other interpretations of experience within his own (rather than arguing against them), but he ties up his materials into a package too neat for their realities. Quite often, he becomes the victim of his own ideas, conjuring his interpretations through highly resistant evidence.

Much of his prophecy stems from the speculation that as man overcomes his slavery to literacy, he will attain a sensibility similar to that of primitive man; thus, McLuhan creates a dialectical vision of history by continually referring to pre-print experience (thesis) for his images of the present and future (synthesis) that contrasts with the age of print (antithesis). He notes in *The Gutenberg Galaxy* that soon after the impact of print, music became divorced from its origins in song (and speech); therefore, by expecting that all important contemporary music will complete the circle, McLuhan asserts in *Media* that not only does jazz have its origins in speech but also that 'Schoenberg and Stravinsky and Carl Orff and Bartók, far from being advanced seekers of esoteric effects, seem to have brought music very close to the conditions of ordinary human speech.' This may be true for Orff, it might be somewhat true for Bartók; but as for Schoenberg, the remark has nothing to do with his central contribution to contemporary musical thought. In fact, serial music is so abstract, so divorced from speech, that an accurate description of its methods forbids extrinsic analogies.

At another point, McLuhan conjures that since pre-print art was corporate and anonymous in authorship, so will be post-print art. However, TV is corporate less because of the nature of the medium than the existing practices for making programs, and the greatest films, except perhaps the Marx brothers', reveal the touch of an individual director. The point is that once society develops a certain mode of conceptual awareness, it will not necessarily disappear when that society (or its communications technology) changes; historical memory persistently survives new situations. In one sense, McLuhan admits this tendency to exaggerate, insisting that as his ideas are just explorations he feels no need to defend them as scrupulously as a Ph.D. candidate would his thesis. On the other hand, as his dogmatic style and messianic tone subvert his more modest intentions, his lack of rigor makes him an easy target for debunking marksmen.

The point is that other forces beside media shape human experience, both contemporary and historical, as well as the experience of media. The drive for money, for instance, seems to be a universal quality, doled out in unequal measure; and McLuhan's ideas are unable to explain why they should be so. His chapter on money, probably the foggiest in *Media*, makes the obvious prediction that the credit card will replace printed money as the 'currency' of the new age. However, these remarks fail to cope with the real importance of money in media; after all, as Harry J. Skornia demonstrates in *Television and Society* (1965), a book McLuhan curiously blurbed, the major inspiration behind television practice today is the possibilities of enormous profits, not the potentialities of the medium; and as McLuhan's commentary eschews the crucial question of media ownership, it cannot explain the vast and real differences between British radio and television and American.

Since McLuhan attempts to downgrade the power of politicians and political structures, he has little awareness of how they can, in fact, shape a considerable portion of our existence, even our relationship to the media. People cannot have television unless their state permits it; and governmental politics, as we note, often influence, if not control, the content of the programs, usually with scant awareness of the nature of the medium. Likewise absent from *Media* is any elaboration of Harold A. Innis' version of 'the medium is the message' – that each new form of communication initiates a shift in political power. Furthermore, it is simply preposterous to say, 'The Cold War is largely a conflict between cultures where different sense priorities prevail. The U.S. is eye-oriented. The Soviet Union, with its limited traditions of literacy, is ear-oriented.' Similarly naïve is McLuhan's prediction, perhaps self-ironic, that 'If the "Voice of America" suddenly switched to jazz, the Kremlin would have reason to crumble.' In the end, McLuhan's insights into experience are, as I suggested before, more acceptable as a complement to, rather than a replacement for, other interpretations. He is innocent to omit economic activity, sexual desire and political forces in modern society; merely forgetting them will not make them go away.

Although McLuhan eschews political directives, *Understanding Media* strikes me as implicitly a most persuasive polemic for the necessity of communicatarian anarchism. McLuhan continually predicts that the electronic media and cybernation will produce the decentralization of society (perhaps because it fits into his dialectical scheme); however, he never quite explains how, in the age of networks and expanding government power, this 'uniqueness and diversity' and 'new world of autonomy and decentralization in all human affairs' will occur. Indeed, by implication, particularly in their images of a possible future, his books suggest that the only way to overcome the incipient nightmare of *1984* is through the dismantling of society to its natural boundaries of existing communities – the political separation of cities from their suburbias and both from the rural areas – and the creation of wholly autonomous communications media within each of these enclaves. McLuhan implies this when he writes, 'Restraints of electric absolutist power can be achieved not by the separation of powers, but by a pluralism of centers.' Such action, it seems to me, is not only a desirable political solution to this age of superpowers but also a spiritual necessity in an era of possible global conformity; and McLuhan confirms this prognostication by suggesting that rebellion will not attract sympathy unless it is instigated by a group for the sake of a *community* opposed to unjust authority.

As intellectual endeavors, McLuhan's books merit nothing but highest praise; in spite of their intrinsically high-definitional quality, they invite participation in their processes of thought, initiating not only dialogues between the reader and the book but between one reader and another. They are among the richest books of our time; and I doubt if any intelligent person can read them without being enlightened, if not influenced, in some way – educated to cope better with his present environment. Indeed, precisely because his thought presumes that mankind, by recognizing technology's importance, can overcome its determining power and shape the social environment to his needs, McLuhan is profoundly humanistic.

Amidst all their chaff, McLuhan's books contain much truth; more important, to many of us, they initiate an education – an awareness of significant dimensions previously hidden to us – as they make invisible visible and the unconscious conscious. Like other great native thinkers, McLuhan embodies that peculiarly North American capacity to push ideas, often derived from others, beyond conventional bounds to the wildest conclusions – literally levels beyond other minds in the same field – creating a book in which enormous good-sense and outright non-sense are so closely entwined; and in our post-Marxist, post-existentialist, post-Christian age, such exploratory thought is more valuable and necessary to our culture than another serving of time-worn ideas.

John Simon Norman Brown's Body

The prophets of the Lord were stoned. In an age that had a God, or batches of rival gods, prophets were a luxury if not a downright redundancy. But in an age that has no God, and that is afraid, prophets are something to fall back on. If Aaron's rod does not perform miracles, it can at least point in some direction, however arbitrary; and if it cannot even be used as a signpost, it might still do as a crutch. Or as something to flagellate ourselves with. Let him who is without fear of the void cast the first stone. There is no God, and Norman O. Brown – or Marshall McLuhan, or Timothy Leary – is his prophet.

When Norman O. Brown's *Life Against Death* appeared in 1959, it was viewed either as a serious critical interpretation of Freud or as a rather endearing piece of eccentricity. A professor of Classics writing ostensibly about 'the psychoanalytical meaning of history' while actually advocating the adult's return to the infant's 'polymorphous perverse' sexuality, and getting it published by a sober university press – well! But no one suspected that this book, which called for 'an erotic sense of reality', would become an underground classic, its content earnestly debated by the reading minority, its catchwords astonishedly mouthed by the quoting majority, its influence considerable – to be sure, mostly on those already inclined toward, or practicing, its preachments.

Life Against Death was mainly about the inability of repression or sublimation – whether in the form of systematic thought, economic security, religion, science, or psychoanalysis – to make life full and death acceptable. The man-made soul, like money which is really feces, is only 'the shadowy substitute for bodily relation to other bodies'. Brown came out for 'the wisdom of folly', for man's accepting his sickness, and endeavoring to 'become once more . . . a body-ego . . . sensing that communication between body and body which is life'. The ultimate solution, then, is 'that Dionysian ego which does not negate any more', i.e. the ability to 'circumvent the limitations imposed by the formal-logical law of contradiction'. This entails 'a willing suspension of common sense', and finally, 'a little more Eros and less strife', the increase of the former, presumably, ensuring the decrease of the latter. Or: Down with the reality-principle, up the pleasure-principle! So Eros and Thanatos will be reconciled.

The book was mostly a nosography of our emotional and spiritual shortcomings, its apparent protagonist Freud, its real hero Jakob Boehme; only in a brief concluding chapter was 'the way out' of our predicament outlined. *Love's Body*, Brown's new book, continues and develops that final section. But whereas the earlier volume was written in the conventional discursive form, the new work – and this is the most remarkable thing about it – is subdivided into sixteen sections with headings like 'Nature', 'Person', 'Boundary', 'Food', 'Fraction', 'Resurrection', 'Fulfillment', 'Nothing', and each of these consists of a series of aphorisms or miniature essays that are loosely connected and that list at the bottom certain books, or passages from books, that have served as inspiration for the foregoing, or have actually been quoted therein. But there are no footnotes (perish the thought of anything so academic!), and it is often hard to tell exactly which of several authorities said what. But, presumably, in a world in which individuation is to be banished and health achieved by a universal merger, questions of authorship become nugatory and pedantic.

Just what the book is about has stumped even that usually omniscient mystagogue, the blurb-writer, who here contents himself with nothing more than listing the chapter headings. Before I venture where he has feared to tread, I had better evoke the form, which, as in all mystico-symbolic works (and, according to McLuhan, in television) *is* the message. In her otherwise extremely cogent review of *Love's Body*, Brigid Brophy[1] commits the one error of deriving its form from Wittgenstein's *Tractatus*. Even the most cursory glance into Wittgenstein, as well as the mere consideration of Brown's antirationalism, would suffice to eliminate anything as rigorously methodical from the parentage of *Love's Body*. The aphoristic-didactic style with its meandering, sometimes footstep-retracing, sometimes subterraneous and unfollowable, progression, and with its cryptically Orphic, Messianic, indeed millenarian utterances, is clearly related to the mystical and prophetic works, the sacred books of all time and all place, whose high-water mark in the modern era was *Thus Spake Zarathustra*, and whose last ripple Miss Susan Sontag's 'Notes on Camp'.

The form, then, is a philosophy preached not by logic and consecutiveness ('the destruction of the law of contradiction is the supreme task of the higher logic') but by gnomic-gnostic snippets relying on such devices as alliteration and assonance, rhyme, punning, anaphora, refrain, repetition, inversion, ellipsis (especially the omission of articles and auxiliary verbs), sudden lapses into vernacular, word play (particularly playing around with etymology, sometimes pseudo-etymology), and, in general, pushing prose toward free verse. 'Wisdom is wit; in play, not in work; in freedom, not in necessity. A vast pun, as in dreams, in the neologisms of schizophrenia, in *Finnegans Wake*, in the Old Testament prophets.' And: 'the original sense is nonsense', so that we must go 'from disguised to patent nonsense'. For 'wisdom is . . . in fooling, most excellent fooling'.

There, I suppose, lies the question: how excellent is Brown's fooling? Here are some samples. 'This cave is grave; this womb is tomb'; 'to be stuck together in eternal coitus; wedlock as deadlock'; 'the potentialities are latent till made patent'. 'The complexities of intellectual systems; a web of deceit, a woof wove called Science. *Hyphen, hymen, hymn, hypnos*. The net or nexus. Networks of affiliation: the filial relation is not natural but artificial, threaded (*filum*).' 'Mother is mold; *modder*, matter;

[1] 'Demolish the Ego', in *New York Times Book Review* (24 July 1966).

Mutter is mud.' (This etymology, by the way, is sheer whimsy.) 'The natural order is our construction, our constriction'; 'the shellfishness of selfishness' – this last, obviously, under the influence of Bacchus, whom Brown repeatedly hails as the true god. 'Mars is . . . martial as well as marital'; 'the altar . . . is both post erected and table spread' (do you get it? 'spread' also as legs are spread, hence both phallic and vaginal). 'The staff that cleaves the waters is the dead man's body, the corpse; the stiff that ejaculates the soul or the semen is the penis. Penis or corpse, stiff as stone; a perpetual erection, or monument.' 'The representative organ is . . . a safety deposit bank; a pocket for the peckers of the public . . . the Pecker, bearing (baring) the Person of them all.'

And now one aphorism in full:

> To reconcile body and spirit would be to recover the breath-soul which is the life-soul instead of the ghost-soul or shadow; breath-consciousness instead of brain-consciousness; body-consciousness instead of head-consciousness. The word made flesh is a living word, not a scripture but a breathing. A line that comes from the breath, from the heart by way of the breath. [I could see from the *lungs* by way of the breath.] Aphorism as utterance: a short breath, drawn in pain. Winged words, birds released from the sentence, doves of the spirit.

What does distinguish Brown's stentorian stenography, these apocalyptic apothegms (you see, it's easy: anyone can do it!) from those of other prophets is that they carry with them, as the Nile does hippopotamuses, quotations from or references to the most numerous and heterogeneous authors imaginable. The last-quoted aphorism, for example, credits Bachelard's *La Poétique de l'espace*, a note by Charles Olson on his poetry, and Robert Duncan's *Letters*. Another, a mere two-liner, gives as credentials Sartre's *Critique de la raison dialectique*, Dante's *Paradiso*, and Matthew xi 12. Yet another cites Lidz, 'Strindberg's Creativity and Schizophrenia', Hopkins's 'The Blessed Virgin Compared to the Air We Breathe', *Chandogya Upanishad*, v ii 1; v xviii 1, and Roheim's 'Das Selbst'. Everything is grist for Brown's Satanic mills, from Kerouac to Höfler's *Germanisches Sakralkönigtum*, from McLuhan to Schlossmann's *Persona und πρόσωπον im Recht und im Christlichen Dogma*. The polymath as miller, the molinary millenarian, the scholar-gipsy, a veritable secular Kahlil Gibran. Yet the curious thing is that Brown is against scholarship and intellectual baggage and repeatedly enjoins us to 'travel light'. But you cannot accuse of contradiction him who is for the transcending of contradiction. Or can you?

What underlies this farrago is fear. Fear of one's weakness, of one's mortality, and, for all I know, fear of one's neurosis or inadequate or unorthodox sexuality. I have nothing against all of these as long as they are not converted into a philosophy or, worse, a religion. And a religion is precisely what Brown is peddling, despite his assertion that what we need is poetry, which, he says, is voluntary mystical participation. But Brown's is a religion because it preaches, hectors, deprecates, anathematizes, and commands. Even while he is against the either/or mentality, his book is a monument to it: banish reason, possession, the self – or perish; even though he is for affirmation, he is haranguing away against the rational, the individual, the precisely defined. Poetry is non-prescriptive; Brown, like other religionists, prescribes.

And what is this religion? Variations on the old *unio mystica*, even if the gap to be bridged is not called that between God and man but between self and not-self, contemplation and violence, Oriental dematerialization of the universe and Occidental hedonism, Christ and Dionysus, Eros (sex) and Thanatos (death), word and silence. Brown continually fluctuates from one to the other, ceaselessly tries, by means of paradox or word play, to reconcile or equate them – or, by finding some *tertium quid* that will act as alkahest, to dissolve them in it, in each other.

The solution is to return to prehistory: history is 'sadistic masturbatory fantasies'. Politics is 'a gang-bang', or 'pissing in public'; the state is 'the primal crime'. Economics, possession are evil because they impose boundaries: even the possession of oneself is harmful delimitation. There must be no social differences; instead, 'every throne a toilet seat, and every toilet seat a throne'. Science and scholarship are merely 'univocation', Procrustean observance of the dead letter. The word must return to the flesh.

But there is the problem: the word must return to the flesh and *also* become symbolic silence. ('A penis in every convex object and a vagina in every concave one' – a charming notion of poetic symbolism.) We have not yet begun to live, but we must look to the end. We must overthrow the reality-principle which is the prince of darkness, but we must awake and stop dreaming. If we abolish the self, there will be no more war, and 'it is only as long as a distinction is made between real and imaginary murders that real murders are worth committing' – yet 'freedom is violence'. The way out of the maze seems to be through these four: the body, unification, madness, silence. The body makes us aware of our identity with one another, but how can we reconcile this with the 'real fire [being] Contemplative Thought'? Well, Brown tells us, upwards is downwards, and vice versa. The head and the penis must become one and the same. How? Through unification with the world in polymorphous perversity, I suppose. But how can we, with the differences we have developed in our various minds and sensibilities, become one? The solution is madness, and Brown repeatedly tells us: 'the insane are closer to the truth', 'it is not schizophrenia but normality that is split-minded; in schizophrenia the false boundaries are disintegrating', 'the norm is not normality but schizophrenia, the . . . crucified mind'. But, alas, there are 'those schizophrenics who treat words as real objects' and suffer from inability to accept 'object-loss' and to settle for the symbol. And that would seem to be the final solution: symbolism, which 'conveys both absence and presence', which lets in silence, the void. 'The obstacle to incarnation is our horror of the void.' But would embracing the void, however that is done, incarnate us? Brown would answer, Yes, if we realize that 'everything is only a metaphor; there is only poetry'.

So, from the fine indulgence in our bodies, we have fallen upon mere recognition of Maya, the world as illusion. But what matter if *Love's Body* is only free association, unresolved contradictions, and occasional erotic sensationalism, usually derived from Melanie Klein, probably the most rabidly doctrinaire hyper-Freudian. (I was amazed not to find her in the bibliography of *Life Against Death*, but this gap, at any rate, has been bridged: the bibliography of *Love's Body* lists twelve items by her.) With this book, Brown takes his rightful place between Marshall McLuhan and Habakkuk. For, like McLuhan, he fulfills the four requirements for our prophets: (1) to span and reconcile, however grotesquely, various disciplines to the relief of a multitude of uneasy specialists: (2) to affirm something, even if it is something negative, retrogressive, mad; (3) to justify something vulgar or sick or indefensible in us, whether it be television-addiction (McLuhan) or schizophrenia (Brown); (4) to abolish the need for discrimination, difficult choices, balancing mind and appetite, and so reduce the complex orchestration of life to the easy strumming of a monochord. Brown and McLuhan have nicely apportioned the world between them: the inward madness for the one, the outward manias for the other. After that, everything works as long as we are sufficiently browbeaten not to ask questions like (1) How do we do it – become polymorphously perverse, resexualize life, give up possessions, unite with one another – exactly how? (2) What if people cannot be added, equated, manipulated – because they are not ciphers or algebraic symbols, but people with radical, valid differences? (3) Why must we eliminate logic and accept contradiction – just because the Eichmanns *may* have been neat little functional mechanisms, does that discredit *ratio* forever?

But, happily, *Love's Body* may defeat itself even among potential proselytes. Unlike such low brow equivalents as Lawrence Lipton's *The Erotic Revolution*, or such middlebrow ones as Susan Sontag's *Against Interpretation*, it leaves too much unsaid. 'The meaning is not in the words but between the words, in the silence' runs Brown's *ars poetica*, and the publishers have provided half-inch spaces between aphorisms to facilitate the ingress of silence, or meaning. Was it not already in the Orphic Hymns that

Oneiros, dream, was invoked 'silently, to the silent souls/ to reveal the shape of the future'? It is precisely Dream, and his brother, Sleep, that silently alight on the reader, between the words and right in them. *Love's Body*, alas, is not Orpheus but Morpheus Descending.

Martin Green **British Marxists and American Freudians**

The circumstances of my life have forced me to compare England with America more than most people do; not so much in formal, large-scale comparisons, with each country taken as a whole, as in involuntary acknowledgements that my life on one side of the Atlantic was different in some way from what it was on the other, and speculations as to why. Such comparisons are necessarily limited to those parts of the two environments that impinge on me, as I am defined by my vocations and professions – for instance, as a teacher of literature – and even as defined by my temperament. These are large limitations. They mean that the comparisons must be very partial, very personal. The only compensation there can be for those limitations is some equivalent of personal sincerity that may at best go with them. The intentions that shape and limit such comparisons are at their best existential – intentions deriving from the struggle to make sense of one person's experience, and therefore (at their best) deriving personal good faith from that struggle. But such good faith is no guarantee against distortion of vision, especially when both ideas to be compared involve oneself.

This comparison is not personal in any ordinary sense, but it is so wide-ranging in its implications that I must remind myself how much it derives from me, from my experience, from my being who I am; for instance, from my interest in literature-and-other-things, but also from my preference for seeing situations in patterns of brightly coloured, simply labelled, alternative choices. However, having reminded myself of that, I still want to offer other people my comparison, for them to make of it what they can.

Since I last returned to live in England I've been struck by how often the name of Marx has turned up in contexts not just of political philosophy, but of cultural criticism, of literary criticism, and even within the arts themselves. Marx and Marxism are a pervasive presence in the plays of John Arden and Arnold Wesker, for instance, in the history of Edward Thompson and E. H. Carr, in the novels of Doris Lessing; while the liveliest new theatrical methods, like those in *US*, derive a lot from Brecht.

Marx and Marxism are in the air generally, then; and seriously so in matters of literary-cultural discussion. Moreover, in that area they mean something different from what they used to. When I was an undergraduate, the Communist Party was a possibility for us in British politics, but Marx himself was not a force in our thinking. He figured there as an outdated economist and a rather crude political philosopher, and not as a cultural philosopher. Nowadays the Communist Party counts for less, but Marx as a cultural philosopher counts for much more. To people who want to connect their study of literature with a general understanding of the world and responsibility for society, I would say he is the most important of all figures today. Englishmen who are *not* influenced by Marx, and who have some liveliness and scope of mind in literary matters, are people resistant to *all* ideological affiliation. Simplifying radically, I'd say that a literary Englishman today either engages with Marx, or settles for aestheticism and scholarship. Whereas in America, as it seems to me, there are many people interested in literature-and-other-things who are strongly influenced by Freud, and the people who aren't influenced by him tend to be ideologically indeterminate or scattered.

I'm talking, I should say, about emergent movements and new voices. Of course in America there are still the New Critics and the Southern Gothic writers, and in England there are still the Leavisites and the Angry Young Men. But if these are still forces on the scene in one sense, then there is another sense in which they are not. I am talking about movements visibly growing and increasing in vitality over the last ten years.

This is an enormous simplification. Because both names are only representative; the line of thought I associate with each of them derives from many thinkers; for instance, from some points of view Freud is less important than Nietzsche to the movement I've labelled post-Freudian. Also because both movements make much the same protests against genteel acceptance culture, against conservatism-reaction, and even against conscientious liberalism-individualism. Both stand for a kind of radicalism. And I'm not talking about movements that are conscious of themselves as limited and organized wholes, much less of each other as alternative movements. I'm talking about tendencies in nearly all the people who react to the current cultural situation in intellectually adventurous and morally indignant ways. There are many places therefore where these two tendencies come together inextricably – in art like *Marat/Sade* and *US*, and in thought like Marcuse's and R. D. Laing's. In such places it is not very profitable to disentangle the two strands and argue that they are mutually hostile – though I think that can be done. But my claim, my defence of this reductive simplification, is that there are a fair number of places where there is no need to disentangle, where people and books are clearly aligned with the one tendency and aimed against the other.

Some of the exceptions will be worth discussing, but most will not, because the value of such generalizations is not to account for the exact position of all the items involved, but to indicate the direction in which they are mostly tending to move. The fact that some of the dots on the graph don't fit into the curve doesn't matter so long as there clearly is a curve. And as well as exceptions there must need be conclusions; some sense of what this means; from what causes this difference derives, and with what consequences. These I will consider at the end. But conclusions are as extraneous as exceptions to the main proposition I am going to try to establish; which is simply that these two movements, in these two countries, do exist, and are interesting, and do, in tendency, contradict each other.

Of the two, let us consider first the British Marxists. The

first thing to say is that these are post-Marxists (and the American Freudians we shall come to are post-Freudians). That is, these Marxists take Marx's thought at its roots, and are interested in what they can make of its largest philosophical implications, and quite uninterested in what most of his political disciples, between then and now, have made of it. There were literary Marxists in the thirties; and being a Marxist seems to have meant most typically the process of belonging to the party and obeying the party, and, in literary matters, haggling over the difference between what Engels wrote to Minna Kautsky in 1885, and what Lenin said, or meant, in 'Party Organization and Party Literature' in 1905. Being a post-Marxist means something different. These people are not concerned with the party, they are not concerned with Russia, they are not primarily concerned with China; it is the Third World on which their gaze is concentrated. And in literary matters they haggle over what Leavis said and what Lawrence said.

Theirs is not the Marx of Lenin, much less of Stalin. It is not even primarily the Marx of *Capital*; it is mostly the early Marx of *Economic and Philosophical Manuscripts*, the philosopher of alienation and dehumanization. In what follows I am reporting (to the best of my ability) what the post-Marxists say of Marx and Hegel, Sartre and Lukacs. I have not read Hegel, and I have not really understood the others. The leading concepts of this line of thought Marx took over from Hegel; self-estrangement or alienation is a result of objectification, the externalization of what man has produced; and the way back to cultural unity is through the re-appropriation of man's productivity – that is, through seeing all man makes as under his own control, a part of his self-expression, and therefore a part of his responsibility and not a thing independent of him. The early Marx blamed Christianity for alienation. He saw Christendom as a fragmented and individualistic culture, in contrast with the unity of the Greek city, which was a political and religious whole; individual and social experience, divine and secular, fitting together. In the Greek city all of man's life was felt as his responsibility, his creation, and so was made beautiful. The religious was integrated with the rest. Christianity, on the other hand, derived from Judaism, which had externalized its religion into the Law. The Jews had reified their religion, made it a thing outside themselves. Christ then re-appropriated religious experience, but only individualistically. He made it each man's responsibility to work out his own salvation as an individual, but not the race's as a collectivity. Thus he left the experience of the divine outside the area of man's political life, and created a religion of otherworldliness.

From this, Marx thought, derived a hundred other kinds of alienation. Thus, in 'On the Jewish Question', in 1843, he wrote:

> Only under the sway of Christianity, which objectifies all national, natural, moral, and theoretical relationships, could civil society separate itself completely from the life of the state, sever all the species-bonds of man, establish egoism and selfish need in their place, and dissolve the human world into a world of atomistic, antagonistic individuals.

In *Economic and Philosophical Manuscripts*, in 1844, he argued that this religious alienation was only an expression of a political alienation, which derived from the contradictions between private and social life in the bourgeois state. And later he found the source of those political contradictions in an economic alienation. Indeed, in *The German Ideology* and *The Communist Manifesto* Marx rejected the idea of alienation as the *source* of evil. But the post-Marxists claim that this was only Hegelian-idealist alienation he rejected; for alienation proper is fundamental to their idea of Marxism.

Although Marx in this phase was obviously hostile to Christianity, he was very interested in it, and his own philosophy was both more 'religious' and more compatible with religion, than it was later represented to be. The Christians among the post-Marxists not only accept his strictures on Christianity, but rejoice in them as a programme for church reform. One of the striking features of the movement is this combination of Marxist with Christian, even Catholic, categories.

The key idea, then, is that man is a species, and that to be a man is to acknowledge membership of that species; to cease to be a merely individual entity. A man is a universal being because he can represent his species, and he can represent it because he can grasp the idea of it, can think it. An animal is inseparable from its life-activity; it exists *an-sich* or *en-soi*; Sartre's phrase is cited as often as Hegel's. A man makes his life-activity the object of his consciousness and will-power; he exists *pour-soi*. But this *pour-soi* cannot be said of the naked individual; for Marx there is no such thing among humans; man is constituted by his relations to other men. It is society which creates, through language and through work, through participation in common activities, man as man. That is, society enables man to treat himself as the species; the individual becomes universal, and potentially free. Material scarcities restricted that freedom temporarily, and the alienation of labour did so essentially, reversing the whole movement of history. But under communism, and with the abundance made possible by automation, man would become entirely free, purely *pour-soi*.

These Marxist ideas have been developed towards their post-Marxist form by European rather than by Russian thinkers. It is Sartre and Lukacs rather than Lenin and Trotsky whom British critics cite. There seems to be general agreement that the two most important books since Marx's themselves are Lukacs' *History and Class Consciousness* (1923), which was condemned in Moscow for its semi-subjectivist interpretation of history and Sartre's *Critique of Dialectical Reason*, of 1960, which is openly contemptuous of Moscow Marxism. Sartre adds to Marx what he feels is lacking in orthodox Marxism, a hierarchy of mediations; to make it possible to grasp just how a person and his work are produced by a given class at a given moment in history. For instance, to show how Flaubert came to choose to be a bourgeois writer rather than doctor, and how he came to write *Madame Bovary*, rather than some other equally bourgeois form of literature, like the Goncourts' books. Sartre sees contemporary sociology and psychoanalysis as realizations of moments in the dialectic, finding their proper shape when incorporated into the Marxist theory of history. Psychoanalysis, for instance, discovers the point of insertion of a man in his class; it helps us understand the family as a mediation between the individual and society; an individual experiences alienation first, and crucially, as a child, through his parents' being exploited as alienated labour, through their experience passed on to him as an infant, not through his own first job.

So much for the general ideas of post-Marxism. In Sartre and Lukacs we begin to approach the specifically literary attitudes that go with this philosophy in England. But strikingly enough, though both of them are literary critics, neither have had much direct influence here in literary matters. The probable reasons are various. In *Theory of the Novel* (1916), Lukacs said that in nineteenth-century novels the heroes had souls larger than the destinies life offered them, and the problem they all reflected was that of how to be reconciled with an inadequate world; and he saw Dostoevsky as pointing the way to a solution. But after he became a Communist his literary sympathies were much narrowed, and he has had little sympathy since with Dostoevsky or with most modernist writers. D. H. Lawrence and Samuel Beckett he has dismissed as decadent; *Ulysses* he has described as merely 'a tape-recorded sequence of a number of associations'; Roger Martin du Gard is preferred to Kafka. It requires no explaining why such judgments should have little influence even among the post-Marxists in England, which has its own lively literary criticism. But neither, so far, have Sartre's huge study of Genet or his lengthy analyses of Flaubert. The biggest reason in this case is probably something within that native tradition of literary criticism. While Lukacs' mind is rigid in ways which Sartre himself has sufficiently exposed, Sartre's criticism is unpalatable to native British taste for its implicit hostility to decent averageness.

This English literary and cultural criticism has a powerful

tradition of faith in the values of simple ordinary community life even under capitalism. This no doubt goes back as far as Carlyle, with his faith in work and moral duty and the native grandeur of character of the Scottish Presbyterian crofter. Perhaps the icon of that faith most people refer to nowadays is D. H. Lawrence's picture of his own home and others like it in *Sons and Lovers*, which shows those simple values surviving the Industrial Revolution. And both the fiction and the criticism of Raymond Williams clearly draw on his own experience of Welsh village life. When Williams says 'Culture is ordinary' he quite explicitly relies on that experience and our response to it.

Sartre belongs to a very different tradition, and when he describes simple ordinary community life it is not to praise it. The peasant family in the Morvan, with whom Genet was boarded out as a child, and who sent him to the reformatory when they caught him stealing, is implicitly blamed for much of Genet's trouble. The badness attributed to the boy and introjected by him was a projection of these good, self-respecting people, a product of their goodness. And these were people who, objectively described, might not be easy to distinguish from Carlyle's crofters and Williams' villagers. Sartre's sympathies, in a major French tradition, are with the anti-social intellectual, with Genet himself; liar, thief, homosexual prostitute, pornographic fantasist. Readers are warned against thinking themselves any 'healthier' or more normal than Genet. When Sartre hears a man saying 'We doctors', he knows that that man is morally and psychologically a slave, with no identity of his own. This socially accepted alienation of the psyche he calls a 'legitimate hell', and he expresses a fierce distaste for these 'inhabited souls'.

This difference in fundamental sympathy divides Sartre from the English post-Marxists in literary sensibility. They acknowledge, of course, the truth that a sick society infects its members, but they tend to associate social sickness with ultra-modern, big-city life, or with the new mass-media, and to imply that the older and smaller forms of social organization still have a life that fosters health in the individual. Their primary stress is on that other truth, that an individual cannot be healthy unless he accepts his being part of a community. They barely at all acknowledge the heroism or the sanctity of a Genet, achieved over and against his society. The native English literary tradition, mediated to the present in the work of Dr Leavis, has been as powerful an influence on the literary men amongst them as Marx himself. Raymond Williams for instance describes his life as affected by two major sources of cultural thought, Leavis and Marx; and all these people, in their literary criticism, plainly start from *Scrutiny*. And one can see good historical reasons for this conjunction. This English tradition, with its strongly normative stresses and its sense of responsibility for national culture, derives from Coleridge and Carlyle, who drew on the same stock of German Idealist ideas as Marx did. Leavis himself, when be began *Scrutiny*, declared himself friendly to Marxism, and a believer in 'some form of economic communism'; his roots are in Ruskin and Morris, with their anti-capitalist vision of an England of arts and crafts communities. His literary criticism has always been preoccupied with the relation of the particular work of art to the cultural life it derives from. It has therefore been easy for our modern post-Marxists to take over his judgments and his methods.

Raymond Williams is pre-eminent amongst them, and his two books on drama are among the few pieces of straight literary study these people have produced so far. There is however a good deal of literary criticism in Edward Thompson's histories; least surprisingly, in his book on William Morris, but also in *The Making of the English Working Class*, and in unpublished essays on Wordsworth and Marx. There is more in two books of cultural thought by Roman Catholics: Terence Eagleton's *The New Left Church*; and *Catholics and the Left*, by a group of writers. The first section of the latter book is called 'Christians against Capitalism', and the whole is essentially Marxist in inspiration. At the same time it is essentially literary, for the writers use poetry and novels as crucial evidence for their social arguments.

We might describe in a little more detail three books; Williams' *Modern Tragedy*, Brian Wicker's *Culture and Theology*, and Terence Eagleton's *Shakespeare and Society*. The first argues – against books like Steiner's *The Death of Tragedy* – that tragic writing *is* possible in our time, because the contemporary experience of political revolution is highly appropriate subject-matter for a tragic writer. We have all shared, publicly, just the kind of experience that demands the tragic form. The last section of the book, Williams' own attempt at such a tragedy, uses the events of the Russian Revolution and the history of the Communist state in Russia. The book also contains a long interpretation of *Doctor Zhivago*, and a contrasting of it with *The Cocktail Party*, as two ways of dealing with the themes of sacrifice and resignation. Williams interprets *Doctor Zhivago* as expressing a painful, a tragic, acceptance of the Revolution, with all the sacrifice it involved of private happiness. Interpreting it this way he finds it infinitely superior to Eliot's play, which has so little sense of the value of human experience, once we define human as deriving from community life. The book as a whole is a survey of the various modern approaches to tragedy, and the titles of some of its main sections outline its analytic method. 'Liberal tragedy' includes Ibsen and Arthur Miller, 'Tragic Deadlock' includes Ionesco, Beckett, and Pinter, 'Private Tragedy' includes Strindberg, O'Neill, Tennessee Williams. All of these are found radically unsatisfactory, deriving as they do from the bourgeois-individualist mind at one or other stage of its development; even *Women in Love* betrays an incomplete understanding of community; the only satisfactory modern artist, apart from Pasternak, is Brecht, who also draws on public, political experience as his subject matter.

Brian Wicker's book has sections on philosophy, and anthropology, and literature. There are critical essays on Dickens and George Eliot, whose novels are taken to represent respectively a sacral and a secularist understanding of life. Secularism is identified with Locke, private citizenship and private consciousness, and the possessive individualism of capitalism; and thus is at an opposite extreme from Marxism. Marx's view of life Wicker calls sacral. Dickens' novels are sacral because they represent both nature and society as possessing a life of their own – Dickens' London, for instance, is an organic entity, an active force acting on its citizens – rather than a merely objective background to the subjective drama of individual consciousnesses, as nature and society are in *Middlemarch*. Dickens' art breaks down that antithesis between the subjective and objective which Wicker regards as a major fallacy of thought since Locke, and the source of 'secularism'. And there is another emblematic contrast, between Orwell and William Golding, with a similar point. Wicker defines Orwell as a contemporary writer, as opposed to a modernist one; and contemporaneity he relates to secularism. Golding he calls an allegorist, using Lukacs' opposition of traditional realism to modernist allegory. He then traces both these writers' artistic failures, in different ways, to the power of the secularist view of life in the culture they work in; and in the philosophical and anthropological sections of the book he tries to refute that view. Secularism derives from, and makes permanent, the failure of western man to achieve community.

In Eagleton's *Shakespeare and Society* the central concern is to find in the plays evidence of both the playwright's interest in conflicts between the individual and society, and his sense that the only solution must be a fusion of the two. Our own age, we are told, is approaching this solution via an abandonment of the old distinctions between the two categories. 'The converging experience of a number of thinkers, in culture and psychology, politics and philosophy, has given us definitions of person and society which make any straight division between individual life, and the social forms within which this is available, unthinkable.' Reason and law and society are shown as opposed to spontaneity and authenticity and individuality, in *Troilus and Cressida, Hamlet*, and *Measure for Measure*; and as fused in the last comedies. Hamlet Eagleton describes in terms very like those Richard Poirier used to praise Emerson (see the second half of this essay), as a man refusing to accept self-definition in any of the roles society offers him; but the 'point', for Eagleton, is that such a man destroys himself; a man who preserves his sense of identity only in opposition to formal social patterns finds that this identity becomes unreal, negative. Hamlet exemplifies a life-pattern we should avoid.[1] *Measure for Measure* Eagleton reads as showing that marriage and law must be understood as equally individual and social realities, to be taken as neither merely personal nor merely impersonal, nor as something combining those two kinds of elements, but as a fusion of them. This is the only way we can give our values constancy. The whole book is an attempt to find in Shakespeare illustrations of a society that has lost its values because it cannot make its members still believe in it as a society; they set up an opposition between themselves and it, between spontaneity and social duty; this is the source of both situation ethics and existential authenticity, Eagleton thinks, and the only answer to them is a reconciliation of individual to society, a reconstitution of community.

The post-Marxists are significant in part because they are in natural alliance with other forces in British intellectual life which are not Marxist at all. For instance, the people who write for the *Cambridge Quarterly* and *The Use of English*; and the people at the Centre for Contemporary Cultural Studies at Birmingham; and, as I have pointed out, some of the most committed among the post-Marxists are Roman Catholics, laymen and priests. All these people, disparate as they are, belong together in their contrast with the other large literary-cultural tendency in England now, which is much more purely aesthetic and anti-ideological. We might identify this with the names of Frank Kermode and Christopher Ricks, John Gross and Tony Tanner. In many ways this cultural split follows the lines of a traditional British opposition, between Oxford and Cambridge. Cambridge being the home of the more austere and strenuous, Puritanical and radical mind; Oxford the more elegant and playful, sophisticated and

[1] The 'point' of Cleopatra is even more strikingly moralistic. She is 'Shakespeare's most complete image of fully authentic life; she cancels and recreates all values in herself'; but therefore the 'result' of the play is 'a new insight into the depth of authentic life which will have to be part of any attempt to make this life responsible, to put it back within society'. How to turn Cleopatras into bigger and better Octavias.

nostalgic. Oxford in one sense of the word right wing, Cambridge left wing. In literary matters Cambridge sees art in relation to society, and in relation to right and wrong. Within the congeries of groups united by this Cambridge tendency, the post-Marxists seem to me the most highly charged with intellectual life, and potentially of great significance.

I said at the beginning that they were anti-Freudian in tendency, but I have no texts to cite to prove that. Except, paradoxically, Sartre. This is a paradox because Sartre *is* profoundly indebted to Freud. Indeed, he is Freudian, in his full acceptance of and use of psychoanalysis. But he is not post-Freudian, because he dismisses as quaint mythologizing those late works of Freud in which we get theories of world history; and it is from those works that the post-Freudians start. Psychoanalysis itself they are not much interested in; indeed they are often contemptuous of it. Being analysed, for the post-Freudian, is as irrelevant as belonging to the national party is to the post-Marxist.

The English post-Marxists, so far as I am aware, have not committed themselves on the issue at all, explicitly. Implicitly, as it seems to me, they are anti-post-Freudian; because they believe in the regeneration of the individual sensibility through the regeneration of community life, through retightening the social bonds between men. Whereas the post-Freudians believe in loosening those social bonds, and in a sense in the degeneration of community life, and the renewing of individual life as a consequence of that. The post-Marxists insist that an individual derives everything that makes him human from his society, from his community; the post-Freudians see the self achieving itself in struggles against system, in the family, the school, the whole culture. It seems to me significant that the one Fabian pamphlet written in protest against Raymond Williams' theory of culture was written by a Freudian, who spoke for a more pluralistic theory, with less insistence on unity of belief and purpose. (Richard Wollheim's *Socialism and Culture* of 1961).

Again let me say I realize how many shades of each opinion there are; how possible it is to share some of them without being significantly post-Marxist or post-Freudian; how possible to combine some varieties of one tendency with some varieties of the other without feeling torn apart. But there remain two tendencies. There are people and books who belong clearly in one and not in the other, whose fundamental energies and aims are aligned with the one and against the other; or in whom the two obviously fight against each other. And these include people who are thinking strenuously about literature and culture today.

The post-Freudians, as I understand them, start from late Freud, speculative Freud. Just as the post-Marxists start not from *Capital* but from *Economic and Philosophical Manuscripts*, so the post-Freudians start not from *The Interpretation of Dreams* but from *Civilization and Its Discontents*. Both groups take their masters' largest world-view statements, and interpret them in the largest style, with vivid implications for literature, past, present, and to come.

The writers I'll briefly mention are Norman Brown, in *Life Against Death* and *Love's Body*, Herbert Marcuse in *Eros and Civilization*, Philip Rieff in *The Triumph of the Therapeutic*, Susan Sontag in *Against Interpretation*, and Norman Mailer in *Advertisements for Myself*. In Norman Brown's work what we begin with are basic Freudian ideas, comparable with the basic Marxist ideas. 'Sexual instinct is the energy or desire with which the human being pursues pleasure, with the further specification that the pleasure sought is the pleasurable activity of an organ of the human body.' And that energy however disguised or transmuted, is in fact the only human energy. So that philosophy and religion and history, whether as subjects of study or as states of consciousness in the individual or as the activities of parliament or congresses, are all produced by the same instinct. 'The special contribution of psychoanalysis is to trace religious and philosophic problems to their roots in the concrete human body.' And 'Man, the discontented animal, unconsciously seeking the life proper to his species, is man in history; repression and the repetition compulsion generate historical time.' We ought in fact to live outside time; and we would if we were not discontented but contented animals. Infants are naturally absorbed in themselves and their own bodies; they are in love with themselves, and their sexuality is polymorphously perverse. But civilization interferes with their development, in the form, for instance, of toilet-training and the prohibition against masturbation; their sexuality is genitally organized, and the result is repression and neurosis.

But these simply Freudian ideas lead Brown on to a strikingly post-Freudian interpretation of culture and of world history. He asserts a profound opposition within every personality between the interests of the body, including in that all of pre-mental life, the instincts as well as the senses, and the interests of the mind, that is of civilization representing itself inside the personality as morality, productivity, systematic thought, patriotism, religious duty, etc. The spokesman of the body in literature is Blake, 'Energy is the only life, and is from the body', and 'Energy is eternal delight'. Typical spokesmen of the mind are Plato and Descartes, with their worship of the abstract, the ideal, the disembodied, the sublimated.

We are most concerned with the theory of art and literature within this theory of culture, so here are some representative quotations. 'The function of art is to help us find our way back to the sources of pleasure that have been rendered inaccessible by that capitulation to the reality principle which we call education or maturity – in other words, to recapture the lost laughter of infancy . . . Art, if its object is to undo repressions, and if civilization is essentially repressive, is in this sense subversive of civilization.' These ideas, obviously, are very alien to Eagleton's view of literature, and it is because Sartre is not so far from this point of view – that art is subversive of civilization – that he is so different from his English disciples.

In *Love's Body* Brown is more explicit about what we ought to do here and now as a consequence of this understanding of our situation. Salvation lies only in the resurrected body; that is, in a sensuality not genitally organized. And the giving up of genitality will include giving up all heroic individualism, all politics, and indeed all personality. The sign of man's fallen state is the boundaries he draws; the distinction he makes between good and bad, that between me and thee, that between mine and thine. These are the death-breeding boundaries, between persons, between emotions, between items of property, and they are all essentially the same. To have a personality is to have property. The only way out is to give up personality. Then one can escape from the domination of the reality principle and of the mind and morality. Freud, rightly used, can lead one out into the world of free speech, free associations, random thoughts, spontaneous movements. Clearly, this is very bold thinking; and however often Brown may invoke Marx, it recommends a disengagement from community and culture which no loyal interpretation of Marx could encompass.

Herbert Marcuse, in *Eros and Civilization*, combines Freud's account of the repressive civilization he knew – that is, nineteenth-century civilization – with Schiller's theory of what a non-repressive civilization might be. In the organized society of the past happiness had to be subordinated to, for instance, the discipline of monogamic reproduction, and all the systems of established law and order. The methodical sacrifice of libido, its rigidly enforced deflection to socially useful activities and expressions, all this *was* – for Freud – culture. But in a society of abundance and leisure, such as was hypothesized by Schiller and such as is now foreseeable as a result of modern technology, it will be possible to have, in Schiller's words, an indifference to reality, and an interest in 'show', in appearances, in the aesthetic aspect of everything, and an interest in play, in the non-serious, in mere self-expression, which will be a 'true enlargement of humanity'.

Moreover, it is art which has expressed these interests in the past, and so it is art which will be, in the present, our guide in constructing the culture of the future. Orpheus and Narcissus are the mythological representatives of art, and they stand in opposition to Prometheus, who represents competitive economic performance and productiveness, the old reality principle, the unceasing effort to master life. Orpheus and Narcissus, the artist figure and the figure of self-delighting, self-sufficient beauty, stand beside Dionysos, the figure of lawless instinctual energy, in opposition to Apollo and the realm of reason and organization and morality.

But Marcuse is a difficult person to fit into these categories, because in most of his books he is clearly a Marxist or Hegelian thinker, and in all of them he shows a strong political consciousness of a non-Freudian kind. But in *Eros and Civilization* it seems to me that he is post-Freudian in the sense described. He does there proclaim the possibility of a non-repressive civilization in which Eros would replace Logos, and the reality-principle Freud spoke of would be defeated, and the play impulse would abolish time. Six years later, it is true, in the Preface to the Vintage edition of the book, he introduced the idea of repressive de-sublimation; the release of sexuality in modes which reduce erotic energy; making a big distinction between Eros and sexuality, of a surely non-Freudian kind, by means of which he could say something quite different from what he had said in the book itself. He could warn us that in present political conditions the spread of non-repressiveness might be politically stabilizing and indeed culturally regressive. The years between the book and the preface, he said, had refuted all optimism; he had sufficiently (perhaps unduly) stressed the progressive and promising aspects of this development, to be able here in 1961 to accentuate the negative. To put it crudely, he had changed his mind. And in *One-Dimensional Man* it is the second line of thought he follows up. Non-repressiveness in our present society produces the Happy Consciousness, which invalidates Art; for art has traditionally spoken the Great Refusal, the protest against that which is. This idea of art is of course compatible enough with Marxism. I don't myself see that it is compatible with the Freudian Orphic-Narcissist idea of *Eros and Civilization*. And even those who think that it is should be able to agree that the combining of the two is a unique achievement, fairly special to Marcuse. In most people you find one or the other, but not both.

This theoretical position I've described, in Norman Brown and

Marcuse, seems to me vitally related to a contemporary set of attitudes to cultural problems and a contemporary literary sensibility which one finds expressed in, to take some striking examples, Susan Sontag, Philip Rieff, and Norman Mailer. Like Marshall McLuhan, Miss Sontag and Mr Rieff believe that we are at the end of the literary phase of our culture; that literature will decline as a primary art form and along with it will decline, as cultural values, privacy, individualism, liberalism, the conscience, self-sacrifice, self-improvement, standards, culture itself in the Matthew Arnold sense. They see those values as profoundly ascetic, the servants of the nineteenth-century repressive civilization Freud described, and essentially the enemies of art and of the new non-repressive civilization. The classic dilemma of our culture, Miss Sontag says, has been the hypertrophy of the intellect at the expense of energy and sensual capacity. The art of the future will return to art's essential function, of releasing man's sensuality.

Of the two, Miss Sontag is less ready to look forward into the post-literary future, but she is just as glad to see the end of the Matthew Arnold idea of culture, in which literature was so central; she rejoices in the decline of conscience and the rise of aesthetic and formal autonomy in the arts. She and Norman Mailer, who are the more purely literary minds of the four, are perhaps attuned rather to the extinction of our race along with its culture, while Rieff and McLuhan are tuning themselves in to the new culture which will replace ours.

Rieff and McLuhan's view of the future is apolitical and in any ordinary sense amoral. They doubt, in Mr Rieff's phrase, all traditional modes of self-salvation through self-identification with a communal cause. That includes of course all a post-Marxist believes in. Susan Sontag and Norman Mailer say rather that the life of communal causes, in America in the twentieth century, has been made too difficult. They refer us to the murder of the Jews during the war, to the threat of the hydrogen bomb, to the hypocrisy and immorality of American politics at home and abroad. And they report to us, with participatory excitement, the phenomena of decadence. The years in which one could complacently accept oneself as part of an élite by being a radical are forever gone, Mr Mailer says. The only courage that we have been witness to has been the isolated courage of isolated people, sexual adventurers.

Whereas Rieff and McLuhan are more concerned to describe how peaceful everything will be once we have renounced the life of communal causes, and how well we shall like the new state of affairs once we are used to it. They report to us the speed with which our culture is changing, new technologies are being developed, and the ratios between our senses are being transformed. But all four look forward equally to a greater variety of and prestige for sensuality, and to the withering away of the old forms of ethical culture.

In matters of high culture, this sensibility is explicitly hostile to the post-Marxist sensibility. Arnold and Ruskin are figures it reacts against. 'What we decidedly do not need now is further to assimilate Art into Thought, or, worse yet, into Culture', says Miss Sontag. The modern representatives of that tradition, like Dr Leavis, are not mentioned, and could seem only provincial, priggish, and reactionary to Miss Sontag, who refers rather to Artaud, Genet, and Pavese. Even D. H. Lawrence who is, of course, mentioned, is not dwelt on nor unreservedly praised. He is not accepted in the way even Yeats is.

Among intellectual figures, after Freud, Nietzsche is probably the most important to these writers.[1] His manner as well as his message is obviously an important influence on *Love's Body*. Marx's name is often invoked, but not Marxism. As Mr Rieff says, 'Our revolution is more Freudian than Marxist, more analytic than polemic, more cultural than socialist . . . It is a terrible error to see the West as conservative and the East as

[1] Intellectually he may even take precedence of Freud, but culturally I think the latter has been the more important influence, because of the spread of psychoanalytic therapy and permissive child-rearing in middle-class American society. I think that influence is an important explanation of the intenser sense of the self in America, on which these writers rely, and so I have kept the label 'post-Freudian' for them.

revolutionary. We are the true revolutionaries.' The post-Freudians are much more explicit than the post-Marxists about their enmity, and Mr Rieff is one of their sharpest spokesmen. 'The Communist movement belongs to the classical tradition of moral demand systems . . . Our cultural revolution does not aim, like its predecessors, at victory for some rival commitment, but rather at a way of using all commitments, which amounts to loyalty towards none. By psychologizing about themselves interminably, Western men are learning to use their internality against the primacy of any particular organization of personality.' This would include the Communist personality.

Norman Mailer predicts that the revolutionary vision of our age will not follow Marx into political economy but will engage the mass media. This sounds like a foretelling of McLuhan, and Susan Sontag remarks that 'such strongly apolitical critics as Marshall McLuhan have got so much better grasp on the texture of contemporary reality . . . than the Marxist critics'. In fact McLuhan is as much the natural ally of the post-Freudian writers in America, as the orthodox Leavisites are of the post-Marxists in England. He is instinctively apolitical and implicitly on the side of all new, free, sensory mixes and psychological novelties. The artist's job, for him, is to correct the sense ratios before the blow of new technology has numbed conscious procedures. Art *is* precise advance knowledge of how to cope in this way with the psychic and social consequences of the next technology. But it is above all McLuhan's way of writing, his persona as a writer, his defiant gaiety and joking, his evasion of normal seriousness and connectedness, his commitment to aphorism, which seem to me to place him. The post-Freudian creed demands, or at least invites, the aphoristic manner. One cannot go on calling for the end of the old seriousness in the old serious and systematic manner. Aphorism is exaggeration, as Norman Brown tells us in *Love's Body*; it is the road of excess which leads to the palace of wisdom. Intellect *is* courage; the courage to risk its own life, to play with madness. Intellect is the sacrifice of intellect, or fire; which burns up as it gives light.

This is truth as fragments, as opposed to systematic forms or methods. *Love's Body* quotes a good deal from McLuhan, and borrows even more in direct imitation.

Other major allies of the post-Freudians are the formal aestheticians of symbolism. Susan Sontag calls her book of criticism *Against Interpretation* because she thinks the interpretation of art derives from an over-emphasis on its content. When she says we need to recover our senses, one thing she means is that we need to appreciate art formally. 'In place of a hermeneutics we need an erotics of art'; and we note the continual equating of sensuality with formalism. This seems to me arbitrary, for the formal approach to art, especially art in the intellectualized forms Miss Sontag likes, is as abstract an activity as anything human. But in Norman Brown, too, we find a constant reference to such formally self-conscious poets as Rilke and Yeats, and a recommendation specifically of Symbolist methods. And I suspect that McLuhan's formula, the medium is the message, is understood – even by McLuhan himself – as amongst other things a formalist slogan. Certainly Susan Sontag sees her formalism as what sets her apart from Marxist criticism. 'What all the culture critics who descend from Hegel and Marx have been unwilling to admit is the notion of art as autonomous form. And the peculiar spirit which animates the modern movement in the arts is based on, precisely, the rediscovery of the power (including the emotional power) of the formal properties of art . . .' And the Marxists on their side accept the same distinction, putting their own stress on content. Ernst Fischer's *The Necessity of Art* gives 80 pages to a chapter called 'Content and Form' which is an attack on formalism. And the post-Freudians' formalism goes along with aestheticism in the vulgar sense, to some degree. 'The world *is*, ultimately, an aesthetic phenomenon', says Miss Sontag, 'That is to say, the world (all there is) cannot, ultimately, be justified.' She explicitly rejects humanism for being an attempt to justify the world, to make sense of experience.

Another phenomenon of our times, Northrop Frye, is in effect allied with this tendency. Murray Krieger explains him by referring us to two great models, of whom the second is Freud; and historically Blake was the great focus of literary and cultural ideas for him, the great catalyst of his poetic theorizing. For him the individual book is to be related to the whole world of literature, which is a part of the whole world of culture, which is part of the world of dreams. His systems of archetypes and modes are described by his admirers as 'charting the galaxies dreamed of by human desire', 'galaxies whose centres and axes are constantly shifting'. In other words, you can't understand what he means, or you can't understand it rationally. As they say, he has freed the critic from the stringent procedures of critical discourse, as well as the poet from the bondage of sublunary language. This must remind us of McLuhan and Brown, and indeed his taste is, like theirs, for romanticism, transcendentalism, classless democratic individualism, the future. Like McLuhan's, his schemes of thought are an attempt to meet the challenge of tomorrow's conditions – our immensely increased knowledge of so many literatures from so many points of view – by abandoning yesterday's procedures. He is an antithesis to the New Criticism, and most of all to Leavis. He is not concerned with close reading or with evaluation, or with any total encounter with individual works, and he has little interest in irony, realism, tensions of opposite tendencies, or tragedy. Like Brown, his central myth is one of rebirth, his central modes comedy and romance. And all this derives from his association of art with dream, with the transcendence of individual desire over social conditions.[1]

The same emphasis can be seen in the work of two critics who represent the best fruitfulness the post-Freudians can bring to literary studies. I mean Robert Garis in *The Dickens Theatre* and Richard Poirier in *A World Elsewhere*. The second is subtitled 'The Place of Style in American Literature', and its argument is that style has a special place there, because major American writers have used style as a means of self-assertion, and

[1] Frye's novelist is John Barth. Barth's 'anatomy', *Giles Goat-Boy*, exemplifies nearly all Frye's enthusiasms, combined in Frye's kind of synthesis.

because the self thus asserted has not been the sordid sublunary competitive ego, but the transcendental and ideal self; the self Emerson bade us be. The argument is perhaps clearest as it applies to Emerson, whose style is itself an exhortation to freedom, to the defying of traditional limitations, to the imaginative mastery of the universe. And what is granted about Emerson may be taken as proved about Thoreau and Whitman. But Mr Poirier is most interested in fiction, and applies his theory to James, whose style, especially in the late novels, dominates everything it describes, transforming it from that 'real-life' form which is in fact dictated by society into an environment of freedom for the novels' heroes; who, for instance Strether, themselves 'imagine' their experience in defiance of reality. They are in a sense dreaming their lives, and James, Mr Poirier says, is in collusion with them. He makes similar points about Melville and Faulkner, and indeed extends his argument to cover Cooper, Hawthorne, and Twain. But what I have already reported makes it clear how much this depends on the idea of literature as dream, the product of a triumph of self over system. It is worth noting, too, that Mr Poirier thinks that in British literature the self is not always presented as in conflict with society – that the writer's interest is often in the ways the one can enrich and extend the other – but that in American literature you don't find this.

I'll conclude with two quotations from Norman Mailer's 'The White Negro: Superficial Reflections on the Hipster', which demonstrate, I think, an extreme version of post-Freudian sensibility working itself out spontaneously, in independence of its intellectual origins:

> Knowing in the cells of his existence that life was war, nothing but war, the Negro (all exceptions admitted) could rarely afford the sophisticated inhibitions of civilization, and so he kept for his survival the art of the primitive, he lived in the enormous present . . . relinquishing the pleasures of the mind for the more obligatory pleasures of the body . . . For jazz is orgasm, it is the music of orgasm . . . If the fate of 20th century man is to live with death from adolescence to premature

senescence, why then the only life-giving answer is to accept the terms of death, to live with death as immediate danger, to divorce oneself from society, to exist without roots, to set out on that uncharted journey into the rebellious imperatives of the self. In short, whether the life is criminal or not, to encourage the psychopath in oneself, to explore that domain of experience where security is boredom and therefore sickness, and one exists in the present, in that enormous present which is without past or future, memory or planned intention . . . the psychopath may indeed be the perverted and dangerous front-runner of a new kind of personality which could become the central expression of human nature before the 20th century is over.

That I take to be a pretty striking statement of the post-Freudian readiness to recommend disengagement from society and the pursuit of individual salvation. It is impossible to imagine anything like that being said in England in that post-Marxist movement which seems to me its equivalent for intellectual excitement and intensity. And with that I want to ask what conclusions can be drawn from this differentness between the two countries.

In one way it is easy enough to see why the two countries should be so different now, by considering their two histories of cultural thought. England had, as I said, a powerful tradition of cultural criticism all through the nineteenth and twentieth centuries. This was a tradition of speculative thought and aesthetic criticism, but not without a practical social effectiveness, which rooted it in objective social realism and activism. The national education system, for instance, is powerfully influenced by it; the teaching of English in particular is very much in touch with the whole Leavis movement. The teacher training colleges are full of Leavis disciples. So neither literature itself nor literary comment has been presented as the arena of a merely hostile struggle between the individual and society. The stress has been on that fruitful interaction between the two ideally possible. Whereas in America, even that same tradition of cultural thought, in its native manifestations in Emerson and Whitman, has laid much more stress on self-reliance, on the individual's wonderful and sufficient possession of a private self. The individual has not so much defied society, as in one French tradition, or redrawn his contract with it, as in the British, as transcendently evaded it. Philip Rieff, describing psychological man as a new form of humanity only just being born, admits that in America he may have a history, even a nineteenth-century manifestation.

This contrast was obscured in the recent past because of the New Critics' hostility to transcendentalism, and because of the interpretation those critics therefore gave to even nineteenth-century classics of American literature like Hawthorne and Melville. But nowadays we have something of a new Romanticism in America, in criticism and cultural theory as well as in creative art, and the old version of the national identity, the pre-eminent interest of Emerson, for instance, as an American mind, is re-established. If America is again seen as the land of individualism and transcendentalism, albeit re-interpreted in a post-Freudian way, then a contrast with England very relevant to our problem becomes 'clear' again. In fact, however, to focus on this contrast, to revive this tradition, is itself an act of interpretation, which does not derive from evidence alone, nor can be justified by evidence alone, so its 'clarity' or its 'obscurity' are themselves tendentious terms. And I have no theory better based on evidence, no explanation worthy of the name, to offer.

But I have one comment. Putting the two movements face to face mostly makes us aware of the weaknesses of both. Each makes an implicit comment on the other which seems pretty pertinent.[1] Seen from the post-Freudian point of view, the post-Marxists are aridly theoretical and out of touch with the majority of people writing or composing today, with the processes of

[1] In all that follows I use my key terms to refer to the figures I have called representative of those movements, not to those I have called their allies. For example, I do not here include Garis or Poirier as post-Freudians, because they draw on other sources of strength which save them from the weaknesses I ascribe to the movement.

composition, and all too often with processes of reading. The way the post-Freudians talk about the modern situation bears some obvious relation to the way most people in the arts feel and behave. The way the post-Marxists talk relates to that condition only as to something to be cured in other people. They are prescribing an art which ought to exist, and with what does exist they deal rather stiffly, primly, deadly. Raymond Williams' exemplary tragedy, *Koba*, seems to me a non-play.

Conversely, the post-Freudians, once seen from their rivals' point of view, are surely childish in their idea of what culture is. If affluence and automation are making possible a world in which repression will no longer be necessary, first of all the bulk of the world is not sharing in this affluence. Secondly, this affluence even in a rich country is being achieved and maintained by an elaborate technology and elaborate systems of human controls. Power is remaining with those who have sublimated their energies – by repression – into formidable weapons of intelligence and will-power; just as before; not with the self-delighting heroes of Eros. The future the post-Freudians talk of is only a possibility – and only that – in one part of one country; in an America without a Pentagon and without General Motors and without universities. There is no such country. In effect, this theory identifies a culture with its Bohemia.

Both ideas seem to me, for all their energy, strangely incomplete. Or perhaps it is not strange, since they are still young, but signally incomplete. Neither has, for instance, worked out its own literary taste or critical vocabulary. In literary matters the post-Marxists are still Leavisite, and the post-Freudians are still modernist. The artists Susan Sontag recommends to us are Artaud, Rimbaud, Kafka, Bosch; and the artistic virtues, derangement, anguish, distortion, ugliness. Both groups are living on their inheritances – if indeed they may not be said to be usurping those inheritances. First-class literary work is likely to come from their allies, their collateral branches, rather than from them.

However, their mutual criticism does not amount to a cancelling out of either, to my sense. I don't want to feel either set of ideas muzzled and made harmless, for each is more valuable in certain essential functions than my own ideologically inert liberalism. The setting of the two in opposition satisfies me, I think, not because they destroy each other, but because they work out a vivid dialectic between them. And if saying that reveals a personal motive behind the pattern of comparison I've made, I've said plenty of other things which surely bear witness to there being something there which demands patterning.

Bernard Bergonzi Thoughts on the Personality Explosion

Frank Kermode has usefully traced the connections between the principles of the great Modern Movement of fifty or more years ago and the seemingly desperate innovations of the post-Dada, post-surrealist avant-garde of the present day. He has made many things clear; and for that I am grateful. At the same time, I am a little uneasy about his suave and persuasive demonstration that *plus ça change. . . .* It seems to me that there are deeply revolutionary changes going on in our culture, though they are quieter, if more significant, than those associated with the apostles of neo-modernism so agreeably discussed in Calvin Tomkins' *The Bride and the Bachelors*. I think that these changes should find a place within the general discussion of modernism, that Kermode has initiated, even at the cost of somewhat modifying the neatness of his total picture.

What, briefly, I have in mind is a widespread shift from the traditional concept of the work of art (whether 'minority' or 'popular' art is immaterial) as an *artefact* to that of art as *performance*. This change has been intimately associated with the advent of the electronic media – notably, telephone, radio, television, gramophone records, and tape-recording – and the partial supersession of a visual-spatial basis of culture by an oral-aural one. Such notions are more freely circulated in America than in this country, but they will be familiar to readers of Marshall McLuhan's *The Gutenberg Galaxy* (1962) and *Understanding Media* (1964), and Walter J. Ong's *The Barbarian Within* (1962). Professor McLuhan's way of expressing himself is so wild and his thought processes so eccentric that most English reviewers found a convenient excuse to brush aside the challenging and original content of his books; Fr Ong, a polymathic but lively American Jesuit, is a more rational and sober expositor of similar ideas, but his work is less known here. What I want to say will be quite heavily indebted to these two writers.

One of the points that Ong emphasises is the way in which modern criticism is strongly visual-spatial in its terminology; discussion of art is subsumed under the concept of the artefact, or self-sufficient, free-standing object, and 'structure' has become an indispensable term for almost all contemporary critics.[1] The characteristic language of the palaeo-modernist masters was strongly visualist, as with Ezra Pound's 'image', James Joyce's 'epiphany', Wyndham Lewis' 'vortex', and the 'monuments' of T. S. Eliot's 'Tradition and the Individual Talent'. And the central metaphors of the New Criticism have been even more strongly artefactal, as exemplified in Cleanth Brooks' *The Well Wrought Urn* and W. K. Wimsatt's *The Verbal Icon*. Art as performance, on the other hand, exists in time rather than space. It is evanescent rather than an enduring monument (though the devices of modern technology can make the performance almost infinitely repeatable). Above all, the beholders are brought into a much more direct relation with the artist's personality than when they are contemplating an icon.

This last point recalls a debate that took place in the 1930s between C. S. Lewis and E. M. W. Tillyard (published as *The Personal Heresy*). Against Lewis, who advanced the received modern critical opinion that the value of a work of art inheres within it, and is irrelevant to its creator's personality, Tillyard claimed:

> I believe we read Keats in some measure because his poetry gives a version of a remarkable personality of which another version is his life. The two versions are not the same but they are analogous. Part of our response to poetry is in fact similar to the stirring experience when we meet someone whose personality impresses us.

[1] A similar point was made independently by Donald Davie in a broadcast talk, 'Two Analogies for Poetry', in *The Listener* (5 April 1962).

Tillyard did not extract any extreme conclusions from this heavily guarded statement, which, on one level, merely reaffirms the assumptions of pre-modern biographical criticism. And yet it seems a valid implication of his position that one might, in some circumstances, positively prefer the life to the work of art, the personality to the icon which obliquely reflects it. One may compare Picasso's portentous observation:

> It's not what the artist does that counts, but what he is. Cézanne would never have interested me a bit if he had lived and thought like Jacques-Émile Blanche, even if the apples he had painted had been ten times as beautiful. What forces our interest is Cézanne's anxiety, that's Cézanne's lesson; the torments of Van Gogh – that is the actual drama of the man. The rest is a sham.

The prevailing context of twentieth-century critical opinion, with its stress on 'impersonality', makes such sentiments, in themselves so old-fashioned and so reminiscent of Romantic hero-worship, potentially revolutionary and subversive.

Fr Ong has been much exercised by the problem of reconciling the impersonality of the artefact with the personality of the creator. In one of the best essays in *The Barbarian Within*, 'The Jinnee in the Well Wrought Urn', he discusses this question with great penetration. Himself a believer in the New-Critical principles of iconic impersonality, he nevertheless understands why we constantly interrogate a work to discover the personality concealed in it: 'if you so much as whisper that there is a jinnee in the urn, most onlookers will be only too willing to drop the urn without further ado. Broken, it will let the jinnee out, and they can ask him a few questions'. (Anyone with much experience of teaching literature will, I think, confirm that this is a very deep-rooted tendency, however much one may fulminate against the 'intentional fallacy'.) People have an innate desire to enter into communion with other personalities, and remain dissatisfied with the impersonal contemplation of the aesthetic icon. Ong is not happy about the inclination to personalise art, but he implies that it is inevitable:

Anything that bids for attention in an act of contemplation is a surrogate for a person. In proportion as the work of art is capable of being taken in full seriousness, it moves further and further along an asymptote to the curve of personality.[1]

Elsewhere in his book, Ong describes the way in which the electronic media have given a new dominance to sound, and, in particular, to the human voice and thus to personality:

Heightening the oral-aural element in a culture does much more than merely de-emphasise vision. It subtly heightens the personalist element in a culture. For the plenary development of sound, the human voice, is a manifestation of the person. Even more than it is a manifestation of an understanding of objects, speech is a calling of one person to another, of an interior to an interior. Sight presents always surfaces, presents even depth as a lamination of surfaces, whereas sound presents always interiors, for sound is impossible without some resonance. The post-Baconian preoccupation with sight and 'observation' produced the world of the Enlightenment, a world of objects and things without convincing personal presences, giving us the strangely silent universe which Newtonian physics and Deism both supposed. Printing was the harbinger of this Newtonian world, for printing is spectacularly allied with surface or 'object' treatment of reality.

In these few sentences Ong states the approach which McLuhan has copiously adumbrated in his two books. (It is, incidentally, ironic to recall that something very like the Ong-McLuhan analysis was outlined nearly forty years ago by the most strongly visualist of the palaeo-modernists, though from a totally opposed point of view. In *Time and Western Man*, Wyndham Lewis worked out a chain of oppositions between contrasting concepts: the 'good' entities were space, the eye, light, surface, architecture,

[1] Another writer has interestingly developed this discussion by suggesting that works of art should be approached as 'persons' rather than as 'objects'; see G. Ingli James, 'The Autonomy of the Work of Art', in *Sewanee Review* (Spring 1962).

permanence; the 'bad' were time, the ear, darkness, interiority, music, flux.)

Some time ago, a record reviewer in one of the Sunday colour supplements wrote of Bob Dylan: 'A poet? When he does his own stuff, yes; his wry, two-edged delivery gives life to what looks unpromising on paper.' When I read this casual comment, it struck me as at least as revolutionary as anything solemnly spelt out in the modernist manifestos of the last eighty years. And, curiously enough, it had been anticipated by a remark that a friend made to me a year or so before: describing a poetry-reading by Robert Creeley, he said he had found it an impressive occasion, although he guessed that Creeley's poems would not be very good 'on the page'. In both cases the implication seems to be that the 'poetry' is what happens to the poems when they are sung or read by the composer, rather than something inherent in them; the printed words are merely a score from which the author can, as it were, perform himself.

The field of pop music offers many instructive examples of this process. The typical song that moves quickly in and out of the hit charts (or doesn't even make them) is likely to be fragmentary and banal in melody, crude in rhythm, and puerile in its words; it will, in any case, be forgotten in a few weeks. George Melly has remarked: 'Pop music has built-in obsolescence. Like paper cups and cheap ball-point pens, it's meant to be used and thrown away.'[1] The differences between the songs of the present time and those of the thirties can be discussed from a number of viewpoints. There is, initially, the difference in audience: in the 1930s the teenager, economically speaking, had not been invented, and the audience for popular music was basically adult, with vicariously sophisticated tastes. The songs of someone like Cole Porter presumably reflected, both in their musical style and in their

[1] On Hannah Arendt's formulation this fact would decisively exclude such music from the realm of art: 'the proper intercourse with a work of art is certainly not using it; on the contrary, it must be removed carefully from the whole context of ordinary use objects to attain its proper place in the world'. *The Human Condition* (New York, 1959) p. 147.

lyrics, the polished if brittle café-society in which he habitually moved, and which could provide an acceptable, fantasy-tinged focus for the aspirations of the millions who enjoyed his music. Today, by contrast (as Kermode has correctly observed), the prole has become a dominant cultural ideal, and popular music has become correspondingly simplified. A music which directly reflects the deprived life-style of the American urban Negro has been avidly taken up (and subjected in the process to huge commercial exploitation) by the *déclassé* teenagers of the affluent West and turned into a symbol of their own somewhat factitious cultural revolt. The spectacle of, say, The Animals singing 'We Gotta Get Out of This Place', which has the genuine accents of proletarian desperation, to a cool, trend-setting adolescent audience provides a convenient emblem.

But the explanation in terms of the changing audience is not, in fact, sufficient. More important, perhaps, and more relevant to my present intention, are the technological means by which popular music is disseminated. In the thirties, sheet-music was still the dominant medium: the song was subject to typographical codification; it could then be de-coded, sung and played by anyone with the necessary skill. The ensuing performance might be in any particular style; a song may, perhaps, have been made famous by a particular performer, but there was no assumption that his performance had to be the model for all subsequent ones. The song was, in fact, an autonomous, free-standing artefact, offering itself to a variety of interpretations. The pop song of the sixties, on the other hand, is overwhelmingly disseminated by means of the gramophone record, which offers, not a typographical codification of the song, but the song itself, as a direct aural experience. Where the piece is performed by the composers (as is often the case) then one has a magical electronic capturing of a unique occasion, an indissoluble nexus of song, composers, and performance. Here, clearly, the artefact has been overthrown by the performance. And what has been gained in personal immediacy is lost in freedom of interpretation. The objective musical poverty of most present-day songs means that they cannot be subject to a variety of arrangements like the vintage compositions of Porter, Gershwin, or Kern. They are mostly intended as the vehicles of a particular voice and personality. To this extent the song, as a separate art-work, has been radically devalued in favour of the performer-composer. Any edition of *Juke Box Jury* will confirm the truth of this ('I didn't care too much for that one myself, but *anything* these boys do is sure to go to the top').

If melody and structure are much reduced in current pop, there is a certain amount of compensation in the curiously thick aural texture (produced by all the gimmickry of electronics) of many recent songs, which means that at a given moment the ear has quite a lot to take in (a parallel, perhaps, to the cult of retinal painting). One thinks of the bells, tambourines, harmoniums, rattles and other sound-effects that are added to the normal instrumental backing, and even more ambitious combinations, like the violin section of a symphony orchestra that can be heard on certain Tamla-Motown recordings, or the oratorio-like choral noises on The Righteous Brothers' performances. But the preoccupation with texture is most evident in the fascination with vocal quality, the lovingly-amplified, gravelly wail characteristic of Bob Dylan or Mick Jagger or Paul Jones or Sonny Bono. Here we may recall Ong's formulation: 'the plenary development of sound, the human voice, is a manifestation of the person', which the recording engineers might well have made their motto. At all events, we can now see that *personalities* have replaced *songs* as the focus of interest in the contemporary pop scene (the fact that this direct projection of personality is heavily dependent on an impersonal technology is a central and recurring paradox).

The way in which personality has become a self-subsistent value in modern culture has, of course, been noticed by many critics. Daniel J. Boorstin, for instance, devotes a vigorous chapter of *The Image* (1962) to what he calls the 'human pseudo-event', the 'celebrity' who is well known for being well known; and, as Boorstin points out, in the jargon of modern communications 'celebrity' and 'personality' are interchangeable terms. But Boorstin's account, entertaining though it is, suffers from being rather superficial and too purely negative; he shows little inclination to pursue in depth the connections between the cult of pure personality and the media. (McLuhan refers to Boorstin in *Understanding Media* as a writer blinkered by a wholly typographical and literary perspective.) Ong's approach is subtler; while acknowledging the crudity and limitations of a media-fostered personality cult, he is also impressed by the philosophical and theological dimensions of contemporary personalism; and, as he shows, the various strands are not easily separated. He makes some interesting comments on television, undoubtedly the most powerful and influential of all the media at the present time. He remarks that the purely visual detail of television is of poor quality as compared with films or photographs, and is very dependent on the support of the aural elements, voice and music:

> Strangely enough, although it is in part a visualist development, television has moved away from this effect of print. It has been a personalising, not an objectifying, medium. The discussion panel, with its interchange of personalities, is properly a television phenomenon. Such personal interchange was difficult to manage on radio, for there individual persons could only with difficulty be kept distinct. Hence the use of voice was not brought to its fullest fruition.

It is, I think, possible to be in sympathy with Fr Ong's philosophical personalism and still feel that on this specific aspect of television he is being too sanguine. The TV panel may indeed be a good medium for the 'interchange of personalities'; what is not at all clear is whether it is an effective medium for the interchange of ideas. Indeed, I am inclined to say that so far television has shown itself unable to cope with the presentation of ideas as such; the pressure to exploit personality is all too strong. In his debate with Tillyard, C. S. Lewis made the point that human personality demands an affective, not a contemplative response.

To subject a human being to a detached, appraising gaze is simply insulting:

> It is to make of a man a mere thing, a spectacle. We do not wish to be thus treated ourselves. Is there, in social life, a grosser incivility than that of thinking about the man who addresses us instead of thinking about what he says?

Lewis has made a very telling point; the fact remains, however, that what he condemns is precisely what television continually does. A leading expert on, say, trade union law, or the Swiss banking system, or the Japanese theatre, will be brought along to the studio to give his ninety seconds or so of wisdom. But as he talks the camera will be distracting attention from his words by focusing on his left ear or some other physical configuration, while the interviewer asks questions which are not particularly designed to elucidate the truth of what the man is saying, but to 'draw him out', to provoke him into some singular revelation of personality. The viewers are not so much expected to learn something as to see an expert 'perform', to be put through his paces; there may well be an anti-élitist bias implicit in the medium, betraying a democratic suspicion of experts as such and a corresponding desire to put them down. The whole process may be good entertainment, but it is inimical to the free play of ideas. Marshall McLuhan has made much of the slogan, 'the medium is the message', meaning that the overt content of the medium is much less important than the ways in which the medium affects our sensibilities. But one aspect of the Message seems to be (to adapt William Carlos Williams' famous saying, 'No Ideas but in Things'): 'No Ideas but in Persons', which is very nearly tantamount to saying, 'No Ideas'.

The voice-personality-performance nexus, which is one of the major products of the electronic media in the realm of mass culture, can be closely paralleled in the sphere of minority art. I have already referred to Robert Creeley as a performer of his own verse, and in the past few years there has been a considerable revival of poetry as a performed and oral-aural art, often in conjunction with jazz. The parallel with jazz suggests that there is no reason why verse should not be orally improvised and then captured on tape, thus entirely by-passing the print medium. Doubtless this already happens. In fact, I remember in the early fifties, when tape-recorders were much less common than they are now, a young man playing for me a tape of a poem he had composed and recorded. When I asked if I could *read* it, he said apologetically that he hadn't yet got around to writing it out. At the time, I didn't realise the deep cultural significance of the incident. A dominantly oral-aural poetry will, undoubtedly, seem crude and open-textured when read on the page. Clearly, many of the subtle and complex effects of a poetry written to be read, initially, in a spatially extended poem are unsuitable for a poem intended for declamation, and iconic criticism will have little to grasp. Arguably, one might want to call this poetry something else; John Wain has referred to a characteristic piece by Gregory Corso as 'oratory' rather than 'poetry'. Such poetry already has its own aesthetic, laid down in Charles Olson's Projective Verse manifesto, which has been very influential among the American poets of the Black Mountain-San Francisco axis.[1] Olson specifically relates the quality of verse to the unique personal characteristics of its creator, and rejects the whole visualist approach associated with printing:

> And the line comes (I swear it) from the breath, from the breathing of the man who writes, at the moment that he writes, and thus is, it is here that, the daily work, the WORK gets in, for only he, the man who writes, can declare, at every moment, the line its metric and its ending – where its breathing shall come to, termination. . . . What we have suffered from, is manuscript, press, the removal of verse from its producer and its reproducer, the voice, a removal by one, by two removes from its place of origin *and* its destination.

The logic of this is clearly that the recording of the poet reading his own work should replace the printed book as the principal

[1] Particularly those represented in Donald M. Allen's anthology, *The New American Poetry 1945–60* (New York, 1960), which includes Olson's manifesto.

means of dissemination. Olson is, however, enthusiastic about the typewriter as an aid to the poet, since it helps oral composition and reproduction by providing regular and repeatable spaces that correspond to the musician's staves and bars. McLuhan remarks, 'Seated at the typewriter, the poet, much in the manner of the jazz musician, has the experience of performance as composition.' To counter a fairly evident difficulty, he blandly adds: 'That the typewriter, which carried the Gutenberg technology into every nook and cranny of our culture and economy should, also, have given out with these opposite oral effects is a characteristic reversal.'

In visual-spatial terms the equivalent of Olson's verse-line as a breath-unit peculiar to its creator is the personal calligraphic shape we call a signature. The unique touch of a master has a particular value (often a pecuniary value at that: one thinks of the scribble on the tablecloth with which Picasso is said to pay for restaurant meals). The notion of an aesthetic Kilroy-was-here helps to explain much that has gone on in recent years amongst avant-garde painters. As Harold Rosenberg has insisted, Abstract Expressionism, or action painting, does not aim at producing the traditional art-object, or painting as artefact. It looks for a unique encounter of artist with paint and canvas, in other words, an act, an event, or a performance. (Mary McCarthy has complained, 'You cannot hang an event on a wall, only a picture.') In such an encounter the medium and the personality of the encounter are inseparably one. In Rosenberg's gnomic words:

> What is a painting that is not an object, nor the representation of an object, nor the analysis or impression of it, nor whatever else a painting has ever been – and which has also ceased to be the emblem of a personal struggle? It is the painter himself changed into a ghost, inhabiting the Art World. Here the common phrase, 'I have bought an O-' (rather than a painting by O-) becomes literally true. The man who started to remake himself has made himself into a commodity with a trademark.[1]

[1] *The Tradition of the New* (New York, 1962) p. 35. Rosenberg seems to be referring here to 'weak' action painting, in which there is an insufficient element of struggle, but the distinction is not an easy one to grasp.

In the rapid mutations of the New York art world, action painting was succeeded by Pop Art, of which Andy Warhol is one of the high priests:

> If, as it has been suggested, Abstract Expressionists have reduced to a minimum the difference between creator and creation, and Pop has reduced to a minimum the difference between ready-made and hand-made, then Warhol must be the new movement's perfect exponent.[1]

At first sight it would seem that the Pop Artists, with their stress on impersonal, mechanical forms of reproduction, silk-screen printing and so on, and their repudiation of the painting as something essentially hand-made, are moving in a diametrically opposite direction from the Abstract Expressionists, where the calligraphic record of a personal encounter is the unique source of value. And yet it is not difficult to see that the calligraphic element is relevant here, too, if in a different way. The final development of Warhol's love affair with the world of mass-produced artefacts is the real tins of Campbell's Soup which he signs and which then become saleable art-objects. What gives them their market value is, obviously, Mr Warhol's *signature*. An identical tin signed by, say, Frank Kermode or myself would still be a tin of soup, not an art-object. The hyper-sophisticated connoisseurship which goes for such things is basically motivated by that traditional pursuit of the personality-cultist: autograph-hunting. It is the master's transforming, charismatic touch that we are really after.

In discussing the contemporary New York avant-garde, questions of pure aesthetics become inextricably involved with socio-economic considerations: the whole scene only makes sense if it is looked at in a vulgar-Marxist way. Unlimited wealth and an insatiable taste for novelty keep the machine constantly in motion. Styles succeed one another almost with the rapidity of pop records, and in the process everyone is enriched: the artists and dealers by their earnings and profits, and the collectors by the

[1] Mario Amaya, *Pop as Art* (1965) p. 103.

investment value of their art-objects. (Artists who, for whatever reason, persist in painting in an 'out' style do, however, have a thin time of it.) And for all the protestations of many artists that they want to move right away from personality and its manifestations, they have, despite themselves, become personalities (or celebrities), trapped within a promotional machine. A blank canvas by Rauschenberg is not just any old blank canvas (and a 'silence' by John Cage will get more respect than a 'silence' by a less well-known composer). The well-wrought urn may, indeed, be produced by a purely mechanical process, untouched by hand throughout; but it is still the jinnee who commands attention (and, perhaps, gets rich).

Kermode acknowledges, in passing, something of what I am trying to say, when he remarks: 'Blankness and indifference, like the "impersonality" of Eliot, become, from one angle, a kind of egoism, indeed dehumanisation has always been, from this angle, the apotheosis of the *culte du moi*.' This points in the right direction, but I think the emphasis needs to be a good deal sharper. We are facing now, not a mere survival of Romantic egoism, but an infinitely complex multiple concern with personality, ranging all the way from the 'human pseudo-events' manufactured by the PR men to the philosophy of Martin Buber, in which the voice-performance nexus of the electronic media is a crucial (if not the only) element. Fr Ong has summed up the present situation with more serenity than I feel capable of myself:

> The twentieth century, from one point of view the most mechanised of all the ages of mankind, is from another point of view the most personalised. No other age has generated a whole philosophy of personalism such as one finds in the works of Martin Buber, Gabriel Marcel, and others. At a much less reflective, more superficial, and nevertheless significant level, no civilisation before our technological civilisation has given such attention to problems of personnel and personality in matters even of industrial performance. The 'I' and the 'thou' have never been the objects of more explicit treatment than now. In the future, alongside the digital and analogue computers and

other mathematicising developments such as Western culture has specialised in more and more over the past few hundred years, the human person will receive more and more attention, not in every quarter but in significant milieus and ways.

In an age of manifest public dehumanisation, when the 'organic' community has been overthrown by the modern bureaucratic state, and when mass production and, now, automation have banished human beings from many processes with which they were traditionally and intimately associated, one might indeed expect 'free' personality to become an absolute value in itself. Ong's emblematic alignment of the computer and the person may come to characterise two opposed aspects of our culture just as much as Henry Adams' opposition between the Virgin and the Dynamo served to typify two different cultures.

In the process, however, 'art' as we are accustomed to understanding it might disappear. Instead of the artefact, created and permeated by a given personality but ultimately standing apart from it, we may positively prefer the personality itself, without disguise or intermediary; in which case, the aesthetic will have been absorbed by the affective. I am reminded here of the final section of B. S. Johnson's highly ingenious novel, *Albert Angelo* (1964), in which the narrator brutally shatters the carefully composed fictional surface:

> Im trying to say something not tell a story telling stories is telling lies and I want to tell the truth about me about my experience about my truth about my truth to reality about sitting here writing looking out across Claremont Square trying to say something about the writing and nothing being an answer to the loneliness to the lack of loving.

He then goes on to put us right about all the details of his real experience which he has altered for fictional purposes. This recalls the argument about the essential 'untruthfulness' of fiction which Kermode alludes to, but it also has larger implications. It may point to a dissatisfaction with the imposed impersonality of the novel form, which, as David Lodge remarks in his recent

Language of Fiction, 'of all literary genres is the one most firmly fixed in the Gutenberg galaxy. It is the characteristic literary product of the printing press.' One sees a similar dissatisfaction reflected passim in Doris Lessing's *The Golden Notebook*. That Johnson nevertheless remains imprisoned in the typographical dimension is evident from the obtrusiveness of his lack of punctuation.

It is possible that the direct manifestation of personality will not replace art – but that something will persist and be generally accepted as art that nevertheless escapes all our present aesthetic terminology, rooted as it is in the objective, impersonal, and iconic; and which, in Ong's phrase, will move 'further and further along an asymptote to the curve of personality'. We should keep calm about the prospect; but either way, we can expect some revolutionary changes, even if we stop short of calling them 'mutations'. At least, I shall be surprised, though not particularly disappointed, if they fail to appear.

David Lodge Objections to William Burroughs

I

Have we come to handle the avant-garde too gently? From the *Lyrical Ballads* to *Ulysses* our literary history is very much a chronicle of revolutionary works hooted and reviled by the literary establishments of their times, appreciated by a small élite of initiates, and belatedly elevated to classic status by succeeding literary establishments. Since the 1920s, however, the time lag between the publication and the public recognition of such works has got shorter and shorter, until now we are, perhaps, more in danger of mistaking than neglecting masterpieces. Part of the reason is the radical change which has overtaken academic criticism in this period: the groves of academe, that were once enclaves of conservative literary taste, are now only too eager to welcome what is new. Another, and perhaps more important reason is that through the development of the mass media and what one might call the boom in the culture market, the 'small élite of initiates' which in the past has constituted the only audience for experimental art, good and bad, is now able to bring its influence to bear very swiftly and powerfully on the larger public.

Nothing illustrates this latter process more strikingly than the way the reputation of William Burroughs has grown since Mary McCarthy praised *The Naked Lunch* at the Edinburgh Writers' Conference of 1962. (Miss McCarthy has since complained that her words on that occasion were distorted and exaggerated by the press; but it could be argued that writers who participate in such events, which are peculiar to our own cultural era, must expect and accept such treatment.) What is noteworthy about Burroughs' reputation is not so much the encomiums his work has received from such confreres as Miss McCarthy, Norman Mailer ('I think that William Burroughs is the only American novelist living today who may conceivably be possessed of genius') and Jack Kerouac ('Burroughs is the greatest satirical writer since Jonathan Swift'), as the way in which this body of opinion has acted on the public mind so as to secure the smooth acceptance and accommodation of such books as *The Naked Lunch* and *Nova Express*. It seems to illustrate very well what Lionel Trilling has described as the institutionalisation of the adversary culture of modernism; and like him, I do not see this process as a symptom of cultural health. *The Naked Lunch*, whatever else it may be, is a very indecent book, and *Nova Express*, whatever else it may be, is a very tedious book. These novels' pretensions to serious literary significance which, if realised, would justify the indecency and the tedium (or rather force us to redefine these qualities) need to be examined rather more rigorously than our present literary climate generally encourages. Before doing so, it may be advisable to attempt a description of these books. I say 'attempt' because they both resist any conventional summary of character and action.

II

The Naked Lunch begins with the first-person narrative of a drug addict who, pursued by the New York police, travels across America with a companion to Mexico; his account of the journey is mingled with reminiscences of various characters from the drugs underworld. In the second chapter the novel parts with actuality and takes on the quality of dream. The action shifts abruptly from place to place, sometimes between mythical states called Freeland, Annexia and Interzone, which bear a parodic relationship to the actual world. There is no plot, but a general impression of intrigue and pursuit, sometimes on a cops-and-robbers level, sometimes on a political level. The narrative mode shifts from first person to third person to dramatic dialogue. Many of the scenes have a hallucinatory, surrealistic quality reminiscent of the Circe episode in *Ulysses.* The images of the book are primarily of violence, squalor and sexual perversion. There is a notorious orgiastic sequence in which orgasm is achieved by hanging and finally eating the sexual partner. We seem to be sharing the dream, or nightmare, of an addict – perhaps, as Miss McCarthy has suggested, one who is taking a cure and suffering the agonies of 'withdrawal'.

In *Nova Express* the dislocation of narrative and logical continuity is much more radical, for here Burroughs has used what he describes as a 'cut-up' or 'fold-in' technique – that is, a montage of fragments of his own and other people's writings, achieved, for instance by overlapping two pages of text and reading straight across. Basically the book is a science fiction fantasy based on the premise that the earth has been invaded by extraterrestial gangsters, the 'Nova Mob', whose mission is to infiltrate human institutions and encourage all forms of evil in order to accelerate this planet's progress on the path to destruction. They are pursued by the 'Nova Police', who also work invisibly through human agencies, causing, it would seem, almost as much havoc. Only such fantastic suppositions, it is implied, will account for the political lunacy and moral decay of the modern world. That the fantasy is more real than what we take to be actuality is emphasised by such conceits as that life is a 'biological movie' created and manipulated in a 'reality Studio' for the control of which Nova factions are competing.

III

Burroughs has, principally, two claims on the attention of serious readers: as a moralist, and as an innovator. On both counts, it seems to me, he cannot be considered as more than a minor, eccentric figure. Undoubtedly he has a certain literary talent, particularly for comedy and the grotesque, but in both precept and practice he is deeply confused and ultimately unsatisfying. *The Naked Lunch* seems to offer an appropriate epitaph on his work: 'Confusion hath fuck his masterpiece.'

To begin with, there is a deep confusion, not only in Burroughs but in his admirers too, on the subject of narcotics. Much of Burroughs's notoriety derives from the fact that he is a morphine addict, who has been cured, but who still writes very much out of the experience of addiction. He tells us in the Introduction to *The Naked Lunch* that it is based on notes taken during the sickness and delirium of addiction. He is our modern De Quincey; and undoubtedly this accounts for his adoption by the hipster wing of the American literary scene. Herbert Gold has called *The Naked Lunch* 'the definitive hip book' and Burroughs tells us that the title was donated by the arch-hipster Jack Kerouac. 'I did not understand what the title meant until my recovery. The title means exactly what the words say: NAKED lunch – a frozen moment when everyone sees what is on the end of every fork.' These words clearly imply that the drugged state gives access to a special vision of truth – that the junkie, like Conrad's Kurtz, is an inverted hero of the spirit who truly sees 'the horror, the horror' that ordinary, conforming humanity refuses to face. But in other places Burroughs undercuts this argument, which alone could justify his distressingly explicit (so much more explicit than Conrad's) descriptions of the horror. In an interview published in the *Paris Review* (XXXV, Fall 1965) he agreed that 'The visions of drugs and the visions of art don't mix'; and both novels contain a great deal of obtrusive propaganda against the use of narcotics and on behalf of the apomorphine treatment by which Burroughs himself was cured. The interviewer challenged him on this point – 'You regard addiction as an illness, but also a central human fact, a drama?' – and Burroughs' reply is revealing:

> Both, absolutely. It's as simple as the way in which anyone happens to become an alcoholic . . . The idea that addiction is somehow a psychological illness is, I think, totally ridiculous. It's as psychological as malaria. It's a matter of exposure . . . There are also all forms of spiritual addiction . . . Many policemen and narcotics agents are precisely addicted to power, to exercising a certain nasty kind of power over people who are helpless. The nasty sort of power: white junk I call it – rightness . . .

It will be noted how Burroughs slides here from a literal, clinical view of addiction to a figurative or symbolic one. Both views are at odds with the assumption behind *The Naked Lunch* that the junkie's delirium yields truth; and they are also at odds with each other. In the first view addiction is seen as a preventable sickness, in the second it is seen as a metaphor for authoritarianism. On the one hand it is not 'psychological', on the other hand it can be 'spiritual'. In the first place the junkie is a sick man in need of society's protection, in the second place he is a victim of society.

This kind of equivocation is particularly evident in Burroughs' treatment of the police. In *The Naked Lunch* a certain sympathy is generated for the junkies on the run from the police, yet it is difficult to see how the exposure of the individual to drugs, which according to Burroughs is the cause of addiction, could be prevented without the police. In *Nova Express* the Nova Police seem to be the 'goodies' as the Nova Mob are the 'baddies', but Burroughs, in the interview already cited, says, 'They're like police anywhere . . . Once you get them in there, by God, they begin acting like any police. They're always an ambivalent agency.' In this case, how are we to read the following passage about the Nova Police:

> The difference between this department and the parasitic excrescence that often travels under the name 'Police' can be expressed in metabolic terms: The distinction between morphine and apomorphine . . . The Nova Police can be compared to apomorphine, a regulating instance that need not continue and has no intention of continuing after its work is done.

The confusion that surrounds these two novels of Burroughs can, I think, be partly explained by the fact that they are very different works which Burroughs is trying to present as in some sense continuous, two stages in a coherent programme. *The Naked Lunch* is essentially a nihilistic work and as such it must be granted a certain horrible power; but it is prefaced by an Introduction which seeks to justify it on orthodox moral grounds, and to present its hero as a brand snatched from the burning.

> Since *The Naked Lunch* treats this health problem [addiction], it is necessarily brutal, obscene and disgusting. Sickness has often repulsive details not for weak stomachs.
>
> Certain passages in the book that have been called pornographic were written as a tract against Capital Punishment in the manner of Jonathan Swift's *Modest Proposal.* These sections are intended to reveal capital punishment as the obscene, barbaric and disgusting anachronism that it is.

How literature can deal with evil without morally compromising itself is of course a perennial and perhaps insoluble problem, but Burroughs' defence is either naïve or disingenuous. The analogy with Swift won't stand up. Whereas in *A Modest Proposal* Swift maintains a constant logical connection between his fable (the monstrous 'proposal') and his facts (the miseries of the Irish people), so that in revolting from the former we are compelled to revolt from the latter, it is doubtful whether the uninformed reader would see any connection at all between the Orgasm Death Gimmick and Capital Punishment. It may be that the disgust Mr Burroughs feels for Capital Punishment has been transferred to the antics of his sexual perverts, but the reverse process which should occur for the reader is by no means to be relied upon. The power of Swift's piece inheres very largely in the tone of calm reasonableness with which the proposal is put forward, so that we feel obliged to supply the emotion which is missing. In *The Naked Lunch*, instead of this subtly controlled irony we have a kinetic narrative style which suspends rather than activates the reader's moral sense, and incites him to an imaginative collaboration in the orgy. Since I do not propose to quote from this particular scene here, I shall illustrate my point with a rather less offensive passage:

> Rock and Roll adolescent hoodlums storm the streets of all nations. They rush into the Louvre and throw acid in the Mona Lisa's face. They open zoos, insane asylums, prisons, burst water mains with air hammers, chop the floor out of passenger plane lavatories, shoot out light-houses, file elevator cables to one thin wire, turn sewers into the water supply, throw sharks

> and sting rays, electric eels and candiru into swimming pools . . . in nautical costumes ram the *Queen Mary* full speed into New York Harbor, play chicken with passenger planes and busses, rush into hospitals in white coats carrying saws and axes and scalpels three feet long . . .

This is vivid, inventive writing, but it is scarcely satire. There is a note of celebration here, a hilarious anarchism which relishes the mindless destruction it describes; and it extends to the most successfully drawn characters in the book, the brutal surgeon Benway and the inspired practical joker A. J. There *are* patches of effective satire in *The Naked Lunch* (notably a parody of conversation between some 'good old boys' of the Deep South – 'These city fellers come down here and burn a nigger and don't even settle up for the gasoline'), but the tone and structure of the whole will not support the serious moral significance that is claimed for it. Indeed the account of the Nova Mob's subversive activities in *Nova Express* seems damagingly appropriate to *The Naked Lunch*: 'We need a peg to hang evil full length. By God show them how ugly the ugliest pictures in the dark room can be' . . . 'Take orgasm noises sir and cut them in with torture and accident groans and screams sir and operating-room jokes sir and flicker sex and torture film right with it sir'. Burroughs' reference to himself as an undercover agent of the Nova Police who wrote 'a so-called pornographic novel' as a bait to lure the Nova Mob into the open seems an arch evasion of responsibility.

Nova Express itself is a much more 'responsible' book, much more consistent with the avowed moral intentions of its author – and also much more boring. I find Burroughs more impressive (if no more congenial) as a nihilist than as a moralist, and the sick fantasies of the junkie more interesting than the portentous salvationism of the reclaimed addict. While it is good to know that Mr Burroughs has been cured of addiction, his attempt to load this private experience with universal significance, equating morphine with evil and apomorphine with redemption, becomes tiresome. But what most makes for bordeom in this novel is its technical experiment.

IV

First, an example, taken from a chapter vulnerably entitled 'Are These Experiments Necessary?':

> Saturday March 17th, 1962, Present Time of Knowledge – Scio is knowing and open food in The Homicide Act – Logos you got it? – Dia through noose – England spent the weekend with a bargain before release certificate is issued – Dogs must be carried reluctant to the center – It's a grand feeling – There's a lot ended – This condition is best expressed queen walks serenely down dollar process known as overwhelming – What we want is Watney's Woodbines and the Garden of Delights – And what could you have? – What would you? – State of news? – Inquire on hospitals? what?

This seems to be a 'cut-up' of English newspapers, advertisements, public notices etc. One can identify the likely contexts from which the fragments were taken. But does their juxtaposition create any significant new meaning? I think not.

The comparisons which have been canvassed by Burroughs and his admirers between his method and the methods of Eliot and Joyce (Burroughs has described *The Waste Land* as 'the first great cut-up collage', and a reviewer in the *New York Herald-Tribune* has likened *Nova Express* to *Finnegans Wake*) will not bear scrutiny. Compare:

> There I saw one I knew, and stopped him, crying: 'Stetson!
> You who were with me in the ships at Mylae!
> That corpse you planted last year in your garden,
> Has it begun to sprout? Will it bloom this year?
> Or has the sudden frost disturbed its bed?
> Oh keep the Dog far hence, that's friend to men,
> Or with his nails he'll dig it up again!
> You! hypocrite lecteur! – mon sembable – mon frère!'

> riverrun, past Eve and Adam's, from swerve of shore to bend of bay, brings us by a commodius vicus of recirculation back to Howth Castle and Environs.

What these passages have in common, and what is signally lacking in the Burroughs passage, is continuity. In the Eliot passage it is a thematic and dramatic continuity: the lines, incongruous, anachronistic and inconsequential as they are, nevertheless all relate to the idea of the 'Burial of the Dead' and communicate a very lively sense of the speaker's complex mood of surprise, impudence, admonition and complicity. In the Joyce passage it is a narrative or descriptive continuity: we hold on tight to the lightning tour of Dublin's topography, while being dimly aware that it is also a tour of human history from Adam and Eve onwards according to the cyclic theories of Vico. The more you read each passage the more you get out of it, and everything you get out of it thickens and confirms the sense of continuity and hence of meaning (for in the verbal medium meaning *is* continuity: discrete particulars are meaningless).

Burroughs has much less in common, both in precept and practice, with these modern classics, than with the art which Frank Kermode has dubbed 'neo-modernism'. Extreme examples of neo-modernism are the tins of Campbell's soup which Andy Warhol signs and sells as *objets d'art*, or the piano piece *4′ 33″* by composer John Cage, in which the performer sits before a closed piano in total silence and immobility for the prescribed time while the audience, in theory, becomes aesthetically aware of the noises around them, inside and outside the auditorium. Behind all these experiments is the principle of chance. Chance is allowed to determine the aesthetic product and the aesthetic experience; the artist confines himself to providing an aesthetic occasion within which the random particulars of our environment may be perceived with a new depth of awareness. As Kermode points out, 'Artists have always known that there was an element of luck in good work ("grace" if you like) and that they rarely knew what they meant till they'd seen what they said'; but neo-modernism trusts, or tries to trust, completely to luck. Kermode's conclusion seems to me the right one; that neo-modernism, apart from its merely humorous intent and value, is involved in a logical contradiction, for when it succeeds it does so by creating an order of the kind which it seeks to deny. 'Research into form is the true means of discovery, even when form is denied existence. So it becomes a real question whether it helps to introduce indeterminacy into the research.'

This seems very relevant to Burroughs' experiments, about which he is characteristically equivocal. The cut-up or fold-in technique is clearly designed to introduce a radical element of chance into literary composition. You run two pages of text into one another and allow chance to produce new units of sense (or nonsense). Burroughs defends such experiments (in the *Paris Review* interview) by an appeal to experience. Thus, he describes how he was struck, during a train journey to St Louis, by the congruence of his thoughts and what he saw outside the window:

> For example, a friend of mine has a loft apartment in New York. He said, 'Every time we go out of the house and come back, if we leave the bathroom door open, there's a rat in the house.' I look out of the window, there's Able Pest Control.

'Cut-ups', says Burroughs, 'make explicit a psycho-sensory process that is going on all the time anyway.' Precisely: that is why they are so uninteresting. We can all produce our own coincidences – we go to art for something more. One might guess that Joyce's discovery of a Vico Road in Dublin was a lucky break for him, a coincidence like Burroughs' observation of Able Pest Control (which reappears, incidentally, in a piece of imaginative writing, *St Louis Return*, published in the same issue of the *Paris Review*). But in the case of Joyce we are not aware of it *as* coincidence because it is incorporated into a verbal structure in which innumerable effects of a similar kind are created by means that are palpably not due to luck but to art. I do not mean to imply that we value works of literature solely in proportion to the conscious artifice we are able to impute to the process of composition (though this consideration always has some weight). Rather, that in the experience of successful literature we feel compelled to credit all its excitement and interest, whether this was produced by luck or not, to the creating mind behind it.

There is an essay by Paul Valéry, 'The Course in Poetics: the First Lesson' (reprinted in *The Creative Process*, ed. Brewster Ghiselin, 1955), which deals very profoundly with the difficult problem of indeterminacy in artistic creation. Valéry admits, indeed insists, that 'every act of mind is always somehow accompanied by a certain more or less perceptible atmosphere of indetermination'. But he goes on to point out that the finished art-work 'is the outcome of a succession of inner changes which are as disordered as you please but which must necessarily be reconciled at the moment when the hand moves to write under one unique command, whether happy or not'. As a romantic-symbolist, Valéry is prepared to grant the indeterminate a great deal of play – 'the dispersion always threatening the mind contributes almost as importantly to the production of the work as concentration itself' – but the dispersion is a threat, concentration is essential. The cut-up method, by which the writer selects from random collocations of ready-made units of discourse, seems a lazy short-cut, a way of evading the difficult and demanding task of reducing to order the personally felt experience of disorder.

Fortunately Burroughs does not always practice what he preaches. Kermode remarks: 'Admirers of William Burroughs' *Nova Express* admit that the randomness of the composition pays off only when the text looks as if it had been composed straightforwardly, with calculated inspiration.' I would wager that the following passage *was* composed straightforwardly:

> 'The Sumbliminal Kid' moved in and took over bars and cafés and juke boxes of the world cities and installed radio transmitters and microphones in each bar so that the music and talk of any bar could be heard in all his bars and he had tape recorders in each bar that played and recorded at arbitrary intervals and his agents moved back and fourth with portable tape recorders and brought back street sound and talk and music and poured it into his recorder array so he set waves and eddies and tornadoes of sound down all your streets and by the river of all language – Word dust drifted streets of broken music

> car horns and air hammers – The Word broken pounded twisted exploded in smoke –

Here it does not seem inappropriate to invoke Eliot and Joyce. There is continuity here – narrative, logical, syntactical and thematic. The language is disordered to imitate disorder, but it is orderly enough to form a complex, unified impression. It is worth noting, too, that the meaning of the passage is a conservative and traditional one – a criticism of those forces in modern civilization that are mutilating and destroying words and The Word, and the values they embody and preserve. The passage thus contradicts Burroughs' protestations (see the *Paris Review* interview) that his experiments are designed to break down our 'superstitious reverence for the word'.

V

The function of the avant-garde is to win new freedom, new expressive possibilities, for the arts. But these things have to be *won*, have to be fought for; and the struggle is not merely with external canons of taste, but within the artist himself. To bend the existing conventions without breaking them – this is the strenuous and heroic calling of the experimental artist. To break them is too easy.

I believe this principle can be extended to cover not only formal conventions, but also the social conventions that govern the content of public discourse. From the Romantics onwards the revolutionary works have commonly affronted not only their audience's aesthetic standards, but also their moral standards. *Madame Bovary* and *Ulysses*, for example, shocked and dismayed the publics of their respective periods by mentioning the unmentionable. But these works gradually won acceptance because discriminating readers appreciated that their breaches of existing decorums were not lightly or irresponsibly made, and that their authors had substituted for received disciplines and controls, disciplines and controls of their own even more austere and demanding. Much of the work of today's avant-garde, including that of

Burroughs, carries no such internal guarantee of integrity. Its freedom is stolen, not earned. The end product is hence startling and exciting on the first impression, but ultimately boring.

Finnegans Wake deliberately violates the conventions of language: it seeks to overthrow the law that we can only think and communicate lineally, one thing at a time. Most of us can manage the same trick – we can throw off a Joycean pun once in a while (I offer one free of charge to Mr Burroughs: 'fission chips'). But to produce hundreds and thousands of such puns, as Joyce does, and to weld them all into a complex whole – this is to create not destroy convention, and is a task of staggering difficulty. Similarly, most of us can compose a good obscene joke on occasion, or produce a powerful emotive effect by the use of obscene words; but to give these things authority as public discourse we have to ensure that they will survive the passing of the initial shock – we have not merely to violate, but to recreate the public sensibility, a task requiring precise imaginative control. One can't avoid the conclusion that a lot of Burroughs' most immediately effective writing (e.g. 'A.J. the notorious Merchant of Sex, who scandalised international society when he appeared at the Duc du Ventre's ball as a walking penis covered by a huge condom emblazoned with the A.J. motto "They Shall Not Pass"') has the short-lived appeal of a witty obscenity; or, in its more grotesque and horrific forms amounts to a reckless and self-defeating squandering of the powerful emotive forces that great literature handles with jealous care and economy.

Edwin Morgan **Concrete Poetry**

The idea of a 'vanguard' in literature has never had much acceptance in this country, though it's a commonplace on the Continent. The English Channel is a pretty narrow strip of water, but it's remarkable what an effective barrier it has been to the passage of ideas. The native argument is that this doesn't matter – that we prefer in our pragmatic way to get on with the job without worrying whether we're in the van or in the rear. There's a lot to be said for this attitude, but it can lead to a damaging kind of complacency. People may think that the poet is quietly getting on with his self-imposed task when in fact the quietness and absence of ideas and discussion may indicate lazy minds and smallness of spirit. Too many English poets since World War Two have been busy stacking their neat little bundles of firewood, and have stopped planting trees. This is, in the overall cultural context, somewhat surprising, since it puts poetry so much out of step with the great changes which have been taking place in the other arts. The young painter or sculptor, for example, is working today in an atmosphere of marked creative excitement. This doesn't mean that the assemblages of Rauschenberg or the luminous pictures of John Healey represent directions art has to take; it is simply that the artist feels himself to be in the midst of a varied and vigorous range of aesthetic activity. The English poet, on the other hand, has been contenting himself with a narrowed spectrum in which the traditional looms large and the exploratory has been almost forgotten.

The 1960s, however, have seen a tentative widening of the English poet's field of operations. Concrete or spatial poetry (both terms are used) is one of these extensions, and it's interesting that this at once links up with the spatializing tendencies already seen in the other arts. It's as if poets were suddenly becoming aware of a time-lag which has been withdrawing them farther and farther from the cultural experience of their fellow-artists.

Concrete poetry is an international movement. It began about ten years ago in Brazil and almost simultaneously in Switzerland. In Brazil it was connected with the work of three poets, the brothers Augusto and Haroldo de Campos and Décio Pignatari; in Switzerland with the German-Swiss poet Eugen Gomringer. There was from the beginning contact between these poets, and this personal contact has been a characteristic of the movement as it spread from country to country during the 1950s – mainly Germany, France, the Netherlands, Italy, Czechoslovakia, Japan, and (about 1962) Britain and the United States. The movement now has a large body of work in many languages, a fair amount of critical theory behind it, and a growth and development from the original ideas out into a variety of contiguous areas of experiment. To mention a few of these areas: there is phonetic or phonic poetry (sometimes called 'soundpoems'), especially in France in the work of Pierre Garnier and Henri Chopin but also in Austria (Ernst Jandl) and Britain (Bob Cobbing), where the spoken word and the human voice are used 'concretely' as a material and shaped either naturally or electronically into new patterns and sequences of sound rather as musical notes and natural sounds are reshaped in concrete music; then there's the fold-in and cut-up composition techniques of Brion Gysin and William Burroughs; there's computer poetry or the possibility of computer poetry; finally, and most recently, there's kinetic art, and the possibility of involving concrete poems in some situation or environment where physical movement is part of the aesthetic effect.

But to go back to the beginnings. What was concrete poetry trying to do? Let me quote from the Brazilian manifesto, the 'Pilot-Plan for Concrete Poetry' (*Noigandres*, no. 4, São Paulo, 1958):

> Assuming that the historical cycle of verse (as formal-rhythmical unit) is closed, concrete poetry begins by being aware of graphic space as structural agent . . . Hence the importance of the ideogram concept, either in its general sense of spatial or visual syntax, or in its specific sense (Fenollosa/Pound) of method of composition based on direct – analogical, not logical-discursive – juxtaposition of elements.

The main point is clear: the use of graphic space as itself an organizing agent (the meaningful use of space as well as letters) so that the poem becomes a kind of ideogram, a *sign*, a concrete quasi-three-dimensional sign, a sign that exists as far as it can in space. In other words, even if the poem is only lying on the printed page it should give you a consciousness of its spatial rather than its linear existence, so that you look at it as a whole, as a unit, rather than as something that has no meaning unless it is read consecutively from beginning to end; and ideally, of course, the concrete poem would escape from the page and become a sign in the world outside, perhaps engraved on glass, or cut in actual concrete either as a free-standing form or on the wall of a building, or (even better) if it becomes a neon sign in the darkness of a city at night, or is flashed for ten seconds on a television screen.

I think it's necessary here to notice the two polarities of concrete poetry. On the one hand, this central concept of the spatial involves a search for systems of arrangement of the elements of the poem (which may be words or morphemes or even letters or numerals or marks of punctuation or typographical devices), and this search leads concrete poetry in the direction of the objective, the scientific, and especially the mathematical – that's to say, you're often dealing with formulas of repetition or atomization of words, or permutations and combinations, or sets and series of progressive groupings, ungroupings and regroupings of words or parts of words. And this fits in with what the Brazilian group said in their manifesto, that they were 'against a poetry of expression' – the poet was not to be expressing his personality or his individual experience so much as to be doing something concretely with the medium of language. That is one direction, or one aspect of the movement. But on the other hand, many concrete poets have emphasized the *function* of what they are doing within society. Although the basis is not that of wanting to unite people in a warm emotional involvement, there's a widespread desire to get the poem out into society if this can be done.

Obviously this needn't be seen in political terms, even in a wide use of the word political, but the Brazilian poets were, inevitably, politically conscious, and produced concrete poems about Cuba, about governmental oppression, about segregation and so on. They quote approvingly Mayakovsky's statement that 'There is no revolutionary poetry without revolutionary form.' As an example of this sort of concrete poem, I'd like to quote one of my own which was written about Sharpeville. The words are built up on a grid of S and V, taken from the two parts of the name Sharpeville, and they're arranged on a pattern of alternating polysyllables and monosyllables meant to give a statement of dramatic opposition and menace:

starryveldt
  slave
southvenus
  serve
SHARPEVILLE
  shove
shriekvolley
  swerve
shootvillage
  save
spoorvengeance
  stave
spadevoice
  starve
strikevault
  strive
subvert
  starve
smashverwoerd
  strive

scattervoortrekker
  starve
spadevow
  strive
sunvast
  starve
survive
  strive
so: VAEVICTIS

Concrete poets, like other poets, are men who live at a certain time in a certain place and react to their environment. To some, a direct use of contemporary reference or 'committed' material would be anathema because it clashed with the formal aims of the movement; to others, form can itself be seen not as 'formalism' but as an act of comment or protest, even without the coarser help of direct referents. There is no agreement here, nor should we perhaps expect it. But the generally linking, paramount aim of extending the formal field of operations of poetry is clearly not incompatible with an extension of the social field of operations too. Indeed the relevance of such poetry to society was stressed by Eugen Gomringer in a manifesto of 1954 (quoted in *Image*, Cambridge, 1964):

> We ought perhaps to conclude that the language of today must have certain things in common with poetry, and that they should sustain each other both in form and substance. In the course of daily life this relationship often passes unnoticed. Headlines, slogans, groups of sounds and letters give rise to forms which could be models for a new poetry just waiting to be taken up for meaningful use. The aim of the new poetry is to give poetry an organic function in society again, and in doing so to restate the position of poet in society . . . So the new poem is simple and can be perceived visually as a whole as well as in its parts. It becomes an object to be both seen and used: an object containing thought but made concrete through play-activity, its concern is with brevity and conciseness.

A slightly different defence of concrete poetry, but still within the general concern to produce objects for human use, comes from the Scottish poet Ian Hamilton Finlay, who wrote in 1963 (letter to Pierre Garnier, quoted in *Image*, 1964):

> One does not want a *glittering* perfection which forgets that the world is, after all, also to be made by man into his *home*. I should say . . . that concrete by its very limitations offers a tangible image of goodness and sanity; it is very far from the now-fashionable poetry of anguish and self . . . If I was asked, 'Why do you write concrete poetry?' I could truthfully answer 'Because it is beautiful.'

This emphasis which Finlay has on beauty might suggest the strongly visual nature of much concrete poetry and also its closeness to art, to both painting and sculpture. Finlay is himself an artist and a toymaker. He takes great pains to have his poems printed exactly as he wants them, using different type-faces, coloured inks, special dimensions of page and so on. He has Standing Poems which stand on the table like a piece of sculpture. He has kinetic poems where the action of turning over the page is a little reminiscent of the gradual unrolling of a Chinese horizontal scroll painting. Some concrete poems by him and by other poets have analogies to certain kinds of semi-abstract painting, and the words, unconnected syntactically but of course interrelated spatially and by juxtaposition, may suggest the colours and forms and even the tone and atmosphere of a picture. For example, the French poet Pierre Garnier has a 'Calendar' of 12 concrete poems describing or suggesting the months of the year. Here is the first of these, the 'Janvier':

GLACE				CRI	
NEIGE		EPEE		CRI	
BLEUE		EPEE		CRI	
NOIRE		EPEE		CRI	
NOIRE		FUSIL		CRI	
CRI		SABRE		CRI	
LAIT		EPEE		CRI	ACIER
GLAIVE		EPEE		CRI	MIROIR
FEU		EPEE		CRI	SIFFLE
NOIR	NOIR	FUSIL	CAILLOUX	CRI	SIFFLE

BLANCHE	VASTE	MORT	CAILLOUX	CRI	CALME
RIGIDE	VENT	NOIRE	CAILLOUX	CRI	LAME
SEREINE	GRIS	BLEUE	NOIRDUR	CRI	FER
	ROUGE		BLANCDUR	CRI	DUR
	BLUES		CAILLOUX	CRI	ACIER
	GLACE		NEIGE	CRI	ATTENTE
	NUE		BLUES	CRI	ATTENTE
	NUDITE		BLEU	CRI	ATTENTE
	BLANCHE		NOIRE	CRI	
	NOIRE		VERTE	CRI	
	MOLLESSE		ROUGE	CRI	

Garnier has two things to say about this visual poetry in an essay he published in 1963 (*Les Lettres*, no. 30). First he calls it 'a poetry which is desensitized yet sensitizing'. That's to say, all the obvious appeals to sensuous reaction which might have been elaborated through devices of diction and rhythm can be done away with, so that you have nothing but a collocation of individual words unrelated by syntax, and yet you have rising up from this a tingling chilly evocation of landscape and mood. Garnier is fond of talking about the poem as a 'centre of energy', a thing which is itself calm and orderly but which by its construction, its articulation, is able to sensitize the mind of anyone who exposes himself to it. It's perhaps a little like the practice of acupuncture in Chinese medicine: a Chinese doctor will undertake to cure your sciatica or migraine by inserting a series of fine gold needles in carefully selected areas of your body – these needles are not connected to any electric or therapeutic apparatus, they cure you simpy by being the right kind of needle placed in exactly the right spot, or so the Chinese say. In the same way, visual poetry depends on an exact choice and placing of separate words which are not connected to sentences but which in spite of that carry a charge that you feel when you expose yourself to the grid of the whole poem. As Garnier says, 'What a difference there is between: "The tiger is coming to drink at the river bank" and the single name: "TIGER!" '

The second thing Garnier wrote in this essay was: 'Visual

poetry is a happy poetry.' This links up with Ian Hamilton Finlay's comment that 'concrete poetry by its very limitations offers a tangible image of goodness and sanity . . .'

These statements, although they don't apply to all concrete poetry, are an important pointer to where this poetry fits in. It is definitely post-existentialist, it's reacting against the world of Kafka and Eliot and Camus and Sartre. It's more likely to be interested in Yuri Gagarin than in Kafka. It looks forward with a certain confidence. It sees a probable coming together of art and science in ways that might benefit both. It takes *space* as a key-word, whether it's the uses now being made of space in poetry and art and music, or the actual exploration of space which sets Gagarin as the Adam of a new era, or the revolution in our perception which Marshall McLuhan describes in his books *The Gutenberg Galaxy* and *Understanding Media* – the movement away from the printed book, away from the linear, towards the more 'open', instantaneous, spatial experience which technology has presented us with in newspaper and radio, film, television, and advertising. In the symposium *Explorations in Communication* (1960) McLuhan talks about the new mediums which are usually referred to as mediums of communication, and says:

> All the new media, including the press, are art forms that have the power of imposing, like poetry, their own assumptions. The new media are not ways of relating us to the old 'real' world: they *are* the real world, and they reshape what remains of the old world at will.

This, I think, is relevant to concrete poetry. The concrete poem has grown up specifically in this changed world which McLuhan describes and has obvious points of contact with it. It is an art from which science and technology can never be very far away, even when its practitioners hold no brief for science. Without being 'cybernetic poetry', it is very much a poetry in a cybernetic age, and the objection commonly raised to it, that it is 'trivial' and mere 'play', doesn't understand that 'play' has a new meaning in such an age. And as an extension to this, one might consider another remark of McLuhan's in the same book. Speaking about Russian achievements in space technology, rocket engineering, and allied fields of activity not being matched by applications of technology to culture, as for instance in television, newspaper and magazine layout, advertising techniques, and industrial design, he says:

> The Russians are impotent to shape technological culture because of their inwardness and grimness. The future masters of technology will have to be lighthearted; the machine easily masters the grim.

At first sight a curious statement (which perhaps in any case one wouldn't care to bet on), this does fit into the context of the new mood I've tried to describe, the mood *against* grimness and inwardness and angst, and *for* what Garnier calls happiness, what Finlay calls beauty, what Gomringer calls play. These words, *happiness, beauty, play*, all seem slightly suspect today. We find ourselves asking doubtfully whether we ought to take 'seriously' an art form which has such a basis. But even these doubts might warn us that concrete poetry *is* on to something. Relatively easy points of entry into this poetry for sceptics could include Garnier's 'Calendar', where certain obviously evocative effects are produced as well as the non-evocative interest of surprising juxtapositions; or perhaps a beautiful piece of imitative form like Ian Hamilton Finlay's poem 'This is the little burn that plays its mouth-organ by the mill', where the thin winding course of the stream and the sound it makes over its pebbles are simultaneously suggested by a trail of Ms and Xs in different type-founts and colours of ink; or it might be an idea given brief compressed complex existence in concrete form, as in Dom Sylvester Houédard's 'Christmas Poem 1964' in which the two words *sol* and *thalamus* (standing for 'sun' and 'bride's room' in a religious context) are made to interpenetrate step by step in a movement from east to west.

I'd like to finish by quoting three concrete poems of different types which may help to define the areas of value which this kind of poetry is attempting to explore.

The first is a short untitled poem by Eugen Gomringer. This represents a 'pure' form of concrete, with emphasis on the separated individual word. It's a poem about qualities and relations, about what relations are possible and what relations are not, about what relations are natural and what relations exist only in art. It begins with the easy and familiar relationships and moves out perfectly calmly into the mind-teasing ones:

from deep
to deep
from near
to grey
from deep
to near
from near
to grey
from grey
to deep
from two
to four
from three
to one
from one
to four
from deep
to two
from four
to near
from grey
to one

The second poem is one of my own called 'Pomander'. The lines are arranged in the imitative form of a pomander. I take the idea of a pomander as a round object which in some way is opened up (either by having holes in it or by being actually openable) to release its fragrance – I had one in mind particularly which opened like the segments of a cut orange. I use this to bring out the theme of opening up the poem, opening it up spatially, and in a broader sense the theme of opening out life, life itself (or the round world) as a pomander, its secrets and treasures and rare things not to be hoarded but opened up and made available. To keep this wide range viable within a concrete form, the poem uses associative imagery within a deliberately narrowed range of sound-effects:

pomander
open pomander
open poem and her
open poem and him
o p e n poem and hymn
hymn and hymen leander
high man pen meander
o pen poem me and h e r
pen me poem me and him
om mane padme hum
pad me home panda hand
open up o holy panhandler
ample panda pen or bamboo pond
ponder a bonny poem pomander opener
open banned peon penman hum and banter
open hymn and pompom band and panda hamper
o i am a pen open man or happener
i am open manner happener
happy are we open
poem and a pom
poem and a panda
poem and aplomb

And the last poem is an untitled piece by the American poet Robert Lax. It conveys very well, I think, the consciousness of space which in so many senses pervades this poetry as it more and more pervades our lives:

the port
was longing

the port
was longing

not for
this ship

not for
that ship

not for
this ship

not for
that ship

the port
was longing

the port
was longing

not for
this sea

not for
that sea

not for
this sea

not for
that sea

the port
was longing

the port
was longing

not for
this &

not for
that

not for
this &

not for
that

the port
was longing

the port
was longing

not for
this &

not for
that

William Varley Art as art as Art etc.

Visit almost any art-school in the country at the present and chances are that you will still see paintings with titles such as 'Johnny et Sylvie sont mariés' or, 'The Noble Soul of Dionne Warwick', despite the fact that the high tide of Pop painting has now receded, and that most young painters are preoccupied with other, currently more 'valid', developments; Pop Art itself having been invalidated as soon as it became Art History.

Art-school work, of course, doesn't represent painting at the highest point of the aesthetic scale, which is just as well because in such work Pop tends to emerge in its most superficial form. This is 'digging the scene' art, implying the devotional, undiscriminating and addictive attitude to the mass-media of the typical teenager. In the words of Lawrence Alloway, 'The new pop art painters use the mass media in the way that teenagers do, to assert, by their choice of style and goods, their difference from their elders and others . . . Pop art in England has become a game for those who want to tell themselves that they "think young".'[1]

But the two titles of paintings which I've already quoted reveal just how far removed is the 'sophisticated' art-student from the typical teenager. His pop-cultural expertise is far greater, his attitude to the media non-devotional and discriminating; more importantly, what ultimately separates him from the typical teenager is his objective and analytical attitude to contemporary mythology. Only those who have this analytical attitude seem prepared to use the imagery of contemporary pop culture as the subject-matter of their painting. To those whose attitude to the media is genuinely devotional, contemporary myths, images and

[1] *The Listener* (17 Dec. 1962).

heroes are sacred and it would be a blasphemy to degrade them by the differing degrees of formal manipulation or distortion necessary in painting. (This is one reason why 'Fine Pop' will never be popular with the mass audience except at the level of decorative appeal – flags, targets etc.) So that the image of the student-painter as expert teenager often (but not always) disguises a more serious reality; behind the mod gear is the iconographer of cultural anthropology . . .

This iconography, it appears, is Pop Art: an Art about art; a Fine Art which relies for its visual content on the imagery of the urban, industrial, mass communication society. Within this simple general definition though, there are varying types of relationship with the mass-media; like teenagers, some artists have a bland or devotional attitude – one which can lead ultimately to a pictorial folklorism. Folk heroes and heroines, the popular and synthetic foods of the drugstore and supermarket, the gadgets and domestic trivia of the twentieth-century home are recorded for the curious of two hundred years hence. These images are created with various degrees of skill and imagination but the attitude which most of the artists claim to share, one of coolness and detachment, is, as I've already suggested, by no means common to them all.

Before examining these differences of attitude, though, one of the moral objections to Pop should be considered. One might say that in celebrating the imagery of mass culture Pop artists condone the exploitation of the popular audience, an audience whose aesthetic taste in many areas is so simple that it can be easily manipulated for commercial ends. After all, it's not in the interests of commercial providers of popular art to create unstable consumers; for reasons of industrial and commercial necessity the mass public's taste must be predictable. The art-product must sell as well tomorrow as it does today; standardization becomes the norm, and uncritical conformity on the part of the audience is its corollary.

One might oppose this argument by saying that, whatever its content, the picturesque, beautiful ugliness, squalor or violence,

Art has no duty to comment, socially or otherwise, *it need only exist.*

Again, the orthodox Pop apologist would deny the accusation of mass culture's exploitation of a defenceless audience. He would rather emphasize man's superb irrationality and concupiscence and point to their emergence in the tastes of the mass audience. The taste for pornography, personal power, gadgetry, horror fantasies, the lust for speed and flight and, above all, the emotionally loaded image are easily identifiable features of mass culture and so cannot be said to be imposed upon their audience. The taste for them is genuine because they embody timeless human drives, instincts, and obsessions – features of a mythology which has as fruitfully enriched the High Art of the past as the popular art of the present. The eroticism of the girlie mags finds its High Art equivalents (but qualitatively how much better!) in Titian, Greuze and Etty, while sadism can be found in Delacroix and Goya. One could multiply examples of such analogies. Nevertheless, one suspects the Pops of being condescending. Playing it cool, the privileged intellectual with his objectivity and his ability to analyse can make Art from the images, 'quaint', 'amusing' and 'crammed with associations', dear to the Admass.

On the other hand, it might be said that the vivid identification of the banal is the most moral of preoccupations, implying as it does an awareness of its antithesis, the distinctive and unique.

Not all Pop artists, though, are iconographers in the sense of using popular imagery as the expression of man's pagan myths and obsessions or of revealing the 'shared themes between advertisements and art, movies and sculpture, science fiction and constructivism';[1] in some cases, in the nostalgic art of the new folklorists – Peter Blake's for example – the celebration of the popular images of the present or near past suggests an indifference both to their iconographic significance and to their related social situation. I am not suggesting here that Blake is unaware of the significance that the images of his choice have for their first-hand audience; seen at their source, in fan magazines and elsewhere, his movie stars, pop-music idols and wrestlers have a 'religious'

[1] Ibid.

appeal and demand devotion, but it is questionable whether these images, processed through the medium of Blake's technique and sensibility quite achieve the mystic, totemic qualities one would suppose to be his aim or achieve anything more than a highly accomplished nostalgia.

The idea of a creative process which is near-industrial is integral to Pop Art and is frequently three-way. Imagery is produced by the sophisticated (the commercial world) for the unsophisticated (the consumers), it is then re-processed by other sophisticates (artists). Often the process is more direct – popular imagery is just as frequently produced by the simple for the simple and it is perhaps in this area that British Pop has mined the richest material. Graphic art such as that of the strip-cartoon with its cinematic composition – the narrative developed by rapid cuts from long-shot to close-up, high view-point to low, inserts, captions and daring changes of scale have obviously influenced the younger painters, although we are well aware of their other sources (cereal packets, plastic toys, pin-tables etc.).

But I emphasize this process because most of these artists are concerned above all with *images* rather than with tangible reality, images being a processed reality and more meaningful than reality itself. This, of course, parallels the situation in the advertising world and time and again one can witness this dialogue between image and reality in the visual punning of these painters. Some, however, provide more than this: their Art is about art, is about Art . . . At one and the same time they might ironically celebrate the compositional conventions of Renaissance painting, those of contemporary movies, as well as mischievously appropriate the painting 'mark' of another painter or school; or like Rauschenberg work in the 'gap' between art and life. By now, though, this discussion must appear so implicit that perhaps a brief historical recapitulation is necessary.

Lawrence Alloway has suggested that British Pop began in London in 1949 with Francis Bacon's pointed quotation from the 'The Battleship Potemkin' (the nurse from the Odessa Steps sequence), although it is now generally accepted that the Pop ideology was generated by the Independent Group at the I.C.A. in the early fifties, which included Alloway himself, Rayner Banham, the Smithsons, Richard Hamilton, John McHale, and Eduardo Paolozzi.

Alloway divides its development into three phases; the technological, the abstract and the figurative. Phase (1) he dates approximately from 1951 to 1958 and characterizes it by its acceptance of science and the city, and its appeal to common experience, illustrated in the seminal exhibitions of the period, 'Parallel of Life and Art', 'Man, Machine and Motion' and 'This is tomorrow'. It was to be art 'as discourse rather than soliloquy'. Typical of the art-work of this phase were Paolozzi's technological monsters, basically pop-allusive sculptures of the human image.

Phase (2) began in approximately 1957 and lasted until about 1961. Popular source material was retained but its use became even more oblique and allusive and the emphasis within source material itself shifted from twentieth century urban technology to the images of mid-century mass-leisure. The attempt was made to align Abstract and Pop painting and as a result paintings became larger in scale and more brilliant in colour.

Summarizing these two phases, Alloway concludes that the painters of phase (1) 'used, objectively, popular material that modified the image of man with which they were all concerned. But the artists of phase (2) . . . shifted the emphasis to the man-made environment. The basic assumption was that our idea of nature has changed because of the bombardment of our senses by the signs, colours, and lights of the mass media.' Abstract Pop, then, was to 'create an analogue of the man-made environment that we all participate in'.

Phase (3), from 1961 onwards, was marked by a return to figuration with imagery drawn from a broad range of popular sources and techniques and a developing interest in iconography. This phase saw the emergence of the young Royal College painters, Hockney, Boshier, Phillips and the American, R. B. Kitaj. Richard Hamilton, too, achieved increasing recognition at this time with work which was less extrovert than that of the younger artists although a good deal more cerebral and austere. This phase might be said to have lasted until about 1964: by that time the landscape had been changed and for some of these artists the need for development was marked by a move towards abstraction – in Boshier's case towards the perspectival and spatial illusionism of Richard Smith and in Hockney's by a tendency to visual parody and pastiche.

In America, Pop Painting was developed by individuals who, arriving at similar attitudes to Art, were nonetheless unaware of each other's existence and work. The eventual centralization of these artists in New York did not, however, produce a unified style; on the contrary, their approaches are still extremely diverse.

Among the most important influences on their work have been John Cage's 'Theory of Inclusion', Kaprow's 'Happenings', the Merce Cunningham Dance Theatre, the painting of De Kooning, Rauschenberg and Johns, and, it goes without saying, Dada and the Abstract Expressionist movement. In the case of some of these painters Abstract Expressionism was assimilated, in others, rejected.

De Kooning's work was of particular importance, not only because his painting style had particular significance for Rauschenberg and Johns, the true progenitors of American Pop (nor even because his 'Woman' paintings of the mid-fifties were sometimes titled 'Marilyn'), but because his 'environmental' painting embodies a total indifference to traditional canons of subject-matter. Here, each object lying about his studio would take its place in his painting, not by direct reference but by allusion, either of colour or form (each, moreover, had equal importance whether figure or scrap of wool). This, perhaps, is one of the origins of Rauschenberg's decisive step in creating 'combines' although his debt to Picasso, Schwitters and, indeed, the whole history of assemblage must be acknowledged.

The 'combine', literally a combination of painting and 'real' objects from the 'outside' world, was, as Alan Solomon has pointed out,[1] a way of calling into question 'our habit of dis-

[1] *Art International*, VIII 2 (March 1964).

sociating art from life'. Rauschenberg himself maintained that 'Painting relates to both art and life. Neither can be made. (I try to act in the gap between the two.)' The introduction of found objects into his art-works, therefore, was intended to destroy the division between 'the experience of reality and the detachment of art'.

The same concern with art, image and reality characterizes the work of Jasper Johns but, unlike Rauschenberg, he is much more concerned with ambiguities in the perception of image/object and reality. Like Richard Hamilton, the leading theorist of English Pop, he has a particular reverence for the achievements – practical and theoretical – of Marcel Duchamp. Critical observations concerning these two artists are, in fact, almost interchangeable: for example, Hamilton, discussing Duchamp points out that seeing is not believing . . .[1] 'Duchamp resists a static conception of reality by thinking of all forms, all existence as transitional. All his work is an undermining of belief in absolute values,' and here is Solomon discussing Johns, 'The most significant lesson from Johns was the realization that the avoidance of fixed, stated meanings for objects (which his attachment to the principle of ambiguity imposed) not only expanded the range of images suitable as subject matter, but it also permitted these objects to function in a variety of new ways, with limitless possibilities.' The images referred to are, of course, his 'commonplace' flags, targets, and maps which he began in the mid-fifties; and, Solomon continues, 'they came so close to reality, while retaining the free handling which Johns had kept from Abstract Expressionism, that we found our perception shifting constantly from the fact of the image to the fact of the painting and back again. The resulting ambiguity leaves us in an indeterminate state, confronted with an unanswerable question: Is it a flag, or is it a painting?' Johns himself, of course, would answer: both; the painting can be an object and an object a painting. His concern, like Duchamp's, with the 'apparition of an appearance' means that beneath *his* flag/painting there is a flag, 'everybody's' flag – the flag as object.

1 *Art International*, VII 10 (Jan. 1964).

In addition, his paintings and constructions are art historical in that assimilating an Abstract Expressionism freed from the limitations of the private gesture he can appropriate the 'marks' of a De Kooning, Tobey or Guston and emphasize that they, too, can be objects, just as much as can flags, numerals and targets.

Most of the notable American Pop artists are concerned with aesthetic notions deriving from Rauschenberg or Johns – above all in their preoccupation with the interrelationships of image (painted, constructed or 'processed'), and reality. Alan Solomon classifies them in two main groups: first, Lichtenstein, Warhol and Rosenquist, who translate found images from other graphic sources into Art; second, Dine, Oldenburg, Segal and Wesselman, who combine real objects with painted or modelled forms.

Of group (1) Lichtenstein, a former Abstract Expressionist, enlarges, refines and exaggerates the images in comic strip boxes. The formal control in this re-processing of a processed image is most apparent in works such as 'The Kiss' of 1962 and the 'Seascape with Clouds' of 1965. Motifs are obviously carefully chosen and their elements' realignment is often extremely subtle. The formal and mechanical conventions of the strips, the broad black area – defining lines and the Ben Day screen dots are part of the process, magical in itself, which also interests Warhol. In his case, the preoccupation with mechanically produced images is as much a concern with processes which enable art-works to come into existence magically and as far removed from his own conscious intervention as possible. His subject-matter (soup-can labels, flowers, newspaper photographs etc.) is subjected to various processes simply to increase its imageness; it might be enlarged, for example, or subjected to hallucinatory repetition. In his 'Black and White Disasters', for example, the 'terrible' image is eventually nullified by constant repetition. Warhol ultimately emphasizes the processed image for its coldness, mindlessness and lack of comment; Otto Hahn has pointed out that this is the true subject of his painting. My own feeling is that this is an illusion; as I said earlier, the obsessive identification of the vulgar, the banal and the blandly sinister – 'metaphysical disgust' – presupposes an awareness of alternatives. Warhol's art seems to consist of social catharsis; only by obsessively identifying all that is gently sinister in the contemporary scene can he appease society's viciousness, subterranean or otherwise. Perhaps it's more despairing even than that. Cool and detached he cries 'All is pretty'.[1] One feels that this must either be narcoticized optimism or the ultimate acceptance of 'I love Big Brother'.

Of group (2) George Segal reiterates Johns' questioning of the real and unreal. In the 'real' settings which he constructs, the table of a café or the forecourt of a garage for example, his petrified figures (plaster) are always more alive, more real than reality itself. The same confrontation of figure and setting appears in the work of Wesselman, which, though spatially less real and descriptive, was at one time highly reminiscent of Richard Hamilton's 'Just what is it that makes to-day's home so different, so appealing?' of 1956. But Wesselman's early works differ in their more direct references to High Art, through the inclusion of 'old-master' reproductions – vying with those of kitsch[2] – and the analogies between his somewhat erotic figures and those of Matisse; again, a still-life by Cézanne might unobtrusively play its part in the 'real' setting.

Similar confrontations of image, object and reality and the perceptual ambiguities thus generated occur in the objects of Dine and Oldenburg, especially in the latter's environments.

What, then, are the qualities which Pop, both English and American, has contributed to the continuing development of Art? First, the development of the Abstract Expressionist concern for the nature of the creative act. Second, further speculations about the identity and validity of the 'work of art' itself, which were first considered by Duchamp almost fifty years earlier. Lastly, the exploitation of a whole range of new subject-matter and a deliberately inconsistent language of colour and form. In England especially there has been a near miraculous visual

[1] Catalogue of Warhol Exhibition at Ileana Sonnabend Gallery, Paris, May 1965. Notes by Otto Hahn.

[2] Kitsch – the adulteration or dilution of serious art for popular consumption.

liberation from the khaki fog of Euston Road School painting on the one hand and routine abstraction on the other.

Nevertheless, certain reservations remain: one is the moral dilemma implicit in the work of these artists, pinpointed by Max Kozloff.[1] He emphasized that they were not 'quite as dedicated to pictorial self-sufficiency, to sheer energy of form and composition' as one might suppose but that 'on the contrary, they depend too much on the repulsiveness of their imagery, so that artists as naturally desirous of recognition as they are, "hard sell" the public by means only of hard-sell'.

Of the central idea of this art, 'Kitsch', as he defines it, he continues, 'Are we supposed to regard our popular signboard culture with greater fondness or insight now that we have Rosenquist? Or is he exhorting us to revile it, that is, to do what has come naturally to every sane and sensitive person in this country (America) for years. If the first, the intent is pathological, and if the second, dull . . . not only can't I get romantic about this, I see as little reason to find it appealing as I would an hour of rock and roll into which has been inserted a few notes of modern music.' The argument here is slightly over-pitched; as I've already suggested, the formal subtlety and fastidiousness of some of these artists is undeniable. However, my own final objection to this type of romanticization of popular culture is its aura of privilege and condescension. Say what you will, people (you know, 'lowly' folk – not those sophisticated 'trained eyes' in the galleries) are trapped, suppressed and at the same time dissatisfied by the palliative offerings of popular culture (hence the boredom within the 'affluent' society).

Of course, artists and intellectuals remote and socially isolated have had this privilege of creating works of art with other men's misery as their subject-matter for centuries, but for the first time they celebrate, by implication, their 'humbler fellows'' insufficiency and the forces which create it.

[1] 'Pop Culture, Metaphysical Disgust and the New Vulgarians', in *Art International*, VI 2 (March 1962).

Postscript. *Since Mr Varley's article was published early in 1966, he has modified or developed his attitude on three of the questions with which he dealt, and has provided the following additional statement:*

First: my assumption in the closing paragraph of the essay that 'people . . . are trapped, suppressed and at the same time dissatisfied by the palliative offerings of popular culture (hence the boredom within the "affluent" society).' One should in fairness admit that popular culture often does provide the 'mass' audience with genuine, substantial aesthetic experience and that equally potent factors of cultural suppression include brutalising conditions of work, poverty (wealth), a wrecked environment, etc.

Second: my emphasis of the Kozloff quotation tends to ignore art's status as a gratuitous act: one, moreover, which need not necessarily be didactic or edifying. I can best develop this by quoting Susan Sontag who points out that 'The Matthew Arnold notion of culture defines art as the criticism of life – this being understood as the propounding of moral, social and political ideas. The new sensibility understands art as the *extension of life* – this being understood as the representation of (new) modes of vivacity. There is no necessary denial of the role of moral evaluation here. Only the scale has changed; it has become less gross, and what it sacrifices in discursive explicitness it gains in accuracy and subliminal power.'

This applies to the Pop artists' attitude to popular culture. As Miss Sontag says, 'there is plenty of stupid popular music, as well as inferior and pretentious avant-garde paintings, films and music'. It applies more forcibly to their work, however, which might, in her phrase, be said to be 'infra-didactic'. The usual discussion of Pop Art emphasises that 'content' is transcended; the artists are said to suspend cultural and moral judgement of their source material and concentrate solely upon the creation of imagery which moves us through its formal qualities. This is obviously true to a large extent (Lichtenstein, for example, owes as much to Matisse as to comic-strip graphic schemata). One accepts the synthetic nature of the art-work, but to develop the

Lichtenstein analogy: while the painting is on canvas and a hundred times larger than the original comic-strip box and is a formally resolved modification of the original, it still represents (though that's an inadequate word), say, an air-fight. One responds therefore not only to the formal interaction created by the artist but also to the emotional triggering of the image and to the *frisson* caused by our knowledge of its original context. As Lawrence Gowing wrote in the Gulbenkian exhibition catalogue: 'Lichtenstein is portraying, as if in a moment of insight, something unhinged, unfeeling and automatic in the graphic imagery of the strip, and so in the imagery and the sexual connotation of the whole image-ridden environment.' Gowing preceded these remarks by saying that 'The real content of painting is not just the visible motif, the view the easel points at; it is the whole situation in which art finds itself, the life which envelops it as the forest enveloped Altdorfer, and (which) is likely today to seem as menacing.'

What I'm emphasizing is that in addition to the Pop artist's preoccupation with formal problems, he is not mindlessly detached from his social situation and that his 'vivid identification of the banal is the most moral of preoccupations'.

Third: De Kooning's influence is overemphasised in the essay. He was indeed a friendly rival of the New York painters, but in Rauschenberg's case Duchamp's influence was probably more significant. In the mid-fifties Rauschenberg lived with Johns (a close friend of Duchamp) in New York, and while for Johns the Duchamp influence was that of a relativistic attitude, for Rauschenberg the introduction into his work of common objects (thus producing 'combines') clearly relates to Duchamp's nomination of 'ready-mades'.

Elenore Lester **Happenings and Happiness**

Cheetah. Trips Festival. The World. Plastic Inevitables. Strange names for places young people go to for fun and dancing. What do they mean? Perhaps only the initiate, those born into what Marshall McLuhan has christened 'the electronic age', can get the full message. But even squares over 30 can catch some of the suggestions in the names of the new 'mixed media' discothèques – the reference to the reputed mystic psychic journey induced by LSD in *Trips*, the reference to the mysteries of the elemental or the primitive in Cheetah. *The World*? This is evidently an expansive scene of action – yet a private place since it exists within the large, general lower-case world open to everyone, even non teen-agers. *Plastic Inevitables* (Andy Warhol's touring group, sometimes referred to as the *Velvet Underground Erupting or Exploding Plastic Inevitables*) – Can this be a sinisterly attractive glistening vinyl hallucination induced by technological hysteria? As the silvery plastics inevitably pop, the initiates watch, paralyzed, transfixed, in wonder.

Strange names – names that suggest mysticism, hallucination, cultist waves-of-the-future, all mysteriously shimmering in the neon glare of faddist commercialism. There's a whole new vocabulary to describe what's happening, Baby, where the action is. It's in a 'switched on' 'environment' where Marshall (the-medium-is-the-message) McLuhan, Dr Timothy (LSD) Leary, Andy (Pop art and underground movies) Warhol, Murray the (teen-age idol) K, and the fashion business all come together. No, Baby, taking LSD isn't part of the scene. The idea is to create a fun reflection of the hallucinatory effects of the drug by 'turning on' a 'blow-your-mind' barrage of strobe lights, films and unbelievably amplified sound. The initiates participate in this 'happening' by doing free style orgiastic dancing in futuristic carnival get-ups.

The vocabulary, like the scene itself, represents the end of distinctions once important to the over-30 Old Guard. Classifications like highbrow, middlebrow and lowbrow, and the difference between High Art and Popular Culture dissolve right into the mixed media of the new discothèques. Show biz entrepreneurs snatch lingo and ideas from the academic Mr McLuhan and avant-garde artists create as happily for the teenage market as do any of the fashion designers. The young people, from early teens to late 20s, joyfully embrace what is being sold to them as the dark, faintly sinister glamor of the esoteric. The result is a scene that looks very much like an op art Dante's Inferno, with 'switched on' devils in black-and-white-striped vinyl union suits wearily pricking, with TV antennae, a population explosion of gyrating, taunting, giggling girls and boys in peep-hole nude outfits.

And everyone wants to get in on the act – especially those over 30 (they, who have been dubbed as untrustworthy by the Berkeley leftists; they, who have learned from Mr McLuhan that they are anachronisms out of the mechanical age – the age of getting the message from print instead of TV). Hungrily, jealously these Untrustworthies, these Linear Conceptualizers (they get that way from reading) gaze from the affluent green pastures of their suburbs into this new multi-colored nether world. Changing from their customary business suits and cocktail dresses into inauthentically 'kooky' go-to-hell outfits, they arrive in droves at the door of Cheetah, 53rd St and Broadway, the likeliest landing spot for Mr and Mrs Square from Mechanical-age-ville.

Mr and Mrs S keep their cool as they glance at the gentlemen, decked out as hangmen in an absurdist play in black suits and black turtleneck pullovers, who stand around the ticket booth. They know a bouncer when they see one. (Ironically, the gentlemen's main function is to turn away those who can't prove they are 18.) But Mr and Mrs S go into a state of culture shock when they spot the sign, 'No Liquor Served'. They beg for a denial from one of the Absurdist hangmen. No, it's not a put-on. It's a fact – soda pop and hot dogs for the 'turned on' generation. This sends many couples straight back to Mechanical-age-ville.

But the hardier souls pass into the fake fur lobby and run into, of all things, a boutique! They peer curiously at the girls and boys (over 18, of course) busily trying on funny vinyl hats and big leather belts and going behind silver curtains hung from silver chains to sample complete outfits, managing to frug buoyantly to the rock'n'roll music as they change clothes, laughing as they exchange shirts, ties, belts, suspenders and even pants with another. Yes, some of them do buy complete new outfits on the spot.

Leaving this curious limbo, Mr and Mrs S move toward the fiery gates themselves and are greeted by head-busting sound, increased in impact by the brightening, dimming, flashing, wavering play of colored lights. The lights are keyed to the sound. Sharp notes get yellow flashes, more subdued tones get violet. On stage, before a huge mirror-like screen reflecting the lights is one of the three long-haired rock combos that alternate during the night (there are *no* silent intervals). The typical rock 'singer', writhing in a standard fit, mike in hands, howls. The words are indistinguishable, but out of an evening of listening it is possible for Mr and Mrs S to grasp, gasping, one memorable phrase: 'Do it again, Baby!'

On the floor (designed to hold 2000) the palpitating yellow, orange, red, blue, green and violet lights catch the whiplash of long, free hair, the frenzied angles of elbow and kneecap, the agonized thrust of arms and hands, the uninhibited gyration of rump and belly. The frenzy is considerably increased at the World in Roosevelt, Long Island, at Trips Festival on St Mark's Pl. in the East Village, and at the Plastic Inevitables by the movies and color slides flashed on all walls, and by a white screen, lit by strobe light reflecting the black shadows of the dancers. The dances, of course, are derivations of Watussi and frug. The latest thing is just 'to do whatever you want'. Many dancers stand in place, gently shuffling and gyrating while their partners flip off into wild acrobatics. Partners simply dump one another if the spirit moves and take adventurous solos around the dance floor. It is acceptable to get up and dance by oneself. And exhibitionism on scattered dancing platforms is encouraged.

And the clothes! Sock-in-the-eye colors in bold, jagged patterns that run amok when the lights hit them are favorites (they call them psychedelic prints). So are dizzying black and white stripes and polka dots and dazzling gold, silver and mirror-like plastics. The girls wear tight, tight bell-bottom pants, thigh-high skirts, tinsel-threaded white stockings, little girl pumps or short boots, very long or very short hair. They reveal their belly buttons in hip-hugging pants, their entire anatomies in nude-look dresses and random special parts in cut-out dresses. They also like a beruffled, mock-demure little girl look and a dandyish lesbian look.

The boys wear tight, tight pants, loose colorful flowered shirts, open at the throat, flowered ties and many have Beatle haircuts. They, too, like the dandyish lesbian look. Plastics and leathers are worn by both boys and girls. So are funny accessories – caps, flowered or sequined suspenders, huge-buckled belts and far out buttons (Psychedelicize the Suburbs, Anarchists Unite).

The Untrustworthies, the Linear Conceptualizers are quickly exhausted. What is it all about? 'It's fun,' says a young girl tossing a golden shower of hair from her face and turning her Mona Lisa smile toward the mesmerizing images on the wall. Her escort, wearing a black-and-white polka dot, flowing-sleeved blouse, shrugs – a shrug for the up-tight probing of Untrustworthies.

Rocketed back into our place in the mechanical age, we continue to look for cause and effect, to think in the patterns of our time, the patterns Mr McLuhan tells us were set with the invention of movable type. But what is it like to be of *them*, to have been saturated in electronic media since birth? What do they think, what do they see when they look at all those different images on various walls – a young man in boots doing a whip dance (at the Plastic Inevitables show), details from Bosch paintings (at the World), an apparent badly focused orgy at Trips? They don't seem to be thinking anything in particular. They just dance and seem to love it. We ask more questions.

'You don't watch it. You exist in it,' tartly states Gerd Stern, a poet member of USCO (Us Company), a group of artists and film-makers with whom Mr McLuhan worked at one time, and who created a special show for the World. 'It's an environment,' patiently explains Jackie Cassen, who created the slide patterns projected at Trips. 'It gives people a chance to create part of the environment with their shadows on the screen.'

And Jonas Mekas, guru of the Underground movies, says (in the *Village Voice*), speaking of the Plastic Inevitables: 'It is the last stand of the Ego before it either breaks down or goes to the other side.' And at Cheetah, Mr Mekas experiences the feeling 'of being OUT . . . in those regions where both the mystic pre-occupations and the ego are abandoned, where you disappear and become a zero'.

A strange vocabulary and strange speculations about young people having fun on a dance floor. But new words, new speculations are needed. Old words fizzle and die under the barrage – words like, it's all simply show biz, an entertainment fad, puffed up by the fashion industry and further inflated by hungry journalists. Of course. But what makes a fad? Unless what is being sold connects decisively with the inner yearning of the potential buyer, it passes unnoticed. In the market place of the soul nobody gets fooled. We buy what we crave.

But what exactly is being bought and sold on that dance floor? An entrance ticket to the future, to the age that Mr McLuhan predicts will be an age of tribalism, rather than individualism? Perhaps. Certainly, some loss of personal identity is inevitable under the mammoth bombardment of sensory stimuli. And the break-down of identity is carried a step further by the wearing of masquerade-like clothing.

How square that sounds! How linear conceptualizing can you get? Let's take notes from direct stimuli. Here, on a dance floor that looks like an orgy in hell and on which the visual and auditory senses are given a violent workout, something is missing. The sense of touch. Nobody is snuggling cheek-to-cheek, pelvis-to-pelvis, thigh-to-thigh as they did in the old days. Only at Cheetah did couples dance in one another's arms as they did back in the mechanical age – and then it was done for a few moments as a kind of joke. Suddenly the musical rhythm changed, a curtain was drawn over the metallic screen and lights played over the curtain in heavy, smoky spirals. The couples came together and danced to 'shmaltzy' music briefly, and then flew apart at the parting of the curtain and abrupt change of rhythm and lights. It was a parody of romantic dancing. They were making fun of *us*, Tristan and Isolde, the love myth of *our* world.

So this is what they are up to! They have converted our old mating ground into a playground for some sort of mass psychic hokus pokus. Where dancing once socialized sexual contact, gave it a civilized veneer, made it seem easy to use and master, the new dancing masks the absence of physical contact behind aggressively, brutally sexual dance gestures. Where once music, atmosphere and liquor played a part in dissolving barriers, permitting each couple to connect through talk and touch, the new music, the new setting inevitably sets up barriers between couples (they can have neither eyes nor ears for one another because the audio-visual barrage completely consumes those organs). Where once the background was discreetly designed to shut out the multitude and make each couple an isolated unit, the new background destroys the twosome and makes the individual a fragment of the crowd. Where once clothes reinforced traditional sexual roles – the woman soft and accessible in silks, playing the temptress in perfume and jewelry, the men wearing modern man's battle uniform, the straight-laced business suit – the new clothes are designed to confuse and mask traditional sex roles.

Does it mean they are copping out of meeting and mating –

these sexually-knowing young people, these clever little op art monsters spawned by the electronic age? To a certain extent, perhaps – and only for a while. The signs indicate they eventually manage to make it, in their own way. But today sex can't compete with the glamor of technological and psychic experimentation, with the exhilarating experience of being alone in a seething multitude, a unit, like all other units, tuned in to a gigantic switchboard.

Electronics have finally shattered the myth of Tristan and Isolde. The new Liebestod is a rock-shriek, with Wagner's music-drama, Total Theater concept translated, ironically, into terms of a Niagara of pulsating strobe lights, films and sound.

Over-30s, trembling under the strobes, see Armageddon. Wrong as usual. The little *fleurs du mal* are frugging in nothing more *mal* than the old American pay dirt. They are really engaged in the sensible activity of preparing for their role as consumers in the next technological stage. Their science-fiction homes will have TV screen walls, and dimmers will play complex lighting patterns over the entire scene, while sound will flood from ceiling, floors and walls. No silence, no stillness, no loneliness, no fear for the electronic age family – only a blissful hook-up to all other creatures on the globe and in outer space. One world, endlessly rocking and rolling in the universal electronic cradle.

Contributors

BERNARD BERGONZI is senior lecturer in English at the University of Warwick, and author of *The Early H. G. Wells* (1961) and *Heroes' Twilight* (1965)

LESLIE A. FIEDLER is Professor of English at the State University of New York at Buffalo. He has written *Love and Death in the American Novel* (1960), *Waiting for the End* (1964), and many other works of criticism and fiction

E. H. GOMBRICH is Director of the Warburg Institute and Professor of the History of the Classical Tradition in the University of London. His works include *Art and Illusion* (1960), *Reflections on a Hobby Horse* (1963) and *Norm and Form* (1966)

MARTIN GREEN is a lecturer in English at the University of Birmingham. His writings include *Reappraisals* (1963) and *Yeats's Blessings on von Hügel* (1967)

IHAB HASSAN is Director of the College of Letters at Wesleyan University, Connecticut, and author of *Radical Innocence* (1961) and *The Literature of Silence* (1967)

FRANK KERMODE is Lord Northcliffe Professor of English Literature in the University of London. Among his books are *Romantic Image* (1957) and *The Sense of an Ending* (1967)

RICHARD KOSTELANETZ is a free-lance writer living in New York. He has edited *On Contemporary Literature* (1964) and *The New American Arts* (1965) and written *The Theatre of Mixed Means* (1967)

ELENORE LESTER is a free-lance critic who has written on the theatre for the *Village Voice* and the *New York Times*

DAVID LODGE is a lecturer in English at the University of Birmingham, and author of *Language of Fiction* (1966) and several novels

MARSHALL McLUHAN is Albert Schweitzer Professor at Fordham University, New York. His books include *The Mechanical Bride* (1951), *The Gutenberg Galaxy* (1962) and *Understanding Media* (1964)

LEONARD B. MEYER is Chairman of the Department of Music at the University of Chicago. He has published *Emotion and Meaning in Music* (1956) and *Music, The Arts, and Ideas* (1967)

EDWIN MORGAN is senior lecturer in English at the University of Glasgow. He is the author of *The Cape of Good Hope* (1955) and translations from *Beowulf* and Montale

MORSE PECKHAM is Professor of English at the University of Pennsylvania, and author of *Beyond the Tragic Vision* (1962) and *Man's Rage for Chaos* (1965)

JOHN SIMON is a regular contributor to a number of New York journals, and has published *Acid Test* (1963) and *Private Screenings* (1967)

WILLIAM VARLEY is a lecturer in the Department of Fine Art at the University of Newcastle

Index

Adams, Henry, 198
Aeschylus, 64
Albee, Edward, 38–9, 40, 72
Allen, Donald M., 194 n.
Alloway, Lawrence, 226, 229, 230
Alpert, Richard, 43, 96
Amaya, Mario, 196 n.
Animals, The, 190
Antoninus, Brother, 38
Apollinaire, Guillaume, 68, 76, 98
Aquinas, 28
Arden, John, 159
Arendt, Hannah, 189 n.
Ariès, Philippe, 144
Aristophanes, 112
Aristotle, 28
Arnold, Matthew, 175, 176, 236
Artaud, Antoine, 70, 103, 176, 183
Ashton, Dorée, 58
Auden, W. H., 70, 76

Babbitt, Milton, 48
Bach, J. S., 48, 49, 112, 116
Baldwin, James, 40, 95
Banham, Rayner, 230
Barth, John, 26, 179 n.
Barthes, Roland, 103
Bartók, Béla, 49–50, 51, 146
Baudelaire, Charles, 69, 71, 126
Beardsley, Aubrey, 66, 67
Beardsley, Monroe, 84
Beckett, Samuel, 51, 55, 62, 70, 77 n., 83, 86, 94–106, 108, 164, 167
Beerbohm, Max, 66, 67
Beethoven, 52, 64
Bellow, Saul, 36, 39, 44
Bergson, Henri, 69, 112
Berio, Luciano, 48
Berryman, John, 44
Blake, Peter, 228–9
Blake, William, 68, 172, 179
Blanc, Charles, 111
Blanche, Jacques-Émile, 187
Blanchot, Maurice, 100, 103
Bloch-Michel, Jean, 61
Boehme, Jakob, 151
Bono, Sonny, 191
Boorstin, Daniel J., 191–2
Bosch, Hieronymus, 183, 242
Boshier, Derek, 230, 231
Boulez, Pierre, 48
Brecht, Bert, 159, 167
Brophy, Brigid, 152
Brown, Norman O., 11, 18, 20, 26, 38, 96, 108, 139–42, 144, 150–7, 171–3, 174, 176, 177, 178, 179
Buber, Martin, 197
Burgess, Anthony, 26
Burroughs, William, 11, 14, 20–1, 26, 37, 39, 40, 43, 45, 70, 82, 86, 90, 94, 95, 98, 102, 104, 107–8, 200–12, 214
Bussotti, Sylvano, 47
Butor, Michel, 70, 100

Cage, John, 11, 14, 46–7, 51, 52, 54,

55, 58, 60, 64, 79, 82–4, 85–6, 101, 110, 113, 114, 144, 197, 208, 231
Campos, Augusto di, 214
Campos, Haroldo di, 214
Camus, Albert, 94, 97, 108, 220
Capek, Milic, 130
Capote, Truman, 99
Carlyle, Thomas, 165, 166
Carr, E. H., 159
Carroll, Lewis, 130
Carson, Johnny, 138
Cassen, Jackie, 242
Cézanne, Paul, 187, 234
Chopin, Henri, 214
Cicero, 72
Clarke, Arthur C., 27
Claudel, Paul, 69
Cobbing, Bob, 214
Cocteau, Jean, 109
Coleridge, S. T., 166
Conder, Charles, 67
Connolly, Cyril, 68–71, 74, 88–9
Conrad, Joseph, 203
Coomaraswamy, Ananda, 83
Cooper, Fenimore, 180
Corso, Gregory, 31–2, 39
Crackanthorpe, Hubert, 66
Creely, Robert, 33, 189, 193
Cronin, Anthony, 76 n.
Cunningham, Merce, 231

Dante, 24, 153, 239
Danto, Arthur, 80–1, 88
Darwin, Charles, 68
David, 50
Davie, Donald, 186 n.
Debussy, Claude, 52, 69
Dechert, Charles R., 139
Defoe, Daniel, 126
Delacroix, Eugène, 50, 228
De Quincey, Thomas, 203
Descartes, René, 172
Diaghilev, Serge, 109
Dickens, Charles, 167–8
Dine, Jim, 233, 234
Dostoevsky, Feodor, 164
Drucker, Peter, 122
Duchamp, Marcel, 77–8, 79, 82, 84, 86, 232, 234, 237
Duncan, Robert, 153
Durrell, Lawrence, 94, 107
Dylan, Bob, 189, 191

Eagleton, Terence, 166, 167–9, 172
Easterbrook, W. T., 126
Ehrenzweig, Anton, 112
Eliot, George, 167–8
Eliot, T. S., 69, 70, 71, 72, 75, 77, 78, 92, 104, 126, 143, 167, 186, 197, 207, 208, 211, 220
Ellmann, Richard, 68, 72
Ellul, Jacques, 132
Emerson, Ralph Waldo, 180, 182
Engels, Friedrich, 161
Etty, William, 228

Faulkner, William, 139, 180
Feldman, Morton, 47
Feuer, Lewis, 31
Fiedelson, Charles, 68, 72
Fiedler, Leslie A., 11, 12, 13, 16, 21, 89–91, 96, 104
Fielding, Henry, 24
Finlay, Ian Hamilton, 218, 220, 221
Fischer, Ernst, 178
Flaubert, Gustave, 24, 67, 69, 163, 211
Forster, E. M., 70
Franklin, Benjamin, 30
Freud, S., 20, 28, 32, 37, 69, 73, 90, 140, 151, 160, 170, 171–4, 176, 179
Friedenberg, Edgar Z., 139
Frye, Northrop, 178–9
Fuller, Buckminster, 26, 139

Gard, Roger Martin du, 164
Garis, Robert, 179, 182 n.

Garnier, Pierre, 214, 218–20, 221
Gaudier-Brzeska, Henri, 72
Genet, Jean, 40, 164–6, 176
Gershwin, George, 191
Gide, André, 70
Ginsberg, Allen, 28, 37, 39, 40, 42, 72, 96, 101
Goethe, 74, 112
Gold, Herbert, 203
Golding, William, 26, 168
Goldwater, Robert, 61
Gombrich, E. H., 15, 119–21
Gomringer, Eugen, 214, 217, 222
Goodman, Paul, 139
Gould, Glen, 126, 128
Gowing, Lawrence, 237
Goya, 228
Gradenwitz, Peter, 47
Green, Martin, 20
Greuze, Jean-Baptiste, 228
Gross, John, 169
Gustan, Philip, 58, 233

Hahn, Otto, 233
Hall, Edward T., 122
Hamilton, Richard, 230, 232, 234
Hassan, Ihab, 11, 12
Hatch, Robert, 62
Haussmann, Raoul, 77
Havelock, Eric, 129
Hawthorne, Nathaniel, 180, 182
Haydn, Franz Joseph, 49–50, 51
Healey, John, 213
Hegel, G. W. F., 117, 161, 163, 174, 178
Heidegger, Martin, 99, 100
Heisenber, Werner, 57–8, 68
Heller, Erich, 100
Hemingway, Ernest, 33, 36
Hockney, David, 230, 231
Hoffman, Frederick, 94
Hoffnung, Gerard, 79
Hoggart, Richard, 21 n.
Hopkins, G. M., 126, 153
Houédard, Sylvester, 221
Hulme, T. E., 71
Hume, David, 57
Husserl, E., 99
Huxley, Aldous, 26
Huysmans, J.-K., 69, 70
Hyman, Stanley Edgar, 32

Ibsen, Henrik, 167
Innis, Harold A., 148
Ionesco, Eugène, 70, 167

Jagger, Mick, 191
James, Henry, 66, 69, 180
James, Ingli, 188 n.
Jandl, Ernst, 214
Jarrell, Randall, 29
Jarry, Alfred, 69
Jaspers, Karl, 68
Johns, Jasper, 81, 231, 232, 233, 234, 237
Johnson, B. S., 198–9
Jones, Paul, 191
Joyce, James, 64, 69, 75, 103, 104, 126, 135, 139, 143–4, 145, 152, 164, 186, 200, 202, 207, 208, 209, 211, 212

K, Murray the, 238
Kafka, Franz, 75, 100, 164, 183, 220
Kahn, Herman, 139–40
Kandinsky, 111, 119
Kant, Immanuel, 57, 68, 74
Kaprow, Alan, 61, 231
Keats, John, 81, 186
Kenner, Hugh, 97–8
Kermode, Frank, 11, 12, 13, 21, 105 n., 169, 185, 190, 196, 197, 198, 208, 210
Kern, Jerome, 191
Kerouac, Jack, 28, 30, 101, 154, 201, 203
Kesey, Ken, 44, 91
King, Martin Luther, 30

Kinsey, Alfred, 141
Kitaj, R. B., 230
Klages, Ludwig, 112
Klein, Melanie, 156
Klein, Yves, 90
Kooning, William De, 90, 231, 233, 237
Kostelanetz, Richard, 16, 18
Kott, Jan, 86
Kozloff, Max, 235, 236
Krieger, Murray, 178

Laing, R. D., 21, 44 n., 160
Lane, John, 66
Larner, Jeremy, 29, 31
Lawrence, D. H., 37, 69, 93, 95–6, 104, 161, 164, 165, 167, 176
Lax, Robert, 223
Leary, Timothy, 43, 96, 150, 238
Leavis, F. R., 159, 161, 166, 176, 177, 179, 181, 183
Lebel, Jean-Jacques, 14 n.
Lenin, V. I., 161
Lessing, Doris, 159, 199
Lester, Elenore, 17, 19, 21
Lewis, C. S., 186, 192–3
Lewis, Wyndham, 70, 78, 186, 188–9
Lichtenstein, Roy, 233, 236–7
Lipton, Lawrence, 156
Locke, John, 167, 168
Lodge, David, 11, 20, 22, 198–9
Lowell, Robert, 44
Lukacs, Georg, 161, 163, 164, 168

McCarthy, Mary, 29, 195, 200–1, 202
McClure, Michael, 31–2, 43
McHale, John, 230
MacLow, 51
McLuhan, Marshall, 11, 15, 16–19, 20, 26, 44, 74, 134–49, 150, 151, 154, 156, 175–7, 178, 179, 185–6, 188, 192, 193, 195, 220, 221, 238, 239, 241, 242

Mailer, Norman, 20, 31, 38, 44, 96, 98, 100, 171, 175–6, 177, 180–1, 201
Malevich, 111
Mallarmé, Stephane, 69, 75, 103, 106
Malraux, André, 70, 110, 128
Mann, Thomas, 100
Mannheim, Karl, 134, 138
Marcel, Gabriel, 197
Marcuse, Herbert, 139, 160, 171, 173–5
Margenau, Henry, 57
Marx, Karl, 13, 20, 22, 28, 32, 34, 39, 86, 103, 159–64, 166–8, 171, 173, 174, 176, 177, 178
Marx Brothers, 147
Mathieu, Georges, 46, 51, 60, 65, 101
Matisse, Henri, 234, 236
Matthews, Harry, 26, 37
Mauriac, Claude, 103
Mayakovsky, Vladimir, 216
Mead, Margaret, 135
Mekas, Jonas, 242
Melly, George, 189
Melville, Herman, 180, 182
Meredith, George, 66, 72, 73
Meyer, Leonard B., 12, 13
Michelangelo, 64
Miller, Arthur, 167
Miller, Henry, 94–8, 101, 103–6, 108
Milton, John, 24
Monteverdi, 64
Moreau, Gustave, 67
Morgan, Edwin, 21, 72
Morris, William, 166
Morrissett, Bruce, 53, 55
Mozart, Wolfgang Amadeus, 114, 116
Murdoch, Iris, 87
Musil, Robert, 75
Mussolini, Benito, 111

Neumann, Johann von, 102
Nietzsche, Friedrich, 68, 108, 152, 160

O'Brien, Conor Cruise, 68

Oldenburg, Claes, 86, 233, 234
Olson, Charles, 153, 194–5
O'Neill, Eugene, 167
Ong, Walter J., 185–6, 187–8, 191, 192, 197–8, 199
Orff, Carl, 146
Orwell, George, 26, 168
Ossario, Alfonso, 62

Paar, Jack, 138
Paolozzi, Eduardo, 230
Parkinson, C. N., 138
Pasternak, Boris, 167
Pater, Walter, 68
Pavese, Cesare, 176
Peckham, Morse, 14–15, 79, 81, 82, 109–18, 121
Phidias, 64
Phillips, Peter, 230
Picasso, 50, 64, 135, 187, 195, 231
Pignatari, Décio, 214
Pinter, Harold, 70, 167
Plato, 129, 172
Podhoretz, Norman, 59
Poe, E. A., 25, 126
Poirier, Richard, 179–80, 182 n.
Pollock, Jackson, 46, 61, 62, 97
Pope, Alexander, 82
Popper, Karl, 117
Porter, Cole, 189, 191
Pound, Ezra, 69, 70, 71, 78, 104, 145, 186, 215
Pronko, Leonard, 106
Proust, Marcel, 69, 75, 77 n., 104
Puvis de Chavannes, 67

Rabelais, François, 30
Rahv, Philip, 32
Raphael, 50
Rauschenburg, Robert, 14, 21 n., 55, 56, 78, 79, 80, 90, 98, 197, 213, 229, 231, 232, 233, 237
Reich, Wilhelm, 26, 37–8, 96, 141
Resnais, Alain, 138
Richardson, Samuel, 24
Ricks, Christopher, 169
Rieff, Philip, 171, 175–7, 182
Righteous Brothers, 191
Rilke, R. M., 71, 178
Rimbaud, Arthur, 103, 105, 106, 126, 183
Robbe-Grillet, Alain, 51, 55, 58, 61, 64, 70, 76 n., 77, 87 n., 99, 100
Robinson, Heath, 79
Rochberg, George, 49, 56 n.
Roethke, Theodore, 44
Rosenberg, Harold, 76, 77, 86, 87, 89, 100, 195
Rosenquist, James, 233, 235
Rossini, 83
Rothko, Mark, 51, 53–4, 61
Rousseau, Jean-Jacques, 54, 103
Ruskin, John, 167, 176
Russell, Bertrand, 69, 133

Sade, Marquis de, 98
Salinger, J. D., 29, 30, 38, 39, 101
Saporta, Marc, 102
Sarraute, Nathalie, 59, 100, 103
Sartre, Jean-Paul, 59, 97, 99, 103, 153, 161, 163, 164–5, 170, 172, 220
Satie, Erik, 80, 101
Saunders, Ed, 32
Schiller, 173
Schoenberg, Arnold, 146
Schubert, 114
Schwitters, Kurt, 80, 98, 231
Scott, Sir Walter, 24
Segal, George, 233, 234
Selz, Peter, 83–4
Seurat, 111
Sewell, Elizabeth, 106
Shakespeare, 64, 168–9
Simon, John, 18, 22
Sitwell, Edith, 70
Skorna, Harry J., 147

Smith, Richard, 231
Smithson, Alison and Peter, 230
Smollett, Tobias, 24
Socrates, 32, 90
Solomon, Alan, 231–2
Sontag, Susan, 14, 15, 20, 152, 156, 171, 175, 176, 177, 178, 183, 236
Spengler, Otto, 116
Stalin, Josef, 161
Stearn, G. E., 17 n.
Steefel, Lawrence D., 78
Stein, Gertrude, 69
Steiner, George, 98, 167
Sterne, Laurence, 24
Stevens, Wallace, 72, 75
Still, Clyfford, 60
Stockhausen, Karlheinz, 47–8, 51, 61, 62, 72, 98
Stravinsky, Igor, 64, 72, 146
Strindberg, 167
Sullivan, Ed, 138
Superville, Humbert de, 111
Swift, Jonathan, 201, 205
Synge, J. M., 139

Tanner, Tony, 169
Tchaikovsky, 115
Theobald, Robert, 139
Thomas, Dylan, 139
Thompson, Edward, 159, 166
Thomson, Virgil, 83, 85
Thoreau, Henri, 54, 180
Tiepolo, Giovanni Battista, 116
Tillyard, E. M. W., 186–7, 192
Tinguely, Jean, 72, 79, 80, 83–4, 100
Tintoretto, 50
Titian, 228
Tobey, Mark, 51, 58, 233
Tomkins, Calvin, 21 n., 79, 83, 85, 185
Toynbee, Arnold, 135
Trilling, Lionel, 76, 107, 201
Trocchi, Alexander, 37
Trotsky, Leon, 163
Tudor, David, 47, 83
Twain, Mark, 180
Tzara, Tristan, 68, 78

Valéry, Paul, 69, 210
Van Gogh, Vincent, 50, 187
Varèse, Edgar, 64
Varley, William, 21
Verlaine, Paul, 73
Villiers de l'Isle-Adam, Auguste de, 69
Vonnegut, Kurt, 26

Wagner, Richard, 49–50, 51, 244
Wain, John, 194
Warhol, Andy, 81, 95, 196, 208, 233–234, 238
Waugh, Arthur, 67
Waugh, Evelyn, 70
Weil, Simone, 92
Wells, H. G., 26
Wesker, Arnold, 159
Wesselman, Tom, 233, 234
West, Nathanael, 33
Whitehead, A. N., 63–4, 130
Whitman, Walt, 36, 39, 96, 180, 182
Wicker, Brian, 166, 167–8
Wilde, Oscar, 66, 68
Williams, Raymond, 20, 165, 166–7, 170, 183
Williams, Tennessee, 167
Williams, W. C., 33, 77, 193
Wittgenstein, Ludwig, 69, 97, 152
Wolfe, Christian, 51
Wolfe, Tom, 21 n.
Wollheim, Richard, 170
Woolf, Virginia, 70
Wordsworth, William, 56, 166
Worringer, Wilhelm, 72

Yeats, W. B., 67, 69, 70, 139, 143, 176, 178

Zolla, Elémire, 42